ANT to a single gen- L., Turner's, fishmonger,

family. From the ter.—L. Y., 18, Berkeley-

nily, Middle-aged. ry preferred.—A. B., 42,

an's or tradesman's ed.—L. C., 1, South-row,

one is kept, where French's, 227, Oxford-st.

man's family. Five -street, Covent-garden.

d on a lady, and do Good character.—G. L.,

man's or gentleman's Age 29.—A. C., 62, South

it upon the lady if n or country.—E. B., 12,

emaid in a small cter.—A. S., Edwards's,

aid in a gentleman's 28. Excellent character.

an's or tradesman's New Kent-road.

Can work well at , Fitzroy-square.

ge 18.—S. P., 45,

A. B., Mrs. Heir's, ammersmith.

From the country ens, Charing-cross.

kept. Good charac- Edgeware-road.

kept. Three years' Remington-st., City-rd.

pt. Good character. -square.

a small family.— East-lane, Walworth.

is kept, a young hill, Woolwich.

kept. 12 months' Gray's-inn-road.

Two years' good Fitzroy-square.

kept. 5½ years' cha- th-place, Gray's-inn-road.

iness. Two years' g's-road, Chelsea.

where a footman is Grosvenor-square.

kept. 12 months' news, Grosvenor-place.

12 months' good ew Oxford-street.

ne years' undeniable ner Clifton-st., Finsbury.

parlourmaid is kept. treet, Camden-town.

kept. Aged 25. Is —A. B., Mr. Goodwin's,

mily, where a foot- ood character. Town or reet, Newington-butts.

parlourmaid is kept. haracter.—H. S., 3, Vic-

nily, where a foot- 12 months' character.—

n's family, where a rs' character.—Y. D., 30,

Works well at her haracter.—E. R., 1, Por-

ng person from the —M. A., Crown Hotel,

ly. Age 22. From 40, Singleton-street, East-

ept, a young person. Barrett's, 11, Duke-street,

kept. Two years' ntry.—A. M., post-office,

ly, where a footman Three years' good cha-

A. person from the country. Will make herself useful. Highly recommended.—E. A., Drew's, 9, Charles-st., Westbourne-terrace, Hyde-park.

GENERAL SERVANT (GOOD). Age 32. Three years' good character.—A. H., 53, Oakley-street, Lambeth.

GENERAL SERVANT (GOOD), or Cook in a tradesman's family.—L. S., 17, King street, Holborn.

GENERAL SERVANT in a small family, where the washing is put out, a confidential person.—A. B., 67, Eaton-place, Belgrave-square.

GENERAL SERVANT to a single gentleman or tradesman, or a Plain Cook in a small family. Age 37. 1½ year's good character.—E. T., 33, Frederick-street, Hampstead-road.

GENERAL SERVANT in a private or tradesman's family, a steady young woman, from the country. Good character.—J. P., 10, St. Andrew's-terrace, Rhodeswell-road, Limehouse.

KITCHENMAID (HEAD), in a small family under a man cook, or Cook in a small family. Good character.—E. P., Lardner's, 57, Coram-street, Russell-square.

KITCHENMAID, in a gentleman's family. Good character.—S. J., 30, North Audley-street, Grosvenor-square.

KITCHENMAID, in a gentleman's family, a young woman.—C. L., 11, New-street, Covent-garden.

KITCHENMAID, or Scullerymaid, in a gentleman's family. Age 20. Good character. No objection to the country.—G. L., 111, Great Portland-street, Portland-place.

KITCHENMAID in a nobleman's or gentleman's family. Age 22. One year's good character. Town or country.—H. B., 13, Ossulston-street, New-road.

KITCHENMAID, or Scullerymaid in a gentleman's family. Age 22.—Excellent character—Y. Z., 35, Duke-street, Grosvenor-square.

KITCHENMAID in an hotel or club-house, a young person. 15 months' good character.—G. L., 6, Seabon-street, West Ham, near London.

KITCHENMAID in a gentleman's family, a strong, healthy girl. 12 months' character.—M. S., 33, Upper Eaton-street, Pimlico.

SCULLERYMAID, or Servant of All-work. Age 20.—E. W., Scotman's, 70, Cromer-street, Gray's-inn-road.

CHAMBERMAID, or Upper Housemaid, in an hotel. No objection to a single-handed place. Two years' good character.—Y. Z., 2, Marchmont-street, Russell-square.

CHAMBERMAID, Waitress, or Housemaid, in an hotel, boarding or lodging-house. Good character.—A. A., 14, Creed-lane, Great Carter-lane, city.

CHAMBERMAID, or Housemaid in an hotel or tavern. Accustomed to the business. Age 28.—A. B., 10, John-street, Hanway-street, Oxford-street.

CHAMBERMAID, or Upper Housemaid in an hotel. Age 27. Well recommended.—G. B., at Mrs. Hill's, 22, Bloomsbury-street.

CHAMBERMAID, or Needlewoman in an hotel. Experienced, age 36. Good character.—A. B., 13, Prospect-row, Walworth-road.

CHAMBERMAID, or Housemaid in a tavern or hotel, a young woman. Three years' character.—A. M., Waite's, London-Bridge Tavern.

WAITRESS in an hotel, tavern, or dining rooms, a young person. Perfectly understands her business.—E. J., Dolphin Tavern, Coleman-street, city.

WAITRESS, or Housemaid, or Waitress in a tavern, hotel, or any other house of business, a young person. Good character.—M. A. R., 9, North-row, Park-lane.

BARMAID, a young person. Good character.—E. W., Mullen's Hotel, Ironmonger-lane, Cheapside.

BARMAID, or Under Barmaid. Good character.—E. H., the Golden Fleece, 7, St. John-street-road.

MAN and WIFE, the care of offices or chambers.—A. B., 24, Victoria-road, Pimlico.

MAN and WIFE. Middle-aged. No family. Thorough In-door Servant and Plain Cook or Housemaid, or care of chambers or offices. Excellent characters.—W. B., 103, High-st., Marylebone.

MAN and WIFE, without encumbrance: man to drive, and can wait at table; woman as Plain Cook. Age 32. Good character.—C. D., 3, Earl-street, Sloane-square, Chelsea.

MAN and WIFE: man as Coachman; wife as thorough good Cook. Together or separately. Town or country. 2½ years' good character.—J. R., 11, Halkin-street west, Belgrave-square.

MAN and WIFE, in a family, or to a single gentleman or lady: man as thorough In-door Servant; woman as good Cook. Age 33 and 34.—L. J., post-office, 37, Devonshire-street, Portland-place.

MAN and WIFE: the man as Coachman; the woman as Good Plain Cook, with two years' good character. Town or country.—A. B., Gail's, jobmaster, New Burlington-mews, Regent-st.

BUTLER and VALET, where a footman or page is kept. Active, single, middle-aged. Can brew. 2 years' character.—Y. Z., Taaffe's, 128, Crawford-street.

BUTLER, where footman or page is kept. Town or country. Single; age 31; height 5 ft. 10. 18 months' good character.—W. M., 7, Lower-terrace, Lower-street, Islington.

BUTLER and VALET, where a footman or boy is kept. 21 months' good character. No objection to a job. Age 33.—B. B., 29, Hasker-street, Brompton.

BUTLER, or Butler and Valet. Age 38. 18 months' good character.—J. C., Puckeridge's, 2, Duke-street, Manchester-square.

BUTLER, Valet, or Single-handed, a young man. Character will bear the strictest investigation.—G. S., Luckie's, 83, Great Portland-street.

UPPER SERVANT where a footman or lad is kept, or single-handed. Thoroughly understands his business. Two years' excellent character.—F. R., Adams's, 7, St. James's-street, Piccadilly.

IN-DOOR SERVANT (UPPER or thorough), where a footman or boy is kept, a steady, single man, age 34. 1½ year's good

mounter's, Holland-place, Holland-street, Kensington.

COACHMAN. Married, no family, age 40. Can manage a garde[n] ... —W. W., Ro...

COACHM[AN] ... [un]derstand ... Good charact...

COACHM[AN] ... his bus... Wall's, 125, ...

COACHM[AN] ... recomm... J. W., Bartle...

COACHM[AN] ... well. N... —M. T., 9, B...

COACHMAN, to drive a brougham, a married man, age 35. Can wait at table and make himself useful in other ways. Excellent character.—A. A., Spratt's, 5, Haverford-ter., Caledonian-road.

COACHMAN, or Groom, to drive one or a pair. Married, age 23. Knows town well. Two years' good character.—J. B., 2, Short-street, York-street, Walworth-road.

COACHMAN. Married, without encumbrance. Eight years' character. Knows town well.—S. L., South's-yard, New Bond-street.

COACHMAN and GROOM, or to drive a brougham. Single. Two years' character. No objection to the country.—J. D., 9, Pall-mall east.

COACHMAN, or Groom and Coachman. Married, age 30, no family. Can wait well at table. Knows town well. Good character.—A. B., Twyman's, 2, Water-lane, Ludgate-hill, city.

COACHMAN. Married. Perfectly understands his business. Knows town well. Good character.—J. B., 13, Grosvenor-street west, Eaton-square, Pimlico.

COACHMAN, or Groom and Coachman. Married, age 34. Light weight. Town or country.—A. B., Watson, 10, Great Windmill-street, Haymarket.

COACHMAN, or Groom and Coachman, to drive one horse or a pair, a single man, age 26. No objection to make himself otherwise useful.—S. S., 4, Charles-street, Grosvenor-square.

POSTILION, or Gentleman's Cab-boy and Groom. Light weight. Thoroughly understands his business.—T. D., 27, Thomas-street, Oxford-street.

GROOM (GOOD USEFUL), or Coachman. Town preferred. Age 26. 18 months' character.—F. P., 16, North Audley-street, Grosvenor-square.

GROOM, or to drive a brougham. Two years' good character. Age 19.—A. B., Squire's, 4, Wellington-terrace, Bayswater.

GROOM, under a coachman, a young man from the country, age 20. Five years' character.—J. G., John Horn's, 15, Derwent-street, East Greenwich.

GROOM, or Groom and Coachman. Married, no encumbrance. Age 24. Perfectly understands the care of hunters. Country preferred.—A. B., 3, Riding-house-lane, Portland-place.

GROOM, or Groom and Coachman, or to drive a brougham. Age 25. 3½ years' good character. Town or country, or to go abroad.—C. B., 31, Ridinghouse-lane, Portland-place.

GARDENER, or Gardener and Bailiff. Married, without family. Can brew, understands timber, land measuring, draining, and keep accounts.—B. A., 7, Napier-street, Ashley-ter., City-road.

GARDENER and COWMAN, age 40. Thoroughly understands his business in forcing, kitchen and flower garden.—M. C., Howe's, baker, Oxford-terrace, World's-end, King's-road, Chelsea.

GARDENER, a single man, age 27, who thoroughly understands his business. No objection to attend a horse. Two years' good character.—A. B., Meaden's, printer, High-street, Clapham, Surrey.

WAREHOUSEMAN, or Packer. Age 26. Six years' good character.—T. B., 6, Greville-street, Hatton-garden.

CARMAN, or Porter, a strong young man from the country, well used to horses. Good character.—G. K., 4, Little Bush-lane, city.

LIGHT PORTER. Age 21. 5 years' good character.—W. W., 4, Ward's-buildings, Paddington-street, Marylebone.

LIGHT PORTER, in a respectable house of business. Age 18. From the country. Knows town. 1½ year's undeniable character.—S. B., 2, Barbican-court, city.

LIGHT PORTER, Messenger, or any other capacity where he can make himself generally useful, a young man. Good references.—J. C., 36, Wellclose-square, London Docks.

LIGHT PORTER, or Messenger, in a warehouse, a young man. Knows town well. Good reference.—E. A., 101, Drummond-street, Euston-square.

LIGHT PORTER, or Messenger, a young man, age 23. Security if required. Three years' character.—R. G. Smith's, newsvendor, Homerton.

PORTER, Messenger, or Carman, or any capacity where he could make himself generally useful to his employer. From the country.—G. C., 12, Queen's-garden, Brompton.

PORTER, and to make himself generally useful, a married man, age 25. Five years' good character.—E. S., 4, Young's-buildings, Paul's-alley, Redcross-street, city.

PORTER, in an hotel, tavern, or respectable house of business. Age 30. Good character.—A. B., 8, Upper Winchester-street, Pentonville.

PORTER, Messenger, or any other employment. Eight years' character.—T. A., 37, Gordon-terrace, Caledonian-road, King's-cross.

WAITER in an hotel, tavern, or chop-house. Single, age 22. Town or country.—T. J., post-office, Nortonfolgate.

WAITER, in an hotel, boarding-house, or any respectable house of business. Hotel character. Age 38.—J. T., 7, William-street, Manchester-square.

WAITER, in an hotel or any respectable house of business. Age 25. Good reference.—A. B., 81, Southwark-bridge-road.

THE COMPLETE SERVANT

Other titles published in the Southover Historic Cookery and Housekeeping Series:

William Verrall's Cookery Book
First published in 1759, with an Introduction by Colin Brent

The London Art of Cookery
First published in 1783 by John Farley, with an Introduction by Stephen Medcalf

THE COMPLETE SERVANT

by

Samuel & Sarah Adams

Edited by Ann Haly
with an Introduction
by
Pamela Horn

SOUTHOVER PRESS
1989

First published in this edition 1989 by
SOUTHOVER PRESS
2 Cockshut Road
Lewes, East Sussex BN7 1JH

British Library Cataloguing in Publication Data
Adams Samuel
The complete servant.
1. Household management
I. Title II. Adams, Sarah III. Haly, Ann
640

ISBN 1 870962 03 6

Jacket design by A. Gammon Art & Design

Phototypeset in Palatino
by Pauline Newton, Chichester

Printed by Antony Rowe Ltd
Bumpers Farm
Chippenham SN14 6QA
England

CONTENTS

CONTENTS

ACKNOWLEDGEMENTS

The Publisher wishes to thank the proprietors of Punch for permission to use the drawings from the early Volumes of *Punch*; Frank Nash for his kindness in reading the sections on the Head Nurse and the Chamber Nurse; Harry Davies for his help with the terms used in the remedies, and Elizabeth Earle, Tom Reeves, and Catharine Bagnall.

SOURCES OF ILLUSTRATIONS

From *Punch* Vol. 1
Drawings on pp47, 65, 69, 89, 93, 96, 99, 101, 104, 108, 118, 184
From *Punch* Vol. 2
Drawings on pp35, 39, 61, 75, 82, 86, 129, 142, 156, 158, 171, 172, 173
From *Punch* Vol. 3
Drawings on pp36, 79, 90, 133, 140, 145
From *Punch* Vol. 20
Drawings on pp11, 50, 146
From *The Water Babies* by Charles Kingsley 1904
Drawing on p161 by Linley Sambourne
From Beeton's *Every-Day Gardening* 1912
Drawings on pp166, 168, 170
From *Dick Doyle's Journal* 1885
Drawings on pp152, 155
Printer's flowers, Henry Caslon 1844

EDITOR'S NOTE

For a first-hand account of backstairs life in the late eighteenth and early nineteenth centuries, *The Complete Servant* is hard to beat; it is a mine of information. First published in 1825, it was the most comprehensive and influential book of its kind and started off a rash of imitations. Some, like *The Servant's Guide and Family Manual*, published in 1830, followed the same successful formula. Although *The Complete Servant* has been often quoted and many times referred to it was not, for some reason, reprinted. Without doubt its popularity and that of its imitators led to the publication of *Household Management* by Isabella Beeton a generation later in 1861.

The Complete Servant is unusual in that more than half the job descriptions in it are for men. The daily rounds of the Butler, Land Steward, Valet, Grooms and Gardeners are described in detail. The work of the Butler as cellarman, and the necessary office of the Groom as Vet, are here. Only the Man Cook, whose duties seem to be outside the experience of the authors, is given somewhat cursory treatment.

Some of the Adamses' advice is extraordinarily pertinent and modern. That on child management has a distinctly contemporary ring to it, with its emphasis on light and air and a sensible regimen. The remedies of the Chamber Nurse may not have been very effective, but it must be remembered they were written before the days of scientific medicine.

The very cookable and delicious recipes for cakes seem to have changed very little over a long period; but there is a difference. Many ingredients used in the early nineteenth-century kitchen were adulterated, and great care was needed by the cook to discover this. (Testing for impurities in food was not required by law until the 1860 Adulteration of Food Act.) The Adamses insisted on attention to these matters. But in another respect they stood out from their contemporaries. The cook is enjoined to avoid all cruelty "to the living and sensitive animals" under her care, a most humane gesture in an age when animals were treated with harshness and brutality.

Servants in a large and well-run establishment had a reasonable working life, with the possibility of advancement, but the lot of the lowest menial — the servant of all work — was unremitting drudgery. Just to read the five pages of her duties makes one feel tired. It was this toil, with little hope of escape, which gave service the bad name from which it has not yet recovered.

For reasons of space, a long appendix on market and other prices has had to be left out.

ANN HALY

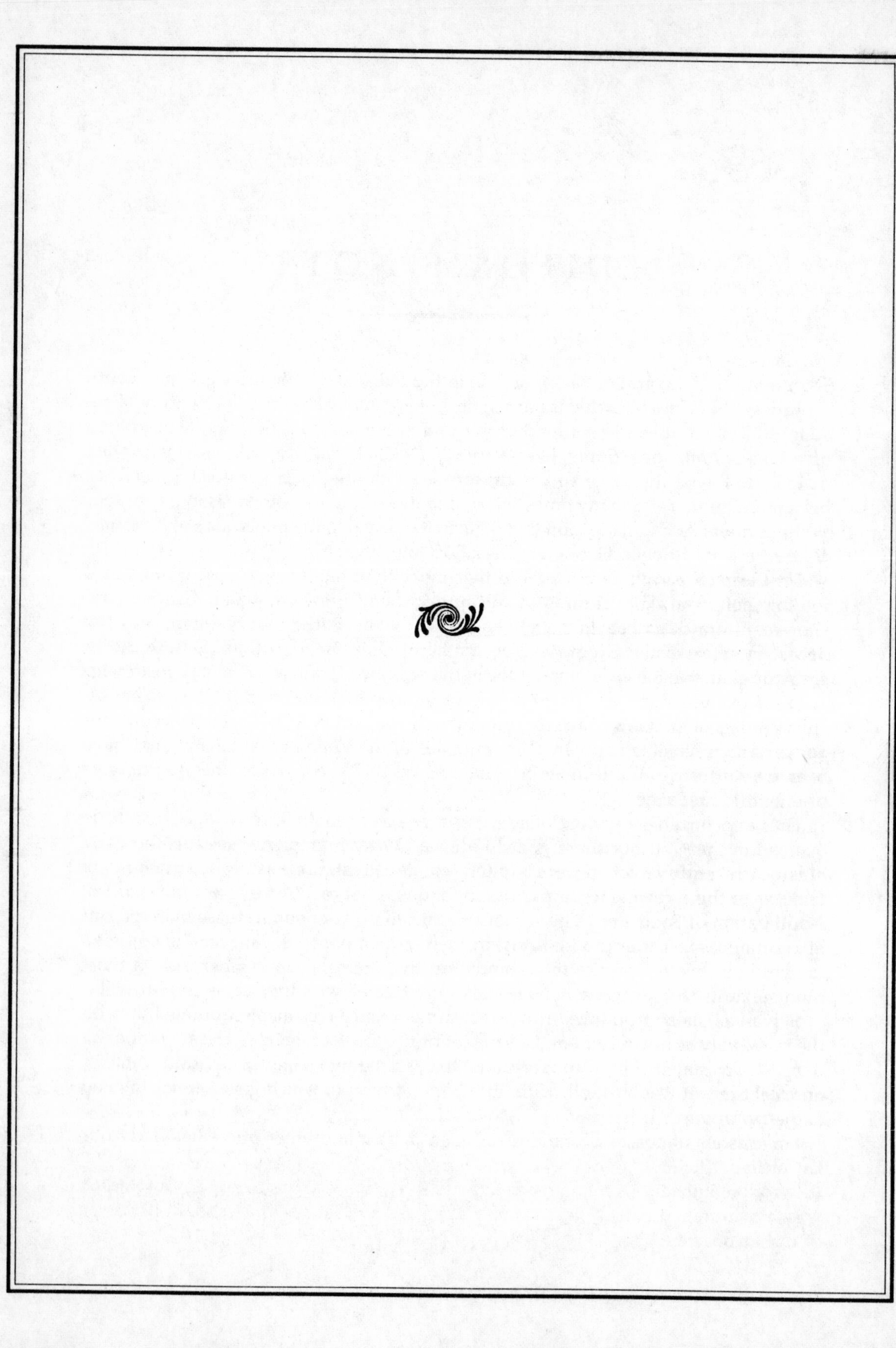

INTRODUCTION

'WANTED, a middle-aged steady Servant, in the capacity of FOOTMAN; he will be required to wait at table, clean plate, and make himself generally useful in the House. No one need apply who has not lived some time in his last place; and it is indispensably necessary that he shall be able to shave his Master.—Apply, post-paid, to A.B., Post Office, Chepstow.'
Advertisement in the *Gloucester Journal*, 24 January, 1825.

When Samuel Adams, joint author of *The Complete Servant*, started work as a footboy in 1770 many of the economic and social changes which were to transform British society were already under way. Commerce and industry were expanding rapidly and agriculture no longer dominated the nation's life. The population was expanding too; from an estimated 5 million people living in England and Wales in the late 1680s, numbers had risen to around 7 million by 1770. In 1801, at the time of the first population census, they had reached 9 million and were to double again in the next fifty years.

With these changes came a new and prosperous middle class recruited from the ranks of merchants, industrialists and professional men, many of whom were anxious to emulate the lifestyle of the traditional leaders of society—the landed aristocracy and gentry, and the clergy. Not only did they demand grander and more luxurious houses and furnishings; they also wanted domestic servants.

Even in the 1750s a correspondent to *The Craftsman* magazine complained there was 'scarce a mechanick in town who does not keep a servant in livery', while a contributor to the *London Chronicle* of 1762 claimed to have known 'many a Doctor or Apothecary . . . starve themselves, that they may maintain their foormen'. Although exaggerated, such comments expressed the ambitions of large numbers of this new, upwardly mobile sector of society. In practice, of course, they were less likely to recruit men servants than women, who were cheaper to employ and easier to discipline.

It was to cater for employers—or servants—who were uncertain precisely what duties were attached to particular household positions that books of advice like *The Complete Servant* (1825) or, a generation later, Mrs Beeton's *Book of Household Management* (1861) were published. Many were extremely popular. Mrs William Parkes's *Domestic Duties: or, Instructions to Young Married Ladies on the Management of their Households*, first published in 1825, had run into three editions by 1828, while Dr William Kitchiner's *The Cook's Oracle* (1817), which was primarily concerned with the work of kitchen staff, had reached its sixth edition by the same year. But neither was as comprehensive as *The Complete Servant*, either in subject matter or in the range of duties described.

In most written accounts of domestic life, the large households of the well-to-do feature prominently because it was there that service was seen at its most spectacular. But at no time during the eighteenth and nineteenth centuries did the bulk of domestic servants work in such establishments. Most households which had servants employed only one or two maids, perhaps supplemented by a washerwoman to help with the laundry. Women predominated at this level; it is noteworthy that in *The Complete Servant* the Adamses suggested a substantial annual income of at least £400 as needed to employ even a young male servant. (Comparisons are difficult, but perhaps the current income equivalent would be one hundred times as great.) More than £500 was required if a footman were to be employed. By contrast, a maiden lady with £100 a year might employ a youthful maid-of-all-work, and some families doubtless managed on far less than that. In Charlotte Brontë's *Jane Eyre*, set largely in the 1830s, the heroine was paid only £30 a year to run the village school at Morton but was also supplied with a young day servant to carry out domestic chores while she was teaching. At the 1851 census more than two-thirds of the nation's female servants fell into the 'general' or maid-of-all-work category. They were expected to do all kinds of jobs, from scrubbing floors and polishing, to preparing vegetables, running errands and helping in the kitchen.

Samuel and Sarah Adams suggested that such servants should be recruited from the ranks of the 'industrious and labouring classes', who had been bred up for the task. Then, if they proved tractable and secured the goodwill of their employers, they might eventually move into 'superior service', as Sarah herself had done. In reality, few made the transition. Most remained in that lowly post for the whole of their working lives, and a lonely, drudging existence it often proved. In 1788 Philip Thicknesse concluded that 'the veriest slaves' he had seen in two hemispheres were the all-work maidservants of London, and more than half a century later similar comments were still being made.

Higher up the scale came the households of substantial farmers, the professional classes, prosperous businessmen, and the smaller country gentlemen. They probably aimed to employ at least three servants, since this was the minimum deemed necessary if a household were to be 'complete in all its functions'. In the early nineteenth century these possibly comprised a cook, housemaid, and young male servant or groom.

Among these comfortably-off employers could be counted the diarist James Woodforde, incumbent of Weston Longeville, Norfolk, from 1774 to 1803, who had an income of around £300 a year. Woodforde employed five servants—two adult males, two females and a boy. One of the men was responsible for the rector's livestock and the other acted as a liveried footman. Woodforde's diaries also show how wages were rising at the end of the eighteenth century, particularly among the males. In 1782 he paid the footman £4 4s. a year, plus 10s. for dressing his wigs, while the 'boy' received 10s. 6d. a year. By 1785 these rates had increased to £5 5s. and £1 1s. respectively. At the same time, the under-maid, to whom he had paid just over £2 in 1782, had advanced to £5 5s. by the later date. By that time she was getting the same amount as her cook-maid colleague, and both women were also supplied with tea and sugar—luxuries not available to all servants at that time. (Some of the rise in this case, however, was due to the woman's competent performance of her duties.)

Woodforde settled his wages bills annually, although occasional interim payments were made to the servants for essential purchases. This practice of yearly or, more commonly, quarterly payments to domestics continued late into the nineteenth century and must have made the servant's personal budgeting difficult.

In larger households than that of Parson Woodforde, or in London itself, still higher wages were expected. In 1772, P. J. Grosley complained that his landlord was having to pay a 'fat Welsh girl, who . . . scarce understood a word of English', and who had only just arrived in the capital, the considerable sum of 6 guineas a year, plus a guinea for her tea, and, of course, her bed and board. 'The wages of a cook-maid, who knows how to roast and boil, amount to twenty guineas a year.'

An individual servant's wage depended both on his or her personal skill and on the wealth of the employer. In 1787 an advertiser for a footman stated that he would pay 13 guineas to an applicant with the usual complement of knowledge, but 15 guineas to a man who could dress hair. These differentials are confirmed by the suggested rates quoted in *The Complete Servant* and in similar books of household management. These works were, of course, published at a time when prices were stabilising once more after the sharp inflation of the French war years from 1793 to 1815, and the deflation which immediately followed the ending of hostilities.

Meanwhile at the summit of the servant-keeping hierarchy were the households of the nobility and gentry. Although, as we have seen, they employed a minority of the domestic labour force, they nonetheless influenced the overall character of domestic service. It was at this prestigious end of the market that Samuel and Sarah Adams's book was aimed. As it makes clear, the social distinctions apparent among employers above stairs applied with equal, or greater, force to those engaged 'below'. Each staff member had to know his or her 'place' in the scheme of things, and woe betide anyone who stepped out of line.

In such households the recruitment of male servants was regarded as an essential symbol of the employer's status and wealth. When the young French aristocrat, François de la Rochefoucauld, son of the Duc de Liancourt, visited London in 1784 he was struck by the way some noble families employed thirty or forty males, to say nothing of numerous females. To the American scientist, Benjamin Silliman, visiting about two decades later, it was 'a great point of emulation' among the well-to-do 'to excel all rivals in the number of footmen'. Some coaches had as many as four footmen standing up and holding on behind the carriage, 'not to mention occasionally a supernumerary one in the coachman's box'. Occasionally this competitive spirit led snobbish employers to dress outdoor servants in livery in order to impress guests at important dinner parties. Elizabeth Grant remembered how, in 1802, when she dined with her clan chief at Castle Grant, there was a 'footman in . . . gorgeous green and scarlet livery behind every chair, but they were mere gillies, lads quite untutored . . . brought in for the occasion . . . fitted into the suit that they best filled'.

The 'luxury' aspect of the male servant was underlined in 1777 when an annual tax of a guinea per man was imposed. Although originally intended to help finance the War of American Independence, it was retained in modified form until 1937. In addition, between 1795 and 1869 a tax on hair-powder was levied and this, too, added to the cost of employing footmen and coachmen in full regalia. Samuel and Sarah Adams suggested an income of over £3,000 a year if more than one footman were to be afforded. The same inflated income was likewise needed to employ a housekeeper to head the female staff; a butler could be afforded by those with over £2,000 a year. It was not the pay and board of the staff members themselves that made such high incomes necessary, but rather the general scale and luxury of the establishment.

Nevertheless many upper servants enjoyed valuable perquisites to supplement their money earnings. Cooks were often allowed to dispose of 'kitchen stuff', including dripping, bones and chunks of fat, while butlers retained candle ends, used cards and old bottles. The valet and lady's maid had their employer's cast-off clothing, and the coachman was given half-worn carriage parts. In many large households these legitimate perquisites were swollen by nefarious practices. Cooks would order extra butter which they then melted down to increase the weight of the 'dripping' they were allowed to sell, while butlers surreptitiously disposed of their master's wine.

In these large establishments, it was common for senior staff to have juniors to wait on them. The stillroom maid, for example, usually attended to the wants of the housekeeper, as well as helping to make the preserves, cordials, and special items of confectionery so lovingly described in *The Complete Servant* when the housekeeper's role is discussed. Similarly, the kitchenmaid waited on the cook—and, often enough, received the blame if anything went wrong—while the most junior housemaid frequently worked entirely for the staff.

In such households the upper servants rarely ate with the juniors. Usually the main course of the dinner only was consumed in the servants' hall by the seniors, who then repaired to the housekeeper's room, or, in the grandest households, the steward's room, to eat their pudding. They entered and left the hall in strict order of precedence while the lower servants stood respectfully to attention. Seating, too, was decided by status, and a visiting valet or lady's maid, near the top of the domestic hierarchy, would be accorded the rank of his or her employer. The housekeeper's or steward's room where these privileged servants took some of their meals was nicknamed the 'Pug's Parlour' by irreverent juniors.

Nursery staff lived very much apart from the rest of the household, and often a nanny formed bonds of affection with her charges which lasted for the rest of their lives. The Adamses stressed the nurse's responsibility for the safety of the children and included several hints on how this could best be achieved.

In most large households contacts between employers and junior servants were minimal. It was the seniors who were the juniors' real employers, and often they treated beginners as a sergeant treated recruits, drilling them by dint of much scolding. In the eighteenth century beatings might even be administered from time to time. At Englefield House in Berkshire, the housekeeper was expected to keep 'order & quiet in the Family', that is among the servants, and 'not let the Maids go out without your leave, & to take care that they are dressed quietly'. Many large households imposed fines for misbehaviour and these, and other rules, would be displayed prominently in the servants' hall. At Wasing Place near Reading even at the end of the nineteenth century a fine of 1d. was imposed for swearing, and of 2d. for cutting more bread than was necessary or wiping 'knives and forks on the table cloth, or hand towel'.

Yet, despite the restrictions, life in these large establishments had many compensations. Food was usually plentiful and varied, staff enjoyed some of the reflected glory of their employers' superior social status, and provision was made for their leisure time, including the organising of occasional parties or balls. It was a world away from the lonely, monotonous daily round pursued by most maids-of-all-work in small town households.

There is little doubt that in some cases ties of friendship grew up between masters and servants which lasted for years. Sarah Adams herself not only remained housekeeper in a very large establishment for over twenty years but was able to call upon the help of a number of her employer's family for help and advice when she and her husband came to write their book.

Long-serving domestics would also often be remembered in their employer's Will. Thus when the Rev. David Davies, rector of Barkham, Berkshire, died in 1819, he left his housekeeper of more than twenty years the sum of £234 exclusive of all inheritance duty, his wine, and his 'Great Elbow Chair'. She and the man-servant, David Horne, shared between them the pigs and poultry, while Horne secured £129 in cash, plus the rector's wearing apparel, his watch, and his seals and buckles. The maid, Elizabeth Beesley, who had joined the household seven years before, obtained a bequest of £20. In each case, Davies carefully noted that these sums were to be 'exclusive of their full wages for the current year'. He was clearly anxious tht his executors should not be tempted to deprive them of any of their dues.

Occasionally, as at Abbotsford, the home of Sir Walter Scott, portraits of well-loved servants would be hung on the walls of employers' houses. Portraits of the author's coachman and gamekeeper are still at Abbotsford. At Erddig, a landed estate near Wrexham in North Wales, the Yorke family not only had numerous portraits of their servants painted but also composed verses in their honour. One who received this attention was Jane Ebbrell, a housemaid, who apparently joined the staff in the 1720s and was still there about seventy years later, having in the interim married the coachman and produced a son who also worked in the stables at Erddig. Her portrait was commissioned in 1793.

In general, relations between masters and servants in the eighteenth and early nineteenth centuries were less formal than they were to become in the reign of Queen Victoria. At Weston Longeville, Parson Woodforde let his male servants go out coursing on their own, and both the men and the women were allowed to attend nearby fairs and festivals. In 1776 he also paid for his two men-servants to be taught to read and write by the village schoolmaster. Similarly, James Wissman, an oyster-merchant of Paglesham, Essex, allowed his maids to attend fairs at Paglesham, Rochford, and Burnham in the 1780s and 1790s, and made cash advances out of their wages so that they might buy ribbons, combs, and other small items.

Moral attitudes, too, were less censorious than they later became. When one of the Weston Longeville maids was found to be pregnant, although Parson Woodforde did not re-engage her at the end of her annual hiring, he gave her an extra 4s. 'on going away', to supplement her wages. And as late as 1835, Jane Welsh Carlyle, wife of the famous author, learned with equanimity that a prospective Scottish maid had already had a child. 'It would be difficult,' she wrote, 'for me to say that an Annandale woman's virtue is the worse for a misfortune. I am certain that, in their circumstances, with their views and examples, I should have had one too, if not more!'

However, not all employers were so tolerant even before Victoria ascended the throne. In 1779, Mary Hardy, wife of a Norfolk farmer and maltster, had no hesitation in dismissing 'both the maids . . . for raking with Fellows & other misdemeaners' (*sic*). Later, another maid was despatched when she was found to be 'with child by old Richard Mayes', while a fourth lost her place when she left the back door unbarred 'for the chimney sweep and then was saucy'.

As small shopkeepers, tradesmen and clerks moved in growing numbers into the servant-keeping classes during the nineteenth century, the stricter attitude adopted by Mary Hardy became more widespread, as employers sought to keep a social distance between themselves and their domestics. Nowhere was this more obvious than in the matter of female servants' dress. In the eighteenth century it was common for maids to wear their mistresses' cast-offs, and there were complaints that when they attended the mistress in the streets, it was difficult to distinguish employer from servant. But by the 1820s, a kind of uniform was emerging consisting of a stuff gown, a cap, and a neck-handkerchief pinned corner-wise. Gradually this merged into the outfit of print dresses, white caps and aprons for mornings and black dresses for afternoons, the characteristic maid's attire for decades to come.

Samuel and Sarah Adams contributed to this sartorial trend by emphasising that servants should not seek to imitate their 'betters' by dressing above their station. Intemperance in dress was 'an evil that ought to be carefully guarded against', they declared firmly. In men-servants it was sheer affectation, but in females it opened 'a door to temptation and extravagance which but too frequently ends in ruin'. At Englefield House, Berkshire, all the servants had to be of the Protestant religion and were expected to attend morning prayers. They were told firmly that if they were ill their employer would not meet apothecaries' bills. In addition, the under butler and the footmen were required to wear hair powder, which they purchased for themselves, and they were not allowed to go out without wearing livery. In return, they were given, as well as their wages, a suit of livery each year, plus two working suits, and a hat and great coat when needed.

By the nineteenth century, the distinctions between the servants' quarters and the family's were becoming clearer. This growing stress on privacy, very different from the sense of community in many eighteenth century households, was clearly conveyed by Parson Woodforde in his diary when he referred to his servants as 'my people' or 'our folks'.

Not all servants, of course, accepted their lot in the meek fashion recommended by the authors of household management texts. Men-servants, in particular, were the frequent subject of bitter complaint, especially in the eighteenth century, because of their insubordinate and avaricious behaviour. Even Parson Woodforde eventually had to dismiss his footman after nearly nine years' service, for persistent drunkenness. The final break occurred in April 1785 when the man returned home at 11 p.m. 'in Liquor' after spending the evening out. He then behaved 'very rudely and most impudently . . . I told him that I was determined never more to bear with such behaviour'.

In the nineteenth century such defiance was curbed but never entirely eliminated. It was also influenced by the fact that there were more and more jobs for men in industry and commerce, and fewer were attracted to a life in service. This became particularly apparent during the Victorian era, and increased the bargaining power of those who did enter domestic employment. In 1831, 104,730 male servants were recorded in the population census. By 1851 the total of men in private indoor service had dropped to 74,323 and the decline continued thereafter, to reach 47,893 half a century later.

Meanwhile, in the early years of the nineteenth century, employers continued to express discontent at the pretensions and insubordination of male servants. In 1809, a correspondent to the *Gentleman's Magazine* even complained that it was impossible for respectable families to attend the theatre, because of the doubtful company they might encounter. Well-to-do employers were apparently paying for their liveried servants to sit in the pit, while the upper boxes were filled with prostitutes.

The diary of William Tayler, a footman employed by a wealthy London widow, Mrs Prinsep, and her unmarried daughter, also confirms that problems persisted in the 1830s. Apart from drinking heavily and spending much time playing cards with fellow servants or visiting family and friends in the neighbourhood, Tayler periodically skimped his duties and defied his employers. Thus on 19 May 1837, he went in the carriage with Miss Prinsep, and because she kept him out longer than he thought she should, he 'gave her a little row for it. I hope it will do her good. I served the old lady the same way the other day and it did her a deal of good'. Far more congenial, from his point of view, was the routine followed on 15 February in the same year. This was described as 'a delightful day', in which he took a short walk in the morning, spent the afternoon drawing for his own amusement and the evening in writing and playing cards.

The custom among male servants of demanding vails or tips from their employers' visitors was widespread in both the eighteenth and early nineteenth centuries. Although efforts were made to end it from the 1760s, it proved impossible to eradicate entirely. William Tayler periodically referred to the shillings he received from visitors to the Prinsep household, as well as gratuities from tradesmen when he want to settle the family's bills. In all, he estimated that his annual wages of £42 were supplemented by these 'perquisites' to the tune of £10 or £15 a year.

Other householders dealt with the problem by substituting women servants for the men. Females were cheaper and more tractable. But they, too, could display independence, usually by frequent changes of place. Jane Carlyle, in what was basically a single-servant household, had six different maids between June 1834 and October 1835, to say nothing of three or four weeks' temporary help from a charwoman 'who has her family in the workhouse'. Sometimes the change was made because Jane herself dismissed the maid. In other cases it was because of the maid's own reaction, as with Isabella from Edinburgh. She departed after three weeks in 1846, declaring that 'no one woman living' could do the work expected of her, and that she would 'never slave herself for anybody's pleasure'. Maids as forthright as this were rare. Fear of a bad character reference kept most of them outwardly submissive. Instead they preferred to show their discontent by moving to another post.

Such flighty conduct would certainly have been condemned by the Adamses; indeed, a desire to induce greater moral rectitude among domestics seems to have been one of the reasons they wrote their book. Their view was that the social order had been divinely ordained, and young people entering service for the first time were firmly advised to submit themselves 'to the controul (*sic*) of those whom they engage to serve'. In this ideal world there was no place for backsliders like William Tayler or the Carlyles' recalcitrant Isabella. *The Complete Servant* was designed to produce a meek, well-informed and skilful domestic labour force, devoted to the interests of the employer, and fully conversant with the duties and responsibilities which were attached to any particular post. Guidance was given on legal rights and obligations, and advice proffered on the virtues of thrift.

With the help of carefully accumulated savings, a retired servant might perhaps run a lodging-house or an inn, like the ex-butler who advertised in the *Gloucester Journal* of 1781 that he was taking over the King's Head Inn, Ross, Herefordshire, after having it fitted up 'in a genteel Manner'. Similarly, Adam Care, 'late Coachman to the Bishop of Gloucester', announced in the same newspaper that he had taken over the business of William Walker, a Tewkesbury haulier. 'He engages to haul any Sort of Goods upon the same terms William Walker used to charge'.

By the late eighteenth century, with rare exceptions, even the most senior domestic posts were filled by the children of labourers, artisans, and small farmers, rather than by the offspring of reduced gentlefolk and substantial farmers, as had often been the case earlier in the century. Both Samuel and Sarah Adams rose to the highest positions in a well-to-do household from lowly beginnings as footboy and maid-of-all-work, respectively—in Samuel's case after attendance at an endowed charity school. However, as *The Complete Servant* amply demonstrates, their humble origins certainly did not mean that they were badly educated. In the text there are several references to leading literary and political figures, including William Shakespeare, Samuel Johnson, Lord Chesterfield and William Cobbett. It is unlikely that many of their successors a century later would have been so well read.

Landed families in the eighteenth and early nineteenth centuries customarily drew most of their servants from the children of tenants or estate workers. When that supply failed, friends would be consulted, a method widely adopted lower down the social scale. Thus when Parson Woodforde moved to Norfolk in the 1770s he obtained his first two maids on the personal recommendation of a fellow cleric's wife, while his footman came with him from his native Somerset. Mrs Thrale, Dr Johnson's friend, asked an acquaintance to find her a new housekeeper, 'such as you *know* will suit us; a good country housewife, who can salt Bacon, cure Hams, see also to the baking, etc. and be an active manager of and for a dozen troublesome servants'.

The reference to a 'good country housewife' is significant in that most employers preferred to get their servants from rural areas. They were thought to be cleaner, healthier and more honest than their urban counterparts. Indeed, such was the prejudice against servants born in London that there were allegations that those who had lost their places not infrequently left the city, in order to return again posing as new arrivals. Meanwhile, among young villagers, the capital proved so magnetic that according to the *Gentleman's Magazine* of 1793, 'vast numbers' were continually being drawn from the countryside to the metropolis in order to enter 'the service of noblemen and gentlemen'. As a contemporary rhetorically asked, 'What young Damsel that knows of the Lord Mayor's show . . . don't wish to be a witness of its splendour?'

Where personal contacts failed, local tradesmen and shopkeepers might be approached, with inns and beer shops widely used by male servants as informal labour exchanges. In the 1780s the *London Adviser and Guide* considered this one of the best ways of recruiting staff, and that view was echoed almost eighty years later in Mrs Beeton's *Book of Household Management*. In country districts, and especially among farmers' wives, servants were also recruited at hiring fairs, along with male farm workers. Often maids attending these fairs carried some distinctive insignia to indicate their particular skills. Cooks, for instance, wore a red ribbon and carried a basting spoon, while housemaids wore blue and held a broom.

Advertising in newspapers, which was to become popular in Victorian times, was only in its infancy in the late eighteenth century. Nevertheless a few servants were beginning to use this method, like the butler and steward, 'near 40 Years of Age, of unexceptionable Character', whose virtues were proclaimed in the *Gloucester Journal* of 2 April 1781. He was enthusiastically described as 'of an active Disposition, very capable with his Pen, is fond of a Country Life, and . . . would be happy in making himself as serviceable as possible to any Nobleman, Gentleman, or Lady, who might think proper to employ him'.

But it was only when the demand for servants accelerated in the nineteenth century, and the general level of literacy improved, that newspaper advertising came into its own as a major means of recruiting staff. None of the advertisements in the *Gloucester Journal* during the early 1780s was for female servants, probably because it was felt this might encourage prostitution. It was for similar moral reasons that registry offices were frowned upon in the late eighteenth century—'markets for pimps and procuresses', one writer described them. To counter these abuses, in 1813 a free registry was established in Hatton Garden by the London Society for the Encouragement of Faithful Female Servants. No servant could be entered on its books unless she had been at least two years in one place, or had not been out to service before. In this way the reputation of registry offices was gradually improved. By 1842, the *Post Office Directory* of London was listing the names of ten offices, and this had increased to sixteen by 1848. A year later Bristol claimed to have eleven, including one run by a Mrs Mary Millard. She was still in business a decade later and was then describing it as the 'Original and Oldest Established Registry Office in the City of Bristol, Conducted by the same Proprietoress for upwards of 70 Years'. By then the number of registry offices listed in London had almost reached forty.

Although *The Complete Servant* did not ignore the duties and responsibilities of the employer, the main emphasis of the book was on the servant's role. This was entirely appropriate, given the background of the two authors, for both had held a formidable range of domestic posts. In Samuel's case these included footboy, groom, footman, valet, butler, and house-steward, while Sarah rose from maid-of-all-work to become progressively housemaid, laundry-maid, under-cook, housekeeper and lady's maid, and finally housekeeper. They were thus writing from a wealth of practical experience, and had begun to make notes for their book even while they were still in service. Yet after their retirement they remain curiously shadowy figures. Although their book was apparently written while they were living in Edgware Road, London, they were, it seems, in temporary rented accommodation since their names do not appear in the rate books for that area during the mid-1820s. Nor has it been possible to trace any Will. Their sole memorial, therefore, must remain their book, which not only served a useful purpose in its own day, but provides a splendid insight into domestic life and attitudes in Georgian England.

PAMELA HORN

SOURCES

John Beresford ed., *The Diary of a Country Parson 1758–1802 by James Woodforde* (OUP World's Classics edn., 1967).
E. W. Bovill, *English Country Life, 1780–1830* (1962).
Charlotte Brontë, *Jane Eyre* (1973 edn.).
Census of Population, Reports for 1831, 1851 and 1901.
Englefield House Servants' Book at Berkshire Record Office, D/EBy.A.130.
Gentleman's Magazine, 1793 and 1809.
Gloucester Journal, 1781 and 1825.
Mary Hardy's Diary, ed. B. Cozens-Hardy (1968).
Harrison, Harrod & Co., *Directory and Gazetteer of Bristol and Gloucestershire* (1859).
J. Jean Hecht, *The Domestic Servant Class in Eighteenth-Century England* (1956).
Thea Holme, *The Carlyles at Home* (1965).
Pamela Horn, *The Rise and Fall of the Victorian Servant* (1975) (paper back edn. 1986). Macdonald and Gill.
Hunt & Co.'s *Directory of Gloucester and Bristol* (1849).
Dr William Kitchiner, *The Cook's Oracle* (2nd edn. 1818 and 4th edn. 1822).
Dorothy Marshall, 'The Domestic Servant of the Eighteenth Century' in *Economica* No. 25 (April, 1929).
Dorothy Marshall, *The English Domestic Servant in History* (Historical Association pamphlet No. G.13, 1949).
Mrs William Parkes, *Domestic Duties; or, Instructions to Young Married Ladies on the Management of their Households* (1st edn. 1825 and 3rd edn. 1828).
Post Office Directory of London, 1842, 1848 and 1859.
The Servant's Friend (n.d. c.1780).
Merlin Waterson, *The Servants' Hall* (1980).
Dorothy Wise ed., *Diary of William Tayler, Footman, 1837* (1962).

ORIGINAL PREFACE

DEDICATION

ADVICE TO SERVANTS IN GENERAL

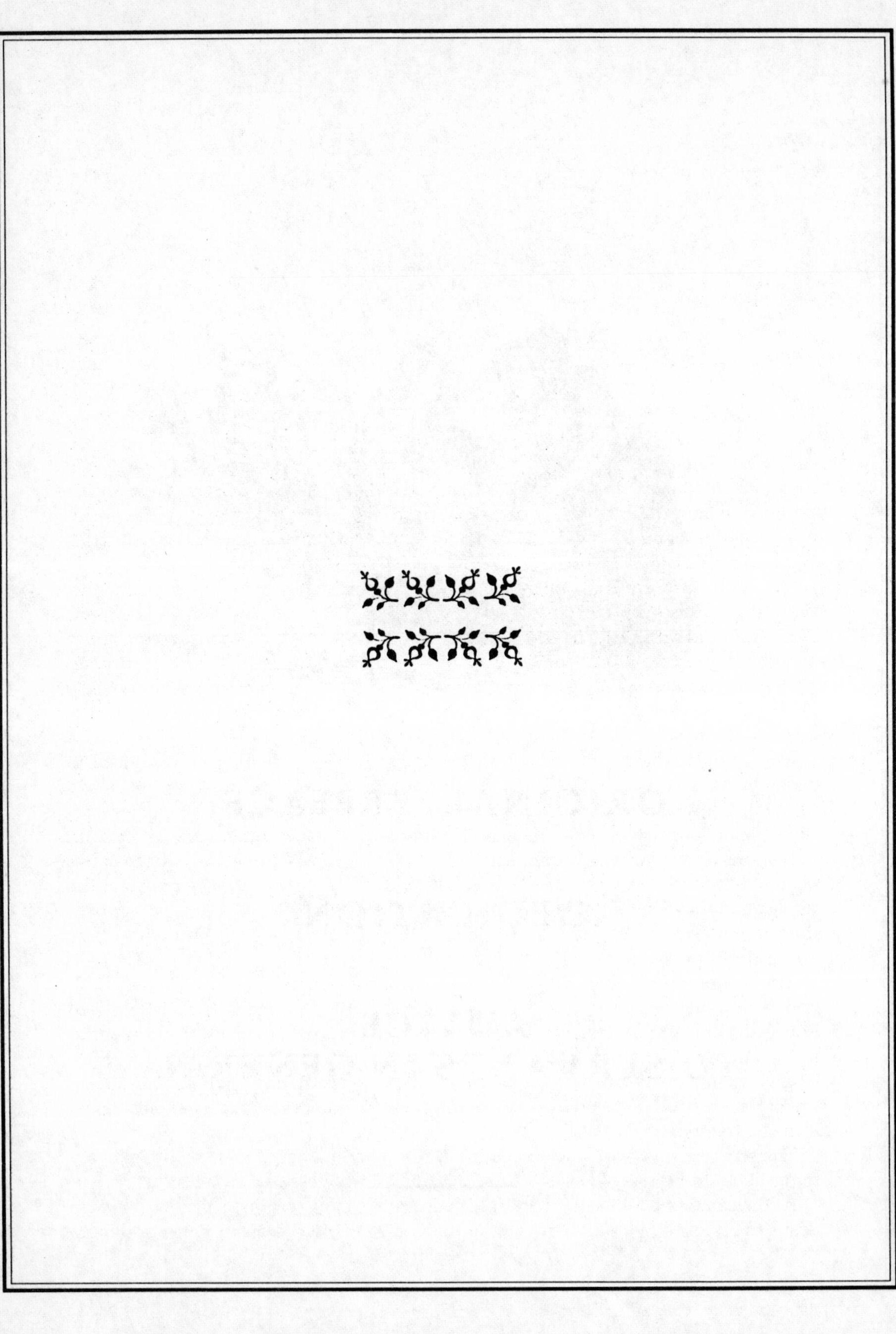

ORIGINAL PREFACE

As no relations in society are so numerous and universal as those of Masters and Servants—as those of Household Duties and the performers of them—so it is proportionally important that they should be well defined and understood. It is a species of knowledge as important to the head of a family as necessary to the servant; and, if thoroughly studied, would relieve life of half its anxieties and vexations.

Yet, till the present book, no special attempt to define these relations, and illustrate these duties has ever been made. We have had Sermons on the moral obligations of masters and servants, and many books of religious advice, addressed to the latter, all good in their way; but we have had no work, which, like the present, addresses itself to the actual personal practice of their duties; which defines them as they actually belong to the various classes; and instructs servants in the way and mode of performing them with skill, advantage, and success.

The want of such a manual of duty and practice having often been noticed in servants' halls, in families in which the authors of this book have resided, it occurred to them, many years since, to make notes, with a view to a work like the present. They hoped long ago to have been able to submit them to the public; but the constant avocations of servitude rendering it impossible to digest their materials, the task has been deferred till they have been enabled to retire on a moderate competency; the publication may therefore be regarded as the legacy of their old age to servants of the present and future generations, and as the last duty which in this world they are likely to perform.

The author, educated in a foundation school, entered service as a footboy, in 1770, and during fifty years he served successively as groom, footman, valet, butler, and house-steward. His Wife began the world as maid of all work, then served as house-maid, laundry-maid, under-cook, housekeeper and lady's maid, and, finally, for above twenty years, as housekeeper in a very large establishment. Their experience is, therefore, such as has fallen to the lot of few, and they have freely and fully displayed it in the following pages.

They profess no skill in authorship, their sole object having been to set down every thing likely to be useful, in language that may be understood by all.

At the same time, important and necessary as the book will be to all Servants who desire to perform their duty with ability, and to rise in their career to higher and more profitable situations, yet it will prove equally useful in the parlour, by assisting MASTERS and MISTRESSES of families in arranging their establishments, advising them of their own duties, and enabling them to estimate the merits of valuable servants. It may, indeed, be a question, whether the volume will not be as desirable to those who are served as to those who serve.

Conviction of its probable use to all classes, led A LADY OF HIGH RANK, in whose family Mrs. Adams resided, to honour her with advice and assistance in some articles, particularly in that of Governess, and it is to be regretted that a delicate reserve prevents the acknowledgement being made by name.

EDGEWARE ROAD,
June, 1825.

DEDICATION

Respectfully addressed to the Heads of Families

OF THE

UNITED KINGDOM

We feel persuaded that the following work, professedly written for the use and instruction of Domestic Servants, may, with great propriety, be dedicated to the Illustrious Heads of Families in the United Kingdom;—to you, who are the immediate *Patrons* of that numerous Class of the Community.

Dr. Johnson held as a *maxim*, that *"Every man's first care is necessarily Domestic."* Independent, therefore, of public Engagements,—of Politics, the Arts, Sciences, and Literature;—of attention to Horses, Hounds, &c. it is considered that the first care, and the peculiar province of the Master of a Family, is his *Revenue;* and that attention to his Land-Stewards, Agents, and Tenants, and to his *Expenditure,* are the principal objects that most immediately solicit his regard; and when a gentleman has satisfied himself that his real or *net* Income exceeds his Expenditure, then, and *not till then,* may he consider himself as an Independent Man;—for, "it is not abundance that maketh rich, but Economy"; and Lord Chesterfield has truly remarked, that "great Fortunes frequently seduce their possessors to ruinous profusion." The great *Bacon* has also observed, "that he who would live *even* with the world should calculate his Expenses at *half* his Income, and he who would grow Rich, at *one-third.*" A few Minutes in every Day, spent in keeping a regular Account of all Monies *received* and *spent, Dr.* and *Cr.* will afford any gentleman the satisfaction of knowing the true state of his affairs,—will operate actively against excess of Expenditure,—will imperceptibly teach him the art of *practical Economy,* and will enable him to appropriate due portions of his Income to the support of his different Establishments.

With a view to this latter point, the following *Rule,* though given in round numbers, may be considered as affording Gentlemen a brief, but tolerably correct, idea of the most eligible and practical mode of appropriating a large Income.—

Viz. 33 per Cent.	or One-third, for Household Expenses, including Provisions and all other Articles of Household Consumption.
25 per Cent.	or One-fourth, for Servants and Equipage including Horses, Carriages, and Liveries.
25 per Cent.	or One-fourth, for Clothes, Education of Children, Medical Assistance, Pocket, Private, and Extra Expenses; including Entertainments, &c.
12½ per Cent.	or One-eighth, for Rent, Taxes, and Repairs of House and Furniture.
4½ per Cent.	as a Reserve for Contingencies.

Smaller Incomes must be appropriated in a different manner; and according to the number of Children in the family: thus the Expense of a family with Children will be from 1-4th to 1-3rd for each of the Principals, and about 1-10th or 1-12th for each Child.

As Hints to the *Formation* of a Household, or the *Reformation* of an Establishment, we insert the following list of the number and description of Servants that are usually employed, according to Income; viz.—

Income per annum	
£100 or guineas.	*A Widow* or other *unmarried Lady*, may keep a *Young Maid Servant*, at a low salary; say from 5 to 10 Guineas a year.
£150 to £180.	*A Gentleman and Lady without Children*, may afford to keep a better *Servant-Maid*, at about 10 or 12 Guineas.
About £200.	*Ditto. A professed Servant-Maid of All-Work*, at from 12 to 14 Guineas.
£300.	*Ditto, with one, two, or three Children*. Two Maid-Servants.
£400.	*Ditto, Ditto*. Three female Servants, or two and a Boy; viz.—A Cook, House-Maid, and Nursery-Maid, or else, instead of the latter, a Boy,—with a Gardener occasionally.
£500.	*Ditto, Ditto*. Three females and a Boy; viz.—A Cook, House-Maid, and Nursery-Maid, with a Boy as Groom, and to assist in the House and Garden. A Gardener occasionally.
£500 to £600.	*A Gentleman and Lady with Children*. Three Females and one Man; viz.—A Cook, House-Maid, and a Nursery-Maid, or other Female-Servant; with a Livery-Servant, as Groom and Footman. A Gardener occasionally.
£600 to £750.	*Ditto, Ditto*. Three Females and two Men; viz.—A Cook, House-Maid, and another Female Servant; a Footman, and a Groom, who may assist in the Garden, and a Gardener occasionally.
£1000 to £1500.	*Ditto, Ditto*. Four Females and three Men; viz.—A Cook, two House-Maids, a Nursery-Maid, or other Female Servant; a Coachman, Footman, and a Man to assist in the Stable and Garden.
£1500 to £2000.	*Ditto, Ditto*. Six Female and five Men-Servants; viz.—A Cook, Housekeeper, two House-Maids, Kitchen-Maid, and Nursery-Maid, or other Female Servant; with a Coachman, Groom, Footman, Gardener, and an assistant in the Garden and Stable.
£2000 to £3000.	*Ditto, Ditto*. Eight Female and eight Men-Servants; viz.—A Cook, Lady's-Maid, two House-Maids, Nurse, Nursery-Maid, Kitchen-Maid, and Laundry-Maid; with a Butler, Valet, Coachman, two Grooms, a Footman, and two Gardeners.
£3000 to £4000.	*Ditto, Ditto*. Nine Female and eleven Male Servants; viz.—A Housekeeper, Cook, Lady's-Maid, Nurse, two House-Maids, a Laundry-Maid, Kitchen-Maid, and a Nursery-Maid; with a Butler, Coachman, two Grooms, Valet, two Footmen, two Gardeners, and a Labourer.

£4000 to £5000. *Ditto, Ditto.* Eleven Female and thirteen Male Servants; viz.—A Housekeeper, Cook, Lady's-Maid, Nurse, two House-Maids, Laundry-Maid, Still-Room Maid, Nursery-Maid, Kitchen-Maid, and Scullion, with Butler, Valet, House-Steward, Coachman, two Grooms, one Assistant Ditto, two Footmen, three Gardeners, and a Labourer.

We have been favoured with the following as the present Household Establishment of a respectable Country Gentleman, with a young family, whose Net Income is from 16,000l. to 18,000l. a Year, and whose expenses do not exceed 7000l.; viz.—

	Guineas
House-Keeper	24
Female Teacher	30
Lady's-Maid	20
Head Nurse	20
Second Ditto	10
Nursery-Maid	7
Upper House-Maid	15
Under House-Maid	14
Kitchen-Maid	14
Upper Laundry-Maid	14
Under Ditto	10
Dairy-Maid	8
Second Ditto	7
Still-Room Maid	9
Scullion	9
A French Man-Cook	80
Butler	50
Coachman	28
Footman	24
Under Ditto	20
Groom.—His Liveries and a Gratuity.	
Lady's Groom	12

Nursery-Room Boy, Clothes and a gratuity.
Head Game-Keeper 70 Guineas a year, and 13s. per Week for Board-Wages;—a Cottage and Firing.
Under Ditto, one Guinea per Week.
Gardener 40 Guineas a year, and 13s. per Week for Board-Wages;—a House and Firing.
Assistant Ditto, 12s. per Week.

The Board Wages of Servants in general, when the family is absent, is 10s. per Week, for the females, and 12s. per Week for males.—Perhaps all the servants on a large establishment may be reckoned at an average of 10s. per head, per Week, expense, for Board. The Men are allowed a Pot of Ale per day, and the Women a Pint, besides table-beer.

Besides the ordinary establishment of servants, noblemen and gentlemen of superior fortune employ land-stewards, bailiffs, woodwards, game-keepers, park-keepers, huntsmen, whippers-in, racing-grooms, jockeys, and others of inferior capacities: also men-cooks, groom of the chambers, page, lady's-coachman, postillion and footman, seamstress, second lady's-maid, chamber-maids, boy for the steward's room, another for the hall, and various other servants.

Having premised thus much as to income, and its proportionate appropriation, we next proceed to offer a few hints on such parts of interior management, as in most families are considered as belonging to the lady, or mistress of the house.

The first is, naturally, the attention due to her husband and children—to make home, *"sweet home"*, the pleasing refuge of a husband, fatigued, perhaps, by his intercourse with a jarring world,—to be his enlightened companion, and the chosen friend of his bosom.

In your manner to your servants, be firm, without being severe, and kind, without being familiar. Never converse familiarly with them, unless on business, or on some point connected with their improvement; but with this reserve, and distance of manner, be particularly careful to maintain kindness, gentleness, and respect for their feelings. Their patience is often unnecessarily exercised, and their tempers wantonly irritated. A lady, who filled every station of life with honour, both to her head and heart, attending the death-bed of an old domestic, who had been thirty years in her service—"How do you find yourself to-day, Mary?" said the mistress, taking hold of her withered hand. "Is that you, my *darling mistress*!" and a beam of joy overspread the old woman's face; "O, yes," she added, looking up, "it is you, my kind, my *mannerly* mistress!" The poor old creature said no more; but she had, by that last simple sentence, expressed volumes of panegyric on her amiable mistress. Human nature is the same in all stations; and if you strive to convince your servants that you have a generous and compassionate regard for their comfort, they will, in return, evince their gratitude. If to protect and encourage virtue be the best preventive from vice, then will your deserving female servants be liberally encouraged.

Let your commands to your servants be consistent and reasonable; and then mildly, but firmly, insist on obedience to them.—"My servants never remember what I tell them to do," is a complaint but too common, but that might, in some degree, be obviated. Let them see that you will not pass over any neglect of orders; and when they find that this decisive measure is accompanied with kindness and consideration, and that you are not to be disobeyed with impunity, they will soon learn to remember what you command them to do. A little effort very easily overcomes a bad memory.

It is very disheartening to a poor servant to be continually found fault with. Praise and reward them when you can;—human nature will not bear constant chiding.

Never keep servants, however excellent they may be in their stations, whom you know to be guilty of immorality.

When servants are ill, their mistress will, doubtless, recollect that she is their patroness as well as their employer, and will not only remit their labour, but render them all the assistance of proper medicine, food, and comfort, in their power.—Tender assiduity is half a cure; it is a balsam to the mind, which has a powerful effect on the body—soothes the severest pains, and strengthens beyond the richest cordial. The poor dependent creatures may have no where to go to—no one else to turn to; and their pale and impaired looks will always have a claim on your sympathy.

"Economy," says Mr. Cobbett, "is management."—The fact is, that management and regularity, is economy verified by practice; and all persons ought to regulate their conduct by circumstances. A moderate income, appropriated to the expenses of housekeeping with prudence and economy, without parsimony, but banishing superfluities and preventing waste, may be made sufficient to furnish every comfort in life; and, strange as it may appear to those in affluence, an income of from 150l. to 200l. a year, will be enough to maintain a man and wife, with two or three children, and a servant girl.

The mistress of a family will always recollect that, in all cases, the welfare and good character of her household depends on her own active superintendance.

Though habits of domestic management are now generally precluded in the education of young ladies of the superior class, yet, happily, attention to family concerns is not unfrequently found in those of less exalted rank, whose minds, amidst the blandishments of modern accomplishments, have been taught to relish, as in days of yore, the more rational, solid, and lasting pleasures, of a social and comfortable home. And were young ladies early instructed in the delights of domestic occupation, before they enter the delusive scenes, presented by modern modes of dissipation, we should probably find the number of votaries to private happiness greatly increased, and a life of domestic employment would become the source of numberless gratifications.

One of the principal objects of the mistress of the house is, the economy or management of the table, the general display of which will evince her judgment and taste; and this will be shown, not so much by the profusion with which the table is covered, as by its neat and pleasing appearance, according to the present fashion, so far as regards elegance, combined with frugality,—the circumstances of fortune and condition being also considered.—People in business should not imitate the pomp and splendour of high rank, nor should those of the higher circles descend to such frugal arrangements as in them would appear to be parsimonious.

The prudent manager will consider the number of her guests, and consult their appetites, rather than feast their eyes; thus will she be enabled to entertain them much oftener, and much better, at the same expense.

It is well understood that the mistress of a family should have, at least, a competent knowledge in the art of carving, not only as it enables her to do the honours of the table with propriety, but with a view to frugality also; and if the young ladies of a family were to practise, under the direction of their mother, when there is no company, they would, in time, become quite *au fait* to this graceful and elegant accomplishment.

An esteemed writer of the present day, has introduced to public view, a pleasing picture of a small and well-regulated family, of which the following is a slight sketch:—

"The mistress of the family is a good manager, without any ostentatious display of it.—Elegantly nice, without being a slave to dress or furniture—Easy and affable with her servants, but firm in her commands,—every one appearing to be contented and happy.—The household business going on regularly, like a good clock;—and every thing being kept in its proper place. No scolding in the kitchen or servants' hall.—The table plentifully covered, but not with incitements to luxury; the food plain and in season, and sent up well dressed;—with a few well chosen luxuries introduced, when company is asked."

Ladies, whose minds are framed for the practical enjoyment of domestic comfort, will admire and copy this beautiful picture!

ADVICE TO SERVANTS IN GENERAL

Young persons, on their first entering into service, should endeavour to divest themselves of former habits, and devote themselves to the control of those whom they engage to serve. They will probably find everything different from what they have been accustomed to at home, or in common life; and as their mode of living will be greatly altered, if not wholly changed, so must be their minds and manners. They should endeavour to discard every low habit and way of thinking, if such they have; and as there will be set before them, by those of superior rank, and cultivated understanding, the best modes of conduct and the most approved behaviour, they will wisely take advantage of the opportunity which Providence fortunately presents to them, to cultivate their minds and improve their principles.

The grand foundation of your good character must be Industry, fidelity to your employers, and an inviolable attachment to truth, both in words and deeds. To utter a falsehood to the prejudice of others, argues malice and baseness—to lie in excuse of one's self, guilt and cowardice;—in both cases it evinces a design to deceive, with a view to benefit one's self by the deceit;—besides, a liar is always in fear of being detected, and if once found out, he sinks into contempt, and is deservedly divested of all credit—all confidence—and all society.

But truth in speech must be accompanied by integrity and fidelity in all your dealings; for it is impossible for a dishonest person to be a good servant; therefore, let no temptation prevail on you to part with these inestimable jewels; nor suffer yourself even to wish to convert the property of another to your own use; more especially when it is confided to your charge; for breach of trust is a heinous aggravation of dishonesty. And, always remember, that "Honesty is the best policy."

Avoid tale-bearing, for that is a vice of a pernicious nature, and generally turns out to the disadvantage of those who practise it. Those who cannot help telling all that they hear, will be supposed to tell more than they know, and will, consequently, be discredited.

Carefully avoid all reproachful, indecent, or even familiar terms in speaking of your master, mistress, or superiors; and, on the other hand, endeavour, at all times, to vindicate them from the open aspersions or latent insinuations of others. There is nothing more detestable than defamation.—Avoid it.

To know— to be thoroughly master of your business in the department you undertake, is indispensably necessary; and not only to know the several branches of your duty, both by theory and practice, but to be determined, from principle, to do it. In order to do this, let your whole conduct be actuated by diligence, and governed by temperance. Banish sloth and the love of ease; and, as poor Richard says, "up, and be doing."

Idleness is a great source of evil, and whilst we give way to its enjoyment, we sacrifice both the duties and the best purposes of our existence.

But, it is not enough merely to avoid sloth, for you must be guarded against the allurements of pleasure—pleasure, when it becomes a business, but too frequently makes business a torment; and as it is impossible to attend to your duty and follow your pleasures, the inevitable consequence must be loss of place, disgrace, and poverty.—Not that you are to debar yourself from innocent amusement, at proper times, and with moderation; it is not, nor can it be expected of you, who are to get your bread by the sweat of your brow, that you are not to reap the harvest of your labours; neither the laws of God nor man exact this of you; but unlawful and intemperate pleasures are interdicted, as alike detrimental to your employers,—your morals,—your character,—your health,—and your purse.

Intemperance, or excess, is a pleasurable evil,—it smiles and seduces—enchants and destroys. It assumes a variety of shapes, all tending to flatter the appetite and inflame desires;—it presents to each the allurement to which he is most prone, and to all a pleasing poison that impairs the body, enervates the mind, and imperceptibly destroys all the energies necessary to our happiness and advancement in life.

Above all things, then—be temperate.—Avoid excess in eating and drinking—"One expensive mouth, will wear out several pairs of hands,"—and, "one shilling will appease the wants of nature as effectually as a pound."

The loss of health and the loss of character are the certain consequences; and the debauch of the evening is followed by pains and sickness in the morning, when that which was before poison, is administered as the cure! Practice becomes habitual, and thus a whole life is frequently wasted in debauchery; poverty itself only cutting off the means, not the inclination; and the unhappy object himself, destitute of health, character, and friends, is left to pine and sink in misery and contempt.

Intemperance in dress is another evil that ought to be carefully guarded against. In most men this argues both weakness and effeminacy; but in men-servants an affectation of this kind is unpardonable—and in females it opens a door to temptation and extravagance, which but too frequently ends in ruin.

The virtue of silence is highly commendable, and will contribute greatly to your ease and prosperity. Those who talk much cannot always talk well; and many much oftener incur censure than praise. The best proof of wisdom is to talk little, but to hear much—Remember, "A silent tongue argues a wise head." Never talk of yourself, —but when others speak of themselves, listen to them;—such attention will please them, and probably profit yourself, as it is a chance but something escapes them that may afford a clue to their whole character. If it be thus dangerous to speak much of one's self, it is much more so to take freedoms with others. A jest may tickle, but if it hurt any one, resentment may follow, that in some way or other may be injurious. —Always remember to hold the secrets of the family sacred, as none, not even the least of these, may be divulged with impuntiy.

Quarrels are much more easily avoided than made up; let it not, therefore, be in the power of trifles to ruffle your temper. A weathercock is the sport of every wind; and a choleric man is sometimes exposed to the scorn, at others to the resentment, and always to the abhorrence of all around him. For these reasons rather wink at all small injuries than study to avenge them—"He that to destroy a single bee that has offended him, should throw down the hive, instead of one enemy will have made a thousand."

It is abundantly better to study the good will of all, than to excite the resentment of any. Make a trial, therefore, of your affability, and you will find your own happiness and the goodwill of all around you, to be the certain result.

We would further recommend to you to practise frugality; it is a virtue which is intimately connected with, and leads to our best prospects in life.

Whilst on the important subject of frugality, we cannot do better than to recommend to your notice THE SAVINGS BANK. These most useful and excellent establishments are to be found in every district, and offer, to provident and well-disposed servants, a means of depositing small sums, in perfect safety, for the purpose of accumulating with interest, to be resorted to in case of illness,—any unforeseen occurrence,—or for the purpose of establishing themselves in some way of business that may make them comfortable to the end of their days.

What we have already said, may be considered as addressed chiefly to men servants; we have therefore to add a few admonitory precepts, particularly appropriated to our female readers.

One of the most advantageous qualifications in all servants, and particularly in females, is that of preserving a good temper, and endeavouring, to the utmost of their abilities, to give satisfaction. Possessed of a strong desire to please, you will seldom fail of doing so.

Cleanliness is another qualification incumbent on every female servant, and particularly in Cooks, and those employed in the department of the kitchen. These should be very careful to keep themselves,—every place,—and all the utensils used in cooking, perfectly clean and neat.

We have already remarked, that those who are fond of telling all that they hear, are very naturally suspected of telling more than they hear. The best rule is, to do your own duty conscientiously, and leave others to take care of theirs; by this means you will preserve peace and acquire the love of all your fellow servants, without offending your employers; who, even though they may appear to give countenance to your tale, will not in their hearts approve of your conduct.

Take great care how you contract new acquaintances, for to be easily drawn into a familiarity with strangers must be attended with ill consequences to yourselves, and those with whom you live. Never accept the invitations of other servants, nor go to feast at the expense of their masters and mistresses; as you must, in that case, be deemed an interloper, at least;—besides, it lays you under an obligation to return the treat, and induces you, after their example, to make free with the property of your own employers, under a consciousness of guilt, and a continual fear of detection.

Give nothing away without the knowledge and approbation of your employers, nor commit wilful waste, for that is a crime which seldom goes unpunished.

All duties are reciprocal. If you hope to obtain favour, endeavour to deserve it. A steady perseverance in the duties of your station is the only sure course infallibly to promote your progress to independence.

In commencing a new service, determine to do your duty in it; and avoid every thing that you found was displeasing in your former place. Judge of your employers from your own observation, and their behaviour to you, and not from any idle reports you may hear to their prejudice. Should you find yourself in a reputable situation, but yet are uncomfortable, through the unkind or unfeeling tempers of your superiors, double your own diligence and civility, and avoid every thing, as much as possible, that might, however unwarrantably, excite their suspicion. By this you may improve their temper and conduct towards yourself; and the very vexation they have occasioned, may dispose them to make their domestics more comfortable, and themselves more happy.

Endeavour to serve with such good will, readiness of mind, and attention to the lawful interest and convenience of your employers, as to render your services almost necessary to them; that they may know and feel that they are blessed, above many of their neighbours, in having gotten a good servant, one who serves, not with eye-service as a man-pleaser, but in simplicity of heart as a Christian. You will be sure to gain esteem by cheerfully doing any lawful necessary service; though it were not agreed for when you were hired.

Every employer has a right to establish rules for his household; therefore, do nothing in your master's house, or with your mistress's business, that you feel obliged to conceal, to keep your situation; for then, you may depend upon it, whatever it be, it is wrong in itself, and will bring you to harm.

Industry is necessary for ALL, that they may lead a useful life; but it is especially needful to those who engage to serve others. Idleness hath clothed many with rags. Your wages are the yearly pay for your honesty, and your time; therefore lying late in bed, or being over long on errands, or making frivolous excuses to be from home, have occasioned many suspicions—deprived many of good places, and eventually of good characters. "He that is slothful in his work is brother to him that is a great waster." Exercise due diligence as to what are the particular duties of your station. Make it your study to put it out of the power of a reasonable mistress to find fault.

Dress as becomes your station, if you desire to please your employers,—to avoid personal harm, and to diminish the number and power of your temptations. The happiness of society arises from each of us keeping in our station, and being contented with it. Among other ways of shewing your wisdom, dressing clean and neat, is of the greatest importance. By this means, you may save a little money to assist your relations, or yourself when unemployed, or in time of need.

A female servant should never make friendships with, or take the advice of, milk people, butchers' or bakers' servants, keepers of chandlers' shops, green-stalls, charwomen, &c.; for mostly they seek only their own interest and profit in every thing. If any proposal that is new, or unexpectedly profitable, force itself on your notice, do not act on your own opinion, nor hastily, but, confidentially, consult your mistress, or some relation, else you may be as hastily ensnared to your utter undoing.

For want of the confidence and esteem I allude to, there seems to be, in most families, two separate interests—that of the employers, and that of the servants.—Some servants communicate none of their personal affairs to their mistresses, and therefore mistresses are not incited to take any special interest in their future welfare. Hence, although such parties may live a considerable time together, they are almost strangers, and nothing like friendship can take place. This is a great loss to a servant. If you expect to have confidence placed in you, be sincere in all your expressions, and open, explicit, and communicative in all your dealings.

Be very careful of your reputation for virtue and discretion in regard of the other sex; for it is the foundation of your happiness in this world; and the loss of it will bring you to misery. Avoid as much as possible going out in the evening, especially on frivolous errands. Be cautious as to whom you give your company. "Evil communications corrupt good manners." Never go to fairs, dances, nor to the theatres. Ask yourself, before you engage in any pleasuring scheme—what may be the probable end of it?

On all unnecessary occasions, avoid as much as possible being alone with the other sex: as the greatest mischiefs happen from small circumstances. Who that is wise would risk the loss of her virtue and happiness on mere promises, made by men of worthless character, and which are made only to be broken? Never trust entirely to your own fortitude—it can only be tried by opportunity; and if, in this case, it fail but once, you are undone! The best resolve you can form is, never to give opportunity to the tempter. A reserved modesty is the best safeguard of virtue.

If a virtuous affection seems to be rising, be sure you instantly calculate on the age and temper, religious conduct, and probable ability of the man to maintain a family, before you suffer your mind to be carried away, lest your affections run headlong, and at length are taken advantage of, to the complete loss of your comfort.

It is a more serious thing to leave a good situation than many are aware of. You may never obtain such another place, all things considered; and may be long unsettled. "A rolling stone gathers no moss." A servant that is not stationary seldom obtains friends that are able and willing to assist her. You now know all the inconveniences that attend your present situation, but you cannot know whether much greater may not be found in the next you obtain. Most situations have their advantages and disadvantages. Calculate, as far as you can, upon both, as they are found in the place where you now are. Higher wages for another service is no proof that it would be a better one, all things considered.

Nothing is so comfortable and creditable to all parties, as when a servant lives many years in the same family. Such servants never want a real friend. Though you may perhaps obtain a new service by a three months' character, you will be respected if you have lived three years in your situation, but still more, if you have lived seven.

The great master principle of all faithful service is an earnest desire and endeavour is to act according to the WILL OF GOD. The reason why servants as well as others, are so defective and partial in the discharge of their duties, and therefore are so often uncomfortable and distressed, is, that they are not influenced as they ought to be, by this prnciple. Those, who think of their need of God's help, and love him with their hearts, and minds, and strength, he will love and honour. "I love them that love me," saith the Almighty. "They that honour me, I will honour; and those who despise me, shall be lightly esteemed."

HOUSEKEEPER

STILL ROOM MAID

7

THE HOUSEKEEPER

The situation of a housekeeper, in almost every family, is of great importance.—She superintends nearly the whole of the domestic establishment,—has generally the control and direction of the servants, particularly of the female servants—has the care of the household furniture and linen—of all the grocery—dried and other fruits, spices, condiments, soap, candles, and stores of all kinds, for culinary and other domestic uses. She makes all the pickles, preserves, and sometimes the best pastry.—She generally distils and prepares all the compound and simple waters, and spirits, essential and other oils, perfumery, cosmetics, and similar articles that are prepared at home, for domestic purposes. In short, she is the locum tenens, the Lady Bountiful, and the active representative of the mistress of the family; and is expected to do, or to see done, everything that appertains to the good and orderly management of the household.

She ought to be a steady middle-aged woman, of great experience in her profession, and a tolerable knowledge of the world.—In her conduct, she should be moral, exemplary, and assiduous, as the harmony, comfort, and economy of the family will greatly depend on her example; and she must know, that no occurrence can be too trifling for her attention, that may lead to these results, and whereby waste and unnecessary expense may be avoided.

When the entire management of the servants is deputed to her, her situation becomes the more arduous and important. If servants have hardships to undergo, she will let them see, that she feels for the necessity of urging them. To cherish the desire of pleasing in them, she will convince them, that they may succeed in their endeavours to please her. Human nature is the same in all stations. Convince the servants that you have a considerate regard for their comforts, and they will be found to be grateful, and to reward your attention by their own assiduity: besides, nothing is so endearing as being courteous to our inferiors.

Female servants who would pursue an honest course, have numberless difficulties to contend with, and should, therefore, be treated kindly. The housekeeper in a great family, has ample means of doing good; and she will, doubtless, recollect that it is a part of her duty to protect and encourage virtue, as the best preventive from vice.

In families where there is a house-steward, the marketing will be done, and the tradesmen's bills will be collected, examined, and discharged, by him; but in many families, the business of marketing, and of keeping the accounts, devolves on the housekeeper. It is, therefore, incumbent on her to be well informed of the prices and qualities of all articles of household consumption in general use; and of the best times and seasons for procuring them, in order that by comparing prices and qualities, she may be able to substitute those that are most reasonable, but equally to her purpose, and best attainable, for others that are most costly or more scarce.

Before the housekeeper goes to market, she will look over the larder with the cook, especially when company is expected, and on a Saturday, and consider well what things are wanted, not forgetting even the smaller articles, that so there may be no necessity for sending out in a hurry, or on a Sunday, for any thing.

The best and most economical way possible for marketing, is to pay ready money for all that you can, especially for miscellaneous articles, and to deal for the rest with the most respectable tradesmen, whose bills should be settled weekly, or, at any rate, frequently, to prevent mistakes; without these precautions, even those of much experience, may chance to be cheated by unprincipled strangers, with old poultry—stale fish—tough mutton—or cow beef.—It should always be recollected, that without good provisions the skill of the cook will avail nothing.

But, by whomsoever the provisions may be bought, it behoves the housekeeper to examine them as they come in,—to see that in weight and measure they agree with the tickets sent with them,—and to make the necessary arrangements, in conjunction with the cook, for their due appropriation.

Besides being a good market-woman, the housekeeper ought to be ready at figures, and to understand the nature of common accounts, as it will generally be her business to keep the detailed accounts of the family, to examine the tradesmen's bills by the checks, to pay them, and pay for all miscellaneous articles as they are brought in, for which vouchers must be given, to be produced when the account is settled; and to avoid the possibility of mistake, this should be done weekly, or at short and stated periods; for this purpose, a book must be kept, in which entry should immediately be made.

The elegant and tasteful arrangement of the table is a very essential object in every Establishment; and when that department devolves on the housekeeper, will require her very serious consideration; as much of the credit and respectability of the family will depend on her.—Economy, taste, and tact must necessarily be displayed, and its execution involves much judgment, great attention, and unceasing assiduity. In order to have a table well served, and tastefully arranged, the skill and ingenuity of the cook, as well as the housekeeper, will be required—of the cook to dress it according to the fashion, and of the housekeeper, afterwards, to see that it be dished and served up according to the present custom.

The etiquette of the table being arranged by the bill of fare, previously made out, and the dishes laid in order below stairs; it is the province of the housekeeper, when dinner is served up, to see that the butler has placed them properly on the table above; this requires a quick glance of the eye, and a correct taste to measure distances,—and to see that the dishes accord with each other, and thereby form a pleasing, inviting, and well-grouped picture.

The housekeeper will employ the little leisure time she may have before the servants' dinner hour, which in most families is generally early, in preparing the best pastry, or in doing any other things she can assist in, preparatory to the family dinner; at any rate, she will look around and see that the household business is, every where, going on regularly, and the culinary preparations getting forward. She then takes her seat at the head of the table, in the steward's, or her own room, with the principle female servants and the men not in livery. In this situation she will have to carve, and as she will occasionally be required to assist the cook in dissecting a dish to be sent up stairs, it is indispensably necessary that she be proficient in the art of carving: and besides, to carve meat well, is a great saving. It would argue prudence and economy in her, to see that the pieces of bread which are brought down stairs, be eaten at this table, or in the servants'-hall, and it would be extravagance to suffer new bread to be eaten below stairs.

When the dinner is gone up, her attention will be directed to the dessert, which she prepares and lays out in her own room, previous to the removal of the cloth above stairs; when she makes her appearance with it, and arranges it on the dining-room table.

The Housekeeper now begins to find herself at leisure; by this time too, the maids will have done the principal part of their work above stairs, and the cook, kitchen-maid, and scullion, have washed up, and cleared away every thing, and cleaned up the kitchen.—After tea, the provident housekeeper will begin to think about to-morrow; evening being the best time for preparing all things that are likely to be wanted soon.—Small quantities of spices should be pounded and ground, and laid by in bottles, well corked, ready for use.—Much less spices are necessary, in gravies, &c. when thus prepared, than when boiled whole.—Raisins may be stoned, if wanted next day.—Currants may be washed, picked, and perfectly dried. White sugars should be broken, or pounded, rolled with a bottle, and sifted. Some of the oranges and lemons, to be used for juice, should be pared, and the rind put by to dry; and of some, when squeezed, and the pulp scraped out, the rinds may be kept dry for grating.

The Salary of the Housekeeper is from twenty-five to fifty guineas per annum, dependent on the extent of the family, and the nature of the business she undertakes.

Useful Memorandums

Provisions that will keep, should be laid in in quantities when cheapest, to be ready when wanted.—The best of all kinds are the most economical, not only because they are best, but also, because they go furthest.

As sugar is an article of considerable expense, it is to be understood that, of the white sugars, the most refined goes furthest and sweetens best. Choose those that are close, heavy, and shining.—The best sorts of the brown have a bright gravelly look. The coarser sorts are strongest and fittest for wines, sweetmeats, &c.

The only certain road to regularity, is to do every thing in its proper time—keep every thing in its proper place—and apply every thing to its proper use.

Accustom all the servants under your direction to rise early, and let them breakfast at an early hour. If orders be given betimes in the morning, there will be more time to execute them,—servants will perform their work with more ease,—and less hands will be required. If the economy of time were duly considered, and a regular plan of daily employment laid down, much business may be effected without hurry or fatigue.

As some preparation is necessary in all families for accidental visitors, care should be taken to have things in readiness for lunch, chocolate, sandwiches, &c.

An inventory of furniture, linen, china, plate, &c. should be kept, and the articles examined by it twice a year, at least, or oftener if the servants be changed, and a correct list of the articles delivered into the care of the new servants should be kept.

Tin fenders, and other things that are painted, should be painted every year or two.—Tin vessels, if suffered to become damp, soon rust, and are eaten into holes.

DIRECTIONS FOR MARKETING

BUTCHERS' MEAT

General observations respecting it

The best of every kind of provision is cheapest, affords most nourishment, and goes farthest. As this is the most nourishing of all animal food, and constitutes a considerable portion of our constant aliment, a knowledge, not only of the nature and properties of the several kinds of animals destined for our use, but also of the manner in which they have been bred and fed, would be very essential if to be obtained, as it would enable us to judge of their wholesomeness, and their fitness for our healthful support and nourishment.

The flesh of cattle, of all kinds, fatted in confined and filthy places, on oil-cakes, or rank and half-decayed vegetables, should be rejected, as unfit for use. On the contrary, those animals which have been bred and pastured in open situations, on high lands, extensive downs, dry commons, heaths, and large enclosures, where the air is pure, and particularly where the grass is short and sweet, and where they require much exercise to obtain their sustenance, have theirjuices pure, their flavour excellent, and the texture of their flesh delicate, nutritive, and wholesome. Hence the superiority of the Welsh and South Downs mutton, the Scotch and Welsh beef, &c. This fact is clearly evinced in the superior qualities that venison, and the flesh of all wild animals possess over that of tame ones.

Buttocks of beef, fillets of veal, and legs of mutton and lamb, as they have most solid meat and least bone, in proportion, are best for large families.

The most economical way for marketing, is to buy what roasting and boiling pieces you want in one lot. Butchers will sell quantities, thus assorted, much cheaper than they will sell single joints; and prime roasting joints, when bought alone, are always charged extravagantly.

Beef and mutton, of a proper age, is more easy of digestion, and more nutritious, than veal and lamb. The same remark holds with respect to pork; for though young pigs are fat and luscious, yet they are not so nutritive as those of more mature age. The heart and other viscera of animals are nutritious, but hard to digest. Pork is a strong meat, but that which is fed at dairies, is mildest and best. Fat meat is not so easy of digestion as the flesh of well fed animals, though not so fat. The flesh of old animals is dry and hard of digestion, and affords but little nourishment.

BEEF

Instructions for choosing it

An ox is in its prime, for food, at five or six years old.

BEEF is never out of season, but it is in the greatest perfection in November, December, and January.

The lean of the finest ox-beef, if of a proper age, has a fine smooth grain, it is of a bright or carnation red, feels tender, and appears to be marled or intermixed with fat. The fat parts are firm, of a cream colour, and rather white than yellow. This latter distinction is of importance, because, if the beef be old, the fat will be yellow and skinny; and if the ox has been unnaturally fed, or in a confined place, and particularly if it has been fed with oil-cake, it will be very yellow, soft, flabby, and greasy. On the other hand, if the beef be too young, the fat will be white, almost like mutton fat, and the lean will be of a pale colour.

The grain of cow-beef is closer than that of the ox, and the lean is of a darker red.

Heifer-beef has all the appearances and qualities of good ox-beef, except that the grain of the lean is of a finer texture.

Bull-beef is coarser and redder than any other, the fat hard and skinny, and it has a strong, rank smell.

The* JOINTS OF BEEF, *according to the London method of cutting

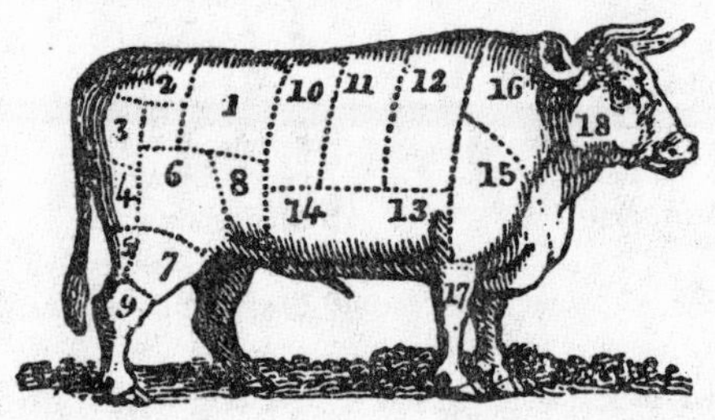

The Hind Quarter

1 Sirloin
2 Rump
3 Edge-bone
4 Buttock
5 Mouse-buttock
6 Veiny-piece
7 Thick-flank
8 Thin-flank
9 Leg
10 Fore-ribs

The Fore Quarter

11 Middle-ribs
12 Chuck-ribs
13 Leg-of-mutton-piece
14 Brisket or Breast-cut
15 Clod
16 Neck or sticking-piece
17 Shin
18 Cheek
A Baron of beef is the two sirloins cut together

The best joints are the sirloin, rump, edge-bone, buttock, and the five or six fore-ribs; and the thin-flank, the sticking-piece, the leg, shin, and cheek, are the worst.

VEAL

Instructions for choosing it

VEAL is best and cheapest from March to July.

Veal ought to be fine in the grain, firm, white, and fat. The leg bone should be small. If fresh, the eyes will be full and bright, the flesh not clammy but dry, and the large vein of the shoulder of a bright red. The kidney taints soonest, and if that be sweet, and neither soft nor slimy, the whole calf is fresh. On the contrary, if any part of the flesh be green or yellow, or feels flabby, it is stale. The fillet of a cow-calf is preferable on account of the udder, but the meat of the bull-calf is generally firmest, whitest, and best, when dressed. The finest calves have the smallest kidneys.

THE JOINTS OF VEAL

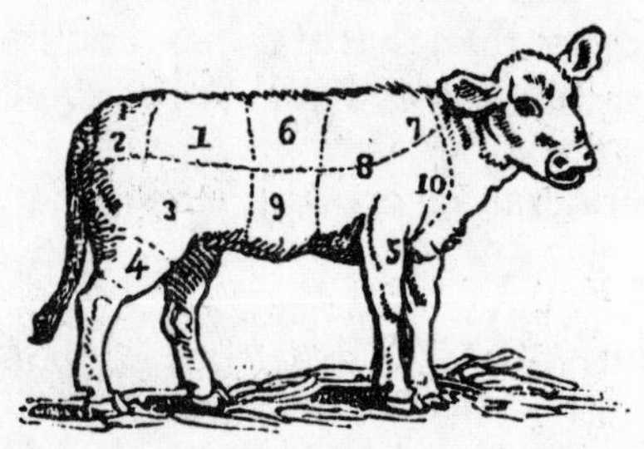

Hind-Quarter	*Fore-Quarter*
1 Loin, best end	5 Fore-knuckle
2 Loin, chump-end	6 Neck, best end
3 Fillet	7 Neck, scrag end
4 Hind-knuckle	8 Blade-bone
	9 Breast, best end
	10 Breast, brisket end

A shoulder is the fore-knuckle and blade-bone together; and a leg is the fillet and hind-knuckle together.

The best end of the loin, the fillet, and the best end of the breast, are the choicest pieces: the knuckle, and scrag end of the neck, are the worst.

MUTTON

Instructions for choosing it

MUTTON is best from Christmas to Midsummer.

When, if in its prime, (that is about four years of age) it will feel tender when pinched with the finger and thumb, but if older, it will feel harder and fibrous. The grain of the lean should be a fine deep red, the colour bright, and the fat firm and white. Wether mutton is the best flavoured, and may be known by a prominent lump of fat at the edge of the broadest part. Ewe mutton is paler than wether mutton, is of a finer texture and of less value; ram mutton is strong flavoured, high coloured, and its fat is spongy.

The mutton of the small Welsh sheep, which are driven up, and fatted on Banstead Heath, and the mutton bred and fed on the South Downs, in Sussex, are the most esteemed in London. At Bath, the short-shanked Dorsetshire, and the Lansdown mutton are most in request; in Yorkshire and the northern counties, the Moor mutton; and in Norfolk and Suffolk the long-shanked is most approved; but the sheep bred in the Fens and deep lands of Lincolnshire, and that neighbourhood, are large, coarse-grained, and ill-flavoured.—Mutton tastes strong of the coat in May and June, or just before shearing.

THE JOINTS OF MUTTON

1 Leg	5 Neck, scrag-end
2 Loin, best end	6 Shoulder
3 Ditto, chump end	7 Breast
4 Neck, best end	

A Chine is the two loins together; and a Saddle is the two necks together.

LAMB

Instructions for choosing it

Lamb, like veal, is fresh when the eyes are full and bright, and the vein in the neck is of a fine blue colour; but if it be green or yellow, or if there be a faint smell about the kidney, it is stale. The earliest house-lamb, in London, is from the Dorsetshire ewes, which are sold in great numbers at Weyhill-Fair, on the 10th October, whence they are driven towards London, quite forward, frequently dropping their lambs on the road. This comes in at or before Christmas, and is generally cut into quarters. Grass-lamb comes into season about Easter, and when large and plentiful is cut up in joints, like mutton.

PORK

Directions for choosing it

The rind of all pork should be thin, and if young and properly fed, the lean will break when pinched, and will be smooth and of a delicate white; the fat will be white and fine, and the joints will look blue; but if the rind be tough and loose, or thick and hard, and the joints look red, it is old. If the flesh be clammy it is stale. The knuckle part taints first. When measles are seen in the fat, the meat is unwholesome, and should not be eaten. A pig is in its prime at two years old.

THE JOINTS OF PORK

1 Spare-rib	4 Fore-loin
2 Hand	5 Hind-loin
3 Belly or spring	6 Leg

BACON

The rind of good bacon is always thin, the fat firm and white, or rather inclined to a pink tinge, and the lean is of a bright red, tender and adhering close to the bone. If there be any appearance of yellow, it is rusty. The Wiltshire and Hampshire bacon is best, but the Yorkshire is much esteemed. Irish bacon is, in general, bad; but this article is now so re-manufactured in London, as to resemble, in appearance, the most beautiful Wiltshire bacon.

Hams.—The Westphalia or bear's hams, are the best; but the Westmorland, Wiltshire, and Yorkshire are the most desirable, of the English curing. Choose these latter short in the shank; and to know whether they are good, thrust a picked-pointed knife under the bone, and if it comes out clean and sweet, the ham is good, otherwise it is not.

GAME

Venison is chosen by its fat, which should be thick, clear, and bright. A knife stuck in under the shoulder or shank will shew whether it be sweet. If venison looks green, or approaching to black, it is stale.

The Joints of Venison are only four; viz. the haunch, neck, breast, and shoulder.

Hares.—The claws of a young hare are smooth and sharp, the ears are tender and will easily tear, and the cleft of the lip is narrow; but the claws of an old hare are blunt and rugged, the ears dry and tough, and the cleft of the lip is wide, and the haunch is thick.—If fresh the body will be stiff. A hare is best when kept ten days or a fortnight, which, in favourable weather, may be done; but it should always be dressed as soon as it begins to bleed at the nose.

Leverets may be distinguished from hares, by their having a knob or small bone on the fore leg, near the foot, which hares have not. Leverets will not keep, therefore should be dressed as soon as possible.

Rabbits.—The age of Rabbits, whether wild or tame, may be known by nearly the same rules as that of Hares: observe also, that if old, their hairs are intermixed with the wool, their claws will be limber, and their flesh, instead of being white, will have a blue cast, and be slimy.

POULTRY

POULTRY is in the greatest perfection when most plentiful. It is generally dearest from February to Midsummer, and cheapest in September

GEESE.—The bill and feet of a young Goose will be yellow, the breast fat and plump, and the fat white and soft; but if old, the bill and feet will be red, and the fat yellow and skinny. If fresh, the feet will be limber, but if stale, stiff and dry. Green-Geese are in season in April, May, and June. They should be scalded. Stubble-Geese come into season in September.

TURKEYS.—Choose cock birds. The very best have black legs, but the white legged birds are nearly as fine. If young their legs will be smooth, and the spurs of the cock will be very short and tender; but if old, the legs will be rough, and the spurs long and hard, unless filed or cut off.

FOWLS.—Young Pullets are in their prime before they begin to lay; but Hen Fowls are best when full of eggs, at which time the vent is soft.

To know whether any kind of Fowl in its feathers is fit to dress, pull the feathers off the vent very gently, and if they come off easily, it ought to be dressed immediately.

DUCKS and DUCKLINGS.—These may be chosen by the same rules as Turkeys and Fowls.

Norfolk is famous for Turkeys, Geese, and Ducks; Surrey and Sussex for Fowls and Ducklings. The Dorking Fowls are in high estimation in London.

PIGEONS.—These birds should be both young and fresh, and when they are so, they are fat and full at the vent; their legs are limber and of a dusky white: young Pigeons have also a yellow down round their necks and heads. If old, their legs and feet are large, harsh, and red, and the vent discoloured and flabby. Tame Pigeons are best, as wood Pigeons are harder and darker coloured.

WILD FOWL

To judge whether these are young and fresh, observe the rules given above for tame Fowls; recollect also that these birds should be fat, and when they are so, they will be hard at the vent; if stale, the skin will peel off when rubbed with the finger.

FISH

General Rules for choosing it

The price of fish depends on the supply; and it will often be found, that one kind of fish, equally as good and seasonable as another, may be bought for much less money; therefore, never buy at an extravagant price.

When fish is fresh, it is firm, bright, and stiff; the gills are of a lively red, hard to open, and smell sweet; and the eyes are full and clear. If stale, the whole fish, and particularly the gills and fins, will always be flabby and limber, the gills will be pale, and the eyes sunk and dull. By these rules alone, good fish may be distinguished from bad.

AN ESSAY ON THE SOLE.

BUTTER, CHEESE, AND EGGS

BUTTER should be chosen by the taste and smell.—The best fresh butter is the Epping, and next the Cambridge; sometimes the potted weekly Dorset is very good. Of tub butter, the Welsh is best, the Dutch next, and the Irish worst. In examining tub butter, and particularly the Irish, look at and smell to the outside next the cask, which is often white in appearance like tallow, and quite rank in smell.

CHEESE. Of the common kinds, Cheshire, North Wiltshire and double Gloucester, are the best. Cheese of the first making, in May, is usually brought to Market in August. Factors have a pernicious practice of sticking brass pins into cheese, which gives it the appearance of blue mould and old age. That cheese which has a smooth, moist coat, is generally good. Spanish arnatto is often used to give the rind a beautiful red colour.

VEGETABLES

All VEGETABLES are best if dressed as soon as gathered; and are in their greatest perfection just before they begin to flower.

Most articles for pickling will be in their prime in July and August; but walnuts not later than the middle of July; and mushrooms and white cabbage in September and October.

HERBS, of all kinds, should be gathered in a dry day; and when the roots are cut off, and the herbs are perfectly well cleaned from dust, &c. they should be divided into small bunches and dried very quick by the heat of a stove, or in a Dutch oven before a common fire, rather than by the heat of the sun, taking care that they be not burnt. When dry put them into bags, and hang them up in a dry place; or pound them and sift them through a hair sieve, and keep the powder in bottles closely stopped.

SWEET AND SAVORY HERBS are best in season from May to August, according to their kinds.

The flavour and fragrance of fresh herbs are much finer than of those that are dried.

Names	When best	Names	When best
Artichokes	July to October	Endive	June & all Winter
Asparagus	May to July	Leeks	Sept. & all Winter
Beans, Windsor &c.	Midsummer to September	Lettuces	April & all Summer
		Onions	June to November
—French	Midsumr. & onwd.	Parsley	All the year
—Scarlet	July to October	Parsnips	Aug. & all Winter
Beetroot	All the year	Peas (green)	June to September
Borcole, or Scotch Kale	November and all the Winter	Potatoes	May & all the year
		Radishes	March to July
Broccoli	October and ditto	Small Salad	All the year
Cabbage	May & all Summer	Salsify and Scarzonera	July and August
—red	July to September		
—Plants	All the year	Sea Kale	April and May
Carrots	May till Winter	Spinach (Sprg.)	March to July
Cauliflowers	June to August	Do. (Winter)	Winter and Spring
Celery	June till March	Turnips	May to September
Corn Salad	May to July	Turnip Tops	February to May
Cucumbers	June to September		

PASTRY, &c.

OBSERVATIONS ON PASTRY

An adept in making pastry, never leaves any part of it adhering to the board used in making it. It is best when rolled on marble or slate. In hot weather the butter should be put in cold water to make it firm; and if the pastry be made early in the morning, and preserved from the air till baked, it will be the better. Salt butter,if good and well washed, makes a fine flaky crust.

Preserved fruit for pastry need not be baked; but the crust should be baked in a tin shape, or on a tin and cut out according to taste.

ON MAKING CAKES

Currants should be nicely washed, dried in a cloth, and then set before the fire. If not quite dry they will make the cake heavy. The cake will be the lighter if a dust of flour be thrown on the currants and then shaken.

Eggs should be beaten very long, the whites and the yolks apart, after which, they must be strained.—Sugar should be rubbed to a powder, on a clean board, and sifted through a fine hair or lawn sieve. Lemon-peel should be pared quite thin, and beaten, with a little sugar, in a marble mortar, to a paste; and then mixed with a little wine or cream, so as to mix easily with the other ingredients. After all the articles are put together in the pan, they should be thoroughly beaten for a long while, as the lightness of the cake greatly depends on their being well incorporated. Yeast, in either black or white plum cakes, makes them require less butter and eggs, and yet be equally light and rich. The dough when made should be set to rise by the fire. If the oven be not *quick* the batter will not rise, and the cake will be heavy: if you think it too quick, put some paper over the cake to prevent its being burnt.

A Rich Plum Cake

Take one pound of fresh butter, one pound of sugar, one pound and a half of flour, two pounds of currants, a glass of brandy, one pound of sweetmeats, two ounces of sweet almonds, ten eggs, a quarter of an ounce of allspice, and a quarter of an ounce of cinnamon.

Melt the butter to a cream, and put in the sugar. Stir it till quite light, adding the allspice, and pounded cinnamon; in a quarter of an hour take the yolks of the eggs, and work them in, two or three at a time; and the whites of the same must by this time be beaten into a strong snow quite ready to work in; as the paste must not stand to chill the butter, or it will be heavy, work in the whites gradually; then add the orange-peel, lemon, and citron, cut in fine strips, and the currants, which must be mixed in well, with the sweet almonds. Then add the sifted flour and glass of brandy. Bake this cake in a tin hoop in a hot oven for three hours, and put twelve sheets of paper under it to keep it from burning.

A Good Plain Cake

The following is a receipt for making a good plain cake, to be given to children, at breakfast, instead of buttered bread.

Take as much dough as will make a quartern-loaf (either made at home, or procured at the baker's), work into this a quarter of a pound of butter, a quarter of a pound of moist sugar, and a handful of caraway seeds. When well worked together, pull into pieces the size of a golden pippin, and work it together again. This must be done three times or it will be in lumps, and heavy when baked.

Icing for Cakes

Put one pound of fine-sifted, treble refined sugar into a basin, and the whites of three new-laid eggs; beat the sugar and eggs up well with a silver spoon until it becomes very white and thick; dust the cake over with flour, and then brush it off, by way of taking the grease from the outside, which prevents the icing from running; put it on smooth with a palette knife, and garnish according to fancy: any ornaments should be put on immediately; for if the icing get dry, it will not stick on. Set it in a cool oven to harden.

A Rich Seed Cake

Take a pound and a quarter of flour well dried, a pound of butter, a pound of loaf sugar, beat and sifted, eight eggs and two ounces of caraway seeds, one grated nutmeg, and its weight in cinnamon. Beat the butter into a cream, put in the sugar, beat the whites of the eggs and the yolks separately, then mix them with the butter and sugar. Beat in the flour, spices, and seed, a little before sending it away. Bake it two hours in a quick oven.

A Plain Pound Cake

Beat one pound of butter in an earthen pan until it is like a fine thick cream, then beat in nine whole eggs till quite light. Put in a glass of brandy, a little lemon peel, shred fine, then work in a pound and a quarter of flour; put it into the hoop or pan and bake it for an hour. A pound plum cake is made the same with putting one pound and a half of clean washed currants and half a pound of candied lemon peel.

Bath Cakes

Mix well together, half a pound of butter, one pound of flour, five eggs, and a cupful of yeast. Set the whole before the fire to rise, which effected, add a quarter of a pound of fine powdered sugar, an ounce of caraways well mixed in, and roll the paste out into little cakes. Bake them on tins.

Shrewsbury Cakes

Mix half a pound of butter well beat like cream, and the same weight of flour, one egg, six ounces of beaten and sifted loaf sugar, and half an ounce of caraway seeds. Form these into a paste, roll them thin, and lay them in sheets of tin; then bake them in a slow oven.

Portugal Cakes

Mix into a pound of fine flour, a pound of loaf sugar, beat and sifted, and rub it into a pound of butter, till it is thick, like grated white bread; then put to it two spoonsful of rose-water, two of sack, and ten eggs: work them well with a whisk, and put in eight ounces of currants. Butter the tin pans, fill them half full, and bake them. If made without currants they will keep a year.

Ginger Cakes without Butter

Take one pound of sugar, a quarter of a pound of ginger, a pint of water, two pounds of flour, and eight caps of orange peel. Pound and sift the ginger, and add a pint of water; boil it five minutes, then let it stand till cold. Pound the preserved orange peel, and pass it through a hair sieve; put the flour on a pasteboard, make a wall, and put in the orange peel and ginger with the boiled water; mix this up to a paste and roll it out; prick the cakes before baking them.

Savoy Cakes

To one pound of fine sifted sugar, put the yolks of ten eggs, (have the whites in a separate pan,) and set it, if in summer, in cold water: if there is any ice set the pan on it as it will cause the eggs to be beat finer. Then beat the yolks and sugar well with a wooden spoon for 20 minutes, and put in the rind of a lemon grated; beat up the whites with a whisk, until they become quite stiff and white as snow. Stir them into the batter by degrees, then add three quarters of a pound of well dried flour; finally put it in a mould in a slack oven to bake.

Queen Cakes

Take a pound of sugar, beat and sift it, a pound of well-dried flour, a pound of butter, eight eggs, and half a pound of currants washed and picked; grate a nutmeg and an equal quantity of mace and cinnamon, work the butter to a cream, put in the sugar, beat the whites of the eggs 20 minutes, and mix them with the butter and sugar. Then beat the yolks for half an hour and put them to the butter. Beat the whole together, and when it is ready for the oven, put in the flour, spices, and currants; sift a little sugar over them, and bake them in tins.

Lemon Cakes

Take one pound of sugar, three quarters of a pound of flour, 14 eggs, two tablespoonsful of rose-water, the raspings and juice of four lemons; when the yolks are well beat up and separated, add the powdered sugar, the lemon raspings, the juice, and the rose-water; beat them well together in a pan with a round bottom, till it becomes quite light, for half an hour. Put the paste to the whites previously well whisked about, and mix it very light. When well mixed sift in the flour and knead it in with the paste, as light as possible; form the biscuits and bake them in small oval tins, with six sheets of paper under them, in a moderate heat. Butter the tins well or it will prove difficult to take out the biscuits, which will be exceedingly nice if well made. Ice them previously to baking, but very light and even.

Banbury Cakes

Take a pound of dough made for white bread, roll it out, and put bits of butter upon the same as for puff paste, till a pound of the same has been worked in; roll it out very thin, then cut it into bits of an oval size, according as the cakes are wanted. Mix some good moist sugar with a little brandy, sufficient to wet it, then mix some clean washed currants with the former, put a little upon each bit of paste, close them up, and put the side that is closed next the tin they are to be baked upon. Lay them separate, and bake them moderately, and afterwards, when taken out, sift sugar over them. Some candied peel may be added, or a few drops of the essence of lemon.

Almond Cakes

Take six ounces of sweet almonds, half a pound of powdered sugar, seven eggs, six ounces of flour, and the raspings of four lemons. Pound the almonds very fine, with whole eggs, add the sugar and lemon raspings, and mix them well together in the mortar. Take it out, put it in a basin and stir it with the yolks of eggs, till it is as white as a sponge paste; beat up the whites of the eggs to a strong snow, mix them very light with the paste, then take the flour and mix it as light as possible; on this the goodness of the paste principally depends, as it is impossible to make a good cake with a heavy paste; butter the mould and bake in a slack oven for an hour, with ten sheets of paper under it and one on the top.

Plain Gingerbread

Mix three pounds of flour with four ounces of moist sugar, half an ounce of powdered ginger, and one pound and a quarter of warm treacle; melt half a pound of fresh butter in it; put it to the flour and make it a paste; then form it into nuts or cakes, or bake it in one cake.

Crumpets

Set two pounds of flour with a little salt before the fire till quite warm; then mix it with warm milk and water till it is as stiff as it can be stirred; let the milk be as warm as it can be borne with the finger, put a cupful of this with three eggs well beaten, and mixed with three spoonsful of very thick yeast; then put this to the batter and beat them all well together in a large pan or bowl, add as much milk and water as will make it into a thick batter; cover it close and put it before the fire to rise: put a bit of butter in a piece of thin muslin, tie it up, and rub it lightly over the iron hearth or frying pan; then pour on a sufficient quantity of batter at a time to make one crumpet; let it do slowly, and it will be very light. Bake them all the same way. They should not be brown, but of a fine yellow.

Muffins

Mix a pint and a half of warm milk and water, with a quarter of a pint of good yeast, and a little salt; stir them together for a quarter of an hour, then strain the liquor into a quarter of a peck of fine flour; mix the dough well and set it to rise for an hour, then roll it up and pull it into small pieces, make them up in the hand like balls, and lay a flannel over them while rolling to keep them warm. The dough should be closely covered up the whole time; when the whole is rolled into balls, the first that are made will be ready for baking. When they are spread out in the right form for muffins, lay them on tins and bake them, and as the bottoms begin to change colour turn them on the other side.

Cross Buns

Put two pounds and a half of fine flour into a wooden bowl, and set it before the fire to warm; then add half a pound of sifted sugar, some coriander seed, cinnamon and mace powdered fine; melt half a pound of butter in half a pint of milk: when it is as warm as it can bear the finger, mix with it three tablespoonsful of very thick yeast, and a little salt; put it to the flour, mix it to a paste, and make the buns as directed in the last receipt. Put a cross on the top, not very deep.

Orange Custards

Boil very tender the rind of half a Seville orange, and beat it in a mortar until it is very fine; put to it a spoonful of the best brandy, the juice of a Seville orange, four ounces of loaf sugar, and the yolk of four eggs. Beat them all together with ten minutes, and then pour in by degrees a pint of boiling cream; beat them until cold, then put them in custard cups, in a dish of hot water; let them stand till they are set, then take them out and stick preserved orange peel on the top; this forms a fine flavoured dish, and may be served up hot or cold.

Orange or Lemon Pie

Rub six oranges or lemons with salt, and put them into water, with a handful of salt, for two days. Put every day fresh water without salt, for a fortnight. Boil them tender, cut them into half quarters, cornerways, quite thin: boil six pippins, pared, cored, and quartered, in a pint of water till they break, then put the liquor to the orange or lemons, with half the pulp of the pippins well broken, and a pound of sugar; boil them a quarter of an hour, then put them into a pot and squeeze in two spoonsful of the juice of either orange or lemon, according to the kind of tart; put puff paste, very thin, into shallow patty-pans. Take a brush, and rub them over with melted butter, sift double refined sugar over them, which will form a pretty icing, and bake them.

Orange Tarts

Grate a little of the outside of a Seville orange, squeeze the juice into a dish, put the peel into water, and change it often for four days, then put into a saucepan of boiling water on the fire; change the water twice to take out the bitterness, and when tender, wipe and beat them fine in a mortar; boil their weight in double refined sugar into a syrup, and skim it, then put in the pulp and boil all together till clear; when cold put it into the tarts, and squeeze in the juice, and bake them in a quick oven. Conserve of orange makes good tarts.

Orange Puffs

Pare off the rinds from Seville oranges, then rub them with salt, let them lie twenty-four hours in water, boil them in four changes of water, make the first salt, drain and beat them to a pulp; bruise in the pieces of all that are pared, make it very sweet with loaf sugar, and boil it till thick; let it stand till cold, and then put it into the paste.

English Macaroons

One pound of sweet almonds, one pound and a quarter of sugar, 6 whites of eggs, and the raspings of two lemons. Pound the almonds very fine with 6 whites of eggs, feel the almonds, and if they are free from lumps, they will do; then add the powdered sugar, and mix it well with the lemon raspings. Dress them in wafer paper of the required shape; bake them in a moderate heat, then let them stand till cold, cut the wafer paper round them, but leave it on the bottoms.

CONFECTIONARY

To prepare Sugar for Candying

The first process is clarifying, which is done thus. Break the white of an egg into a preserving pan; put to it 4 quarts of water, and beat it with a whisk to a froth. Then put in 12 pounds of sugar, mix all together, and set it over the fire. When it boils put in a little cold water, and proceed as often as necessary, till the scum rises thick on the top. Then remove it from the fire, and when it is settled, take off the scum, and pass it through a straining bag. If the sugar should not appear very fine, boil it again before straining it.

To Candy Sugar

After having completed the above first process, put what quantity is wanted over the fire, and boil it till it is smooth enough. This is known by dipping the skimmer into the sugar, and touching it between the forefinger and thumb; and immediately on opening them a small thread will be observed drawn between, which will crystallize and break, and remain in a drop on the thumb, which will be a sign of its gaining some degree of smoothness. Boil it again, and it will draw into a larger string; it is now called bloom sugar, and must be boiled longer than in the former process. To try its forwardness, dip again the skimmer shaking off the sugar into the pan; then blow with the mouth strongly through the holes, and if certain bladders go through, it has acquired the second degree: to prove if the liquid has arrived at the state called feathered sugar, re-dip the skimmer, and shake it over the pan, then give it a sudden flirt behind, and the sugar will fly off like feathers.

It now arrives to the state called crackled sugar, to obtain which the mass must be boiled longer than in the preceding degree; then dip a stick in it, and put it directly into a pan of cold water, draw off the sugar which hangs to the stick in the water, and if it turns hard and snaps, it has acquired the proper degree of crystallization, if otherwise, boil it again until it acquires that brittleness.

The last stage of refining this article is called carmel sugar, to obtain which it must be boiled longer than in any of the preceding methods; prove it by dipping a stick first in the sugar, and then into cold water, and the moment it touches the latter, it will, if matured, snap like glass. Be careful that the fire is not too fierce, as by flaming up the sides of the pan, it will burn, discolour, and spoil the sugar.

To Candy any sort of Fruit

When finished in the syrup, put a layer into a new sieve, and dip it suddenly into hot water to take off the syrup that hangs about it: put it into a napkin before the fire to drain, and then do more in the sieve. Have ready sifted double refined sugar, which shake over the fruit till covered quite white. Set it on the shallow end of the sieve in a warm oven, and turn it two or three times. It must not be cold till dry. Watch it carefully.

Barley Sugar

Take a quantity of clarified sugar in that state that on dipping the finger into the pan the sugar which adheres to it will break with a slight noise; this is called crack. When the sugar is near this, put in two or three drops of lemon juice, or a little vinegar to prevent its graining. When it has come to the crack, take it off instantly, and dip the pan into cold water, to prevent its burning; let it stand a little, and then pour it on a marble which must be previously rubbed with oil. Cut the sugar into small pieces, when it will be ready for use. One drop of citron will flavour a considerable quantity.

Bon-Bons

Provide leaden moulds, which must be of various shapes, and be oiled with oil of sweet almonds. Take a quantity of brown sugar syrup in the proportion to their size, in that state called a blow, which may be known by dipping the skimmer into the sugar, shaking it, and blowing through the holes, when parts of light may be seen: add a drop of any esteemed essence. If the bon-bons are preferred white, when the sugar has cooled a little, stir it round the pan till it grains, and shines on the surface; then pour it into a funnel and fill the little moulds, when it will take a proper form and harden: as soon as it is cold take it from the moulds; dry it two or three days, and put it upon paper. If the bon-bons are required to be coloured, add the colour just as the sugar is ready to be taken off the fire.

TO PRESERVE FRUITS

Some rules are necessary to be observed in this branch of confectionary.

In the first place, observe, in making syrups, that the sugar is well dissolved before it is placed on the fire, otherwise the scum will not rise well, nor the fruit obtain its best colour.

When stone fruits are preserved, cover them with mutton suet rendered, to exclude the air; as air is sure to ruin them.

All wet sweetmeats must be kept dry and cool to preserve them from mouldiness and damp.

Dip a piece of writing paper in brandy, lay it close upon the sweetmeats, cover them tight with paper, and they will keep well for any length of time; but they will inevitably spoil without these precautions.

To Bottle Damsons

Put damsons, before they are too ripe, into wide-mouthed bottles, and cork them down tight; then put them into a moderately heated oven, and about three hours will do them; observe that the oven is not too hot, otherwise it will make the fruit fly. All kinds of fruits that are bottled may be done in the same way, and they will keep two years; after they are done, they must be put away with the mouth downward, in a cool place, to keep them from fermenting.

Grapes

Take close bunches, whether white or red, not too ripe, and lay them in a jar. Put to them a quarter of a pound of sugar candy, and fill the jar with common brandy. Tie them up close with a bladder, and set them in a dry place.

To Dry Cherries

Having stoned the desired quantity of morello cherries, put a pound and a quarter of fine sugar to every pound; beat and sift it over the cherries, and let them stand all night. Take them out of their sugar, and to every pound of sugar, put two spoonsful of water. Boil and skim it well, and then put in the cherries; boil the sugar over them, and next morning strain them, and to every pound of syrup put half a pound more sugar; boil it till it is a little thicker, then put in the cherries and let them boil gently. The next day strain them, put them in a stove and turn them every day till they are dry.

To Preserve Candied Orange Flowers

Free them from their cups, stamina, and pistils,
put four ounces into one pound of sugar boiled to a candy height,
and poured on a slab, so as to be formed into cakes.

To Preserve Fruits in Brandy, or other Spirits

Gather plums, apricots, cherries, peaches, and other juicy fruits, before they are perfectly ripe, and soak them for some hours in hard, or alum water, to make them firm; as the moisture of the fruit weakens the spirit, it ought to be strong, therefore, add five ounces of sugar to each quart of spirit.

Candied Ginger

Put 1 ounce of race ginger grated fine, a pound of loaf sugar beat fine, into a preserving pan, with as much water as will dissolve the sugar. Stir them well together over a slow fire till the sugar begins to boil. Then stir in another pound of sugar, beat fine, and keep stirring it till it grows thick. Then take it off the fire, and drop it in cakes upon earthen dishes. Set them in a warm place to dry, when they will become hard and brittle, and look white.

PICKLING

This branch of domestic economy comprises a great variety of articles which are essentially necessary to the convenience of families.

It is too prevalent a practice to make use of brass utensils to give pickles a fine colour. This pernicious custom is easily avoided by heating the liquor and keeping it in a proper degree of warmth before it is poured upon the pickle. Stone or glass jars are the best adapted for sound keeping.

Pickles should never be handled with the fingers, but taken out by a spoon, with holes in it, kept for the purpose.

The strongest vinegar must be used for pickling. It must not be boiled, as thereby the strength of the vinegar and spices will be evaporated. By parboiling the pickles in brine, they will be ready in half the time they would otherwise be. When taken out of the hot brine, let them get cold and quite dry before you put them into the pickle.

The articles to be pickled should be perforated with a larding pin, in several places, by which means they will the more readily imbibe the flavour of the pickle.

The spices, &c. generally used, are those mentioned in the following receipt for walnuts.

To Pickle Walnuts

Make a brine of salt and water, with a quarter of a pound of salt to a quart of water. Soak the walnuts in this for a week, and if you wish to have them ready the sooner, run a larding pin through them, in half a dozen places, which will make them much softer and better flavoured. Put them into a stew-pan with the brine, and give them a gentle simmer. Lay them on a sieve to drain, then put them on a fish plate in the open air, a couple of days, or till they turn black. Put them into unglazed or stone jars, about three parts full, and fill up the jars with the following pickle; and when they have been done about a week, open them and fill them up again, and so on continually, or else they will be spoiled.*

Onions

Put a sufficient quantity into salt and water for nine days, observing to change the water every day; next put them into jars and pour fresh boiling salt and water over them, cover them close up till they are cold, then make a second decoction of salt and water, and pour it on boiling. When it is cold drain the onions on a hair sieve, and put them into wide-mouthed bottles; fill them up with distilled vinegar; put into every bottle a slice or two of ginger, a blade of mace, and a tea-spoonful of sweet oil, which will keep the onions white. Cork them well up, and keep them in a dry place.

Saur Kraut

Take a large strong wooden vessel, or cask, resembling a salt-beef cask, and capable of containing as much as is sufficient for the winter's consumption of a family. Gradually break down or chop the cabbages (deprived of outside green leaves,) into very small pieces; begin with one or two cabbages at the bottom of the cask, and add others at intervals, pressing them by means of a wooden spade, against the side of the cask, until it is full. Then place

** To every quart of the strongest vinegar, add one ounce each of black pepper, ginger, shallots, and salt; half an ounce of allspice, and half a drachm of cayenne. Put these into a stone jar, covered with a bladder, wetted with the pickle; tie over that some leather, and set the jar on a trivet, by the side of a fire, for three days, shaking it three times a day, and then pour it, while hot, on the walnuts, and cover them down with a bladder, wetted with the pickle, &c.*

N.B. This pickle is the best, easiest prepared, and cheapest of any, for every kind of article.—It is also an excellent savoury sauce for cold meats.

a heavy weight upon the top of it, and allow it to stand near to a warm place, for four or five days. By this time it will have undergone fermentation, and be ready for use. Whilst the cabbages are passing through the process of fermentation, a very disagreeable fetid, acid smell is exhaled from them; now remove the cask to a cool situation, and keep it always covered up. Strew aniseeds among the layers of the cabbage during its preparation, which communicates a peculiar flavour to the Saur Kraut at an after period.

In boiling it for the table, two hours is the period for it to be on the fire. It forms an excellent nutritious and antiscorbutic food for winter use.

To Dry Salt Beef and Pork

Lay the meat on a table or in a tub with a double bottom, that the brine may drain off as fast as it forms, rub the salt well in, and be careful to apply it to every niche; afterwards put it into either of the above utensils; when it must be frequently turned, after the brine has ceased running, it must be quite buried in salt, and kept closely packed. Meat which has had the bones taken out is the best for salting. In some places the salted meat is pressed by heavy weights, or a screw, to extract the moisture sooner.

To Pickle in Brine

A good brine is made of bay salt and water, thoroughly saturated, so that some of the salt remains undissolved; into this brine the substances to be preserved are plunged, and kept covered with it. Among vegetables, French beans, artichokes, olives, and the different sorts of samphire, may be thus preserved, and among animals, herrings.

BRITISH WINES

The different processes in wine making, range themselves under the following heads: Gathering the fruit,—picking the fruit,—bruising the fruit,—and vatting the fruit. Vinous fermentation, flavouring the wine,—drawing the must,—pressing the husks,—casking the must.

Spirituous fermentation, racking the wine,—fuming the wine,—bottling the wine,—bottling and corking the wine.

APPARATUS FOR WINE MAKING

To make wine well, and with facility, persons should have all the requisite apparatus, namely, the *vats, vat-staff, fruit-bruiser, strainer, hair-bags, canvas-bags, wine-press, thermometer, and bottling-machine.*

Gathering the Fruit

Fruit of every description, says Mr. Carnell, in his excellent treatise on wine making, should be gathered in fine weather; those of the berry kind often appear ripe to the eye before they really are so, therefore it is requisite to taste them several times in order to ascertain that they are arrived at the crisis of maturity. If the fruit be not ripe, the wine will be harsh and hard, and unpleasant to the palate, and more so to the stomach; it will also take more spirit and saccharine, and take a longer time to be fit for the table. If the fruit be too ripe, the wine from it will be faint, low, and vapid; it will not be strong and generous; it will also require more trouble, additional spirit, and expense.

Picking

Detach the unripe and bad berries: the result when the wine is drunk, will be greatly superior in richness. Pick the stalks from grapes, currants, and gooseberries, previously to their being placed in the vat.

Bruising

The quantity of fruit for making a vintage of domestic wine, is not so large but it may be bruised in a tub, and from thence removed into the vat, or if the quantity be very small, it may be bruised in the vat. While the fruit is picking by one person, another may bruise it, and as it is bruised remove it into the vat. When Malaga or Smyrna raisins are used, they are to be put into the vat with the water, to soak, and the following day taken out and bruised, then returned into the vat again.

Vatting

The first thing to be done is to place the guard against the tap-hole, to prevent the husks escaping at the time the must or extract is drawn off. When all the fruit is in the vat the water should be added, and the contents stirred with the vat-staff, and left to macerate until the next day, when sugar, tartar, &c. diluted with some of the liquor, is to be put into the vat, and the whole again stirred up. The place where the vat is situated should have a free circulation of air, and a temperature of not less than 58 degrees Fahrenheit. If the vinous fermentation do not take place, in a reasonable time, the contents must be often stirred, and the place made warmer.

Vinous Fermentation

The time of a vinous fermentation commencing is always uncertain; it depends much on the quality and quantity of the contents of the vat, on its local situation, on the season or weather, and most particularly on the greenness or ripeness of the fruit. To produce a medium vinous fermentation, the vats and contents ought to be placed in a temperature from 60 to 70 degrees Fahrenheit. And if this is found not to produce fermentation in a short time, the temperature of the place must be made warmer, and the vat often stirred with the vat-staff.

The commencement of the vinous fermentation may be known by plunging the thermometer into the middle of the vat, for a minute, and when taken out, if a fermentation has commenced, the temperature of the contents will be higher than at the place where the vats are situated. When the vinous fermentation begins, it is very conspicuous, and may be known by its taste, smell, appearance, and effects. The contents will first gently rise, and swell with a slight movement and a little hissing. A considerable motion will take place, and the contents will increase in heat and bulk, while a quantity of air escapes.

It is impossible to lay down an exact time for a vinous fermentation; but for eighteen gallons, two or three days are generally sufficient for white wines; and red wines require a day or two more.

Flavouring

When the vinous fermentation is about half over, the flavouring ingredients are to be put into the vat and well stirred into the contents. If almonds form a component part, they are first to be beaten to a paste and mixed with a pint or two of the must. Nutmegs, cinnamon, ginger, seeds, &c. should, before they are put into the vat, be reduced to powder, and mixed with some of the must.

Drawing the Must

When the must in the vat gives, by tasting, a strong vinous pungency, that is the period to stop the remaining slight fermentation, by drawing off the must, in order to have strong and generous wine. A cock, or spicket and faucet, is to be put into the tap-hole of the vat, and the must drawn off and put into open vessels, there to remain till the pressing is finished.

Pressing the Husks

As soon as all the must is drawn off from the vat, the husks are to be put into hair-bags, and the mouth of each bag is to be well fastened, then put into the press, and the whole pressed without delay. The must that is pressed out is to be mixed with the must that was drawn off from the vat. Many ways may be contrived for pressing a small vintage, for those persons who cannot afford to purchase a proper wine-press; but several wines do not require pressing; and may be strained through a sweet, clean, canvas bag, made with a pointed end downwards.

Casking the Must

Each cask is to be filled, within about an inch of the bung-hole, which should be covered over lightly with a flat piece of wood. The must now is perfectly cool and calm, and will remain in this state until the spirituous fermentation commences.

Spirituous Fermentation

The spirituous fermentation is essentially necessary to the clarification, goodness, and perfection of the wine. If the vinous fermentation has been well conducted, and the wine cellar be not too cold, a spirituous fermentation will commence in a few days, and abate in six or twelve days, the time depending on circumstances, and on the quality and quantity of the wine. The brandy or spirit assigned should at this time be put to the wine by pouring it in gently without disturbing the wine. The cask now, if not full, must be filled up and bunged with a wooden bung covered with a piece of new canvas larger than the bung. In about a month after the spirit has been added, the cask will again want filling up; this should be done with the overplus of the vintage, if not with some other good wine, and the cask re-bunged very tight. The cask should be pegged once a month or oftener to see if the wine be clear and not thick, and as soon as it is fine and bright, it must be racked off its lees.

A SOUND NAP.

Racking

This is an operation highly requisite to keeping the wine good; to its purification, strength, colour, brilliancy, richness, and flavour, and is performed by drawing off the wine and leaving the lees in the cask. A siphon should be used but if not, the cask should be tapped two or three days previously. It may be racked off into another cask, or into a vat or tub, and returned into the same cask again, after it has been well cleaned: and, if requisite, the cask may be slightly fumigated, immediately before the wine is returned into it. If the wine, on being tasted, is found weak, a little spirit is to be given to it, the cask filled up and bunged tight.

The racking off ought to be performed in temperate weather, and as soon as the wines appear clear, a second racking will make them perfectly brilliant, and if so they will want no fining.

Fining

Many wines require fining before they are racked, and the operation of fining is not always necessary. Most wines, well made, do not want fining; this may be ascertained by drawing a little into a glass, from a peg-hole.

One of the best finings is as follows:—Take one pound of fresh marsh-mallow roots, washed clean, and cut into small pieces; macerate them in two quarts of soft water, for twenty-four hours, then gently boil the liquor down to three half pints, strain it, and when cold, mix with it half an ounce of pipe clay or chalk, in powder, then pour the mucilage into the cask, and stir up the wine so as not to disturb the lees, and leave the vent-peg out for some days after.

Or, take boiled rice, two table-spoonsful, the white of one new egg, and half an ounce of burnt alum, in powder. Mix with a pint or more of the wine, then pour the mucilage into the cask, and stir the wine with a stout stick, but not to agitate the lees.

Or, dissolve, in a gentle heat, half an ounce of isinglass in a pint or more of the wine, then mix with it half an ounce of chalk, in powder; when the two are well incorporated, pour it into the cask, and stir the wine so as not to disturb the lees.

As soon as wines are clear and bright, after being fined down, they ought to be racked into a sweet and clean cask, the cask filled up and bunged tight.

MANAGEMENT OF BRITISH WINES

To guard against unripe Fruit

If the season proves bad, so that some fruits are not sufficiently ripe, immediately after the vinous fermentation, and the must of such fruit is put into the cask, it is to be rolled two or three times a day, for a week or two. A spirituous fermentation will soon commence, the bung of the cask must then be taken out, and the hole covered with a bit of light wood or canvas, and as any scum arises, it should be taken away. When the scum disappears, fill up the cask, and bung it up. But a vent-hole must be left open for a week.

To keep and manage Wines

Wines will diminish, therefore the cask must be kept filled up with some of the same wine, or some other that is as good or better.

They must at all times be kept in a cool cellar, if not, they will ferment. If wines are kept in a warm cellar, an acetous fermentation will soon commence, and the result consequently will be vinegar. The more a wine frets and ferments, the more it parts with its strength and goodness: when wines are found to work improperly in the cellar, the vent-peg must be taken out for a week or two.

If any wine ferments, after being perfected, draw off a quart and boil it, and pour it hot into the cask, add a pint or a quart of brandy, and bung up a day or two after.

Or, draw off the wine, and fumigate the cask, with one ounce of flour of brimstone, and half an ounce of cinnamon, in powder. Mix the two together, and tie them up in a rag. Turn the bung-hole of the cask downwards, place the rag under the bung-hole, and set fire to it, so that the gas ascends into the cask. As soon as it is burnt out, fill up the cask with the wine, and bung it up tight.

To restore Flat Wines

Flat wines may be restored by one pound of jar raisins, one pound of honey, and half a pint of spirit of wine, beaten up in a mortar with some of the wine, and then put into the cask.

To remove a musty or disagreeable taste in Wines

Put into the cask three or four sticks of charcoal, and bung up the cask tight. In a month after take them out.—Or, cut two ripe medlars, put them in a gauze bag, and suspend them from the bung-hole into the wine, and bung up the cask air-tight. A month after take them out, and bung up the cask again.—Or, mix half a pound of bruised mustard-seed, with a pint or more of brandy, and stir it up in the wine; and two days after bung up the cask.

To sweeten a foul Cask

Set fire to a pound or more of broken charcoal, put it into the cask and immediately fill up the cask with boiling water. After this, roll the cask once or twice a day for a week; then pour out the charcoal and water, wash out the cask with clean cold water, and expose it to the external air for some days.

To improve Poor Wines

Poor wines may be improved by being racked off, and returned into the cask again; and then putting into the wine about a pound of jar or box raisins, bruised, and a quart of brandy.

Or, put to the wine two pounds of honey, and a pint or two of brandy. The honey and brandy to be first mixed together.

Or, draw off three or four quarts of such wine, and fill the cask up with strong wine.

To improve Wine when lowering or decaying

Take one ounce of roche-alum, make it into powder; then draw out four gallons of wine, mix the powder with it, and beat it well for half an hour; then fill up the cask, and when fine (which will be in a week's time or little more) bottle it off. This will make it drink fine and brisk.

A CORDIAL WISH.

To stop the Fermentation of Wine

It is in the first place necessary to consider whether the existing state of fermentation be the original or secondary stage of that process which comes on after the former has ceased for several days, and is indeed the commencement of acetous fermentation. That of the former kind rarely proceeds beyond what is necessary for the perfect decomposition of the saccharine and other parts of the vegetable substances necessary for the production of spirit, unless the liquor be kept too warm, or is too weak, and left exposed to the air after the vinous fermentation is completed. The means to correct these circumstances are sufficiently obvious. The heat for spirituous fermentation should not be above 60 degrees Fahrenheit; when it is much above that point, the liquor passes rapidly through the stage of vinous fermentation, and the acetous immediately commences. When too long-continued fermentation arises from the liquor having been kept in a warm situation, it will be soon checked by bunging, after being removed into a cold place; the addition of a small proportion of spirits of wine or brandy, previously to closing it up, is also proper. A degree of cold, approaching to the freezing point, will check fermentation of whatever kind. Fermentation of this kind cannot be stopped by any chemical agent, except such as would destroy the qualities of the liquor intended to be produced.

The secondary stage of fermentation, or the commencement of the acetous, may be stopped by removing the liquor to a cool situation; correcting the acid already formed; and if the liquor contain but little spirit, the addition of a proper proportion of brandy is requisite.

The operation of racking is also necessary to preserve liquor in a vinous state, and to render it clear. This process should be performed in a cool place.

PERFUMERY AND COSMETICS

A Natural Dentifrice

The common strawberry is a natural dentifrice, and its juice, without any preparation, dissolves the tartareous encrustations on the teeth, and makes the breath sweet and agreeable.

Eau de Cologne

Take 3oz. of essence de bergamotte
1½ drachms of Neroli
2 drachms of cedrat
3 drachms of lemon
1 drachm of oil of rosemary
12 lbs of spirit of wine
3¼ lbs of spirit of rosemary
2¼ lbs of eau de melissee de Carmes

Mix. Distil in balneum mariae, and keep it in a cold cellar or ice-house for some time. It is used as a cosmetic, and made, with sugar, into a ratafia.

Essence de Jasmin

The flowers are stratified with wool or cotton, impregnated with oil of behn, or nut oil, in an earthen vessel, closely covered, and kept for some time in a warm bath; this is repeated with fresh flowers, until the oil is well scented; the wool, &c. is then put into a sufficient quantity of spirit of wine, and distilled in balneum mariae.

The best Honey Water

Take of coriander seeds, a pound, cassia, four oz., cloves and gum benzoin, each, 20oz., oil of rhodium, essence of lemon, essence of bergamot, and oil of lavender, each, 1 drachm, rectified spirit of wine, 20 pints, rose water, 2 quarts, nutmeg water, 1 quart, musk and ambergris, each, twelve grains. Distil in a water bath to dryness.

Ottar of Roses

The Royal Society of Edinburgh received from Dr. Monro the following account of the manner in which this costly perfume is prepared in the east. Steep a large quantity of the petals of the rose, freed from every extraneous matter, in pure water, in an earthen or wooden vessel, which is exposed daily to the sun, and housed at night, till a scum rises to the surface. This is the ottar, which carefully absorb by a very small piece of cotton tied to the end of a stick. The oil collected, squeeze out of the cotton into a very diminutive vial, stop it for use. The collection of it should be continued, whilst any scum is produced.

English Milk of Roses

Take 2 lbs of Jordan almonds
5 quarts of rose water
1 quart of rectified spirit of wine
½ oz. of oil of lavender
2 oz. of Spanish oil-soap, and
4 oz. of cream of roses

Blanch the almonds in boiling water, dry them well in a cloth, then pound them in a mortar until they become a paste. Pound in the soap and mix it well with the almond paste. Then add the cream of roses. When these are mixed, add the rose-water and spirits, which stir in with a spatula or knife. Strain the whole through a clean white cloth, then add the oil of lavender to the expressed liquid, drop by drop, and stir the whole well. When the mixture has stood for a day, cover it over with a cloth from the dust, then bottle it for use.

Cold Cream Pomatum, for the complexion

Take an ounce of oil of sweet almonds, and half a drachm each, of white wax and spermaceti, with a little balm. Melt these ingredients in a glazed pipkin over hot ashes, and pour the solution into a marble mortar; stir it with the pestle until it becomes smooth and cold, then add gradually an ounce of rose or orange-flower water; stir all the mixture till incorporated to resemble cream. This pomatum renders the skin at once supple and smooth. To prevent marks from the small pox, add a little powder of saffron. The gallipot in which it is kept, should have a piece of bladder tied over it.

Pearl Water, for the face

Put half a pound of best Spanish oil soap, scraped very fine, into a gallon of boiling water. Stir it well for some time, and let it stand till cold. Add a quart of rectified spirit of wine, and half an ounce of oil of rosemary; stir them again.

This compound liquid, when put up in proper phials, in Italy, is called tincture of pearls. It is an excellent cosmetic for removing freckles from the face, and for improving the complexion.

Soft Pomatum

Take 25 pounds of hog's-lard
8 pounds of mutton suet
6 ounces of oil of bergamot
4 ounces of essence of lemons
½ an ounce of oil of lavender, and
¼ of an ounce of oil of rosemary

These ingredients are to be combined in the same manner as those for the hard pomatum. This pomatum is to be put up in pots, in the usual way.

Orange Flower Paste, for the hands

Blanch 5 or 6 pounds of bitter almonds, by boiling in water, and then beat them very fine in a marble mortar, with 2 pounds of orange flowers. If the paste be too oily, add to it some bean flour, finely sifted, but let no water enter the composition. This paste is made abroad, but comes here very damaged, the sea-air destroying its properties.

Coral Tooth Powder

Take 4 ounces of coral, reduced to an impalpable powder
8 ounces of very light Armenian bole
1 ounce of Portugal snuff
1 ounce of Havannah snuff
1 ounce of good burnt tobacco ashes, and
1 ounce of gum myrrh, well pulverized
Mix them together, and sift them twice.

An Astringent for the Teeth

Take of fresh conserve of roses, 2 ounces, the juice of half a sour lemon, a little very rough claret, and 6 ounces of coral tooth-powder. Make them into a paste, which put into small pots; and, if it dry by standing, moisten with lemon juice and wine, as before.

To Clean the Teeth

Take of good soft water, 1 quart
juice of lemon, 2 ounces
burnt alum, 6 grains
common salt, 6 grains.—Mix.

Boil them a minute in a cup, then strain and bottle for use: rub the teeth with a small bit of sponge tied to a stick, once a week.

To make the Teeth White

A mixture of honey with the purest charcoal will prove an admirable cleanser.

Vegetable Tooth-Brushes

Take marine marsh-mallow roots, cut them into lengths of 5 or 6 inches, and of the thickness of a middling rattan cane. Dry them in the shade, but not so as to make them shrivel.

Next finely pulverize two ounces of good dragon's blood, put it into a flat-bottomed glazed pan, with four ounces of highly rectified spirit, and half an ounce of fresh conserve of roses. Set it over a gentle charcoal fire, and stir it until the dragon's blood is dissolved; then put in about thirty of the marsh-mallow sticks; stir them about, and carefully turn them that all parts may absorb the dye alike. Continue this until the bottom of the pan be quite dry, and shake and stir it over the fire, until the sticks are perfectly dry and hard.

Both ends of each root or stick should, previous to immersion in the pan, be bruised gently by a hammer, for half an inch downwards, so as to open its fibres, and thereby form a brush.

They are generally used by dipping one of the ends in the powder or opiate, and then, by rubbing them against the teeth, which they cleanse and whiten admirably.

  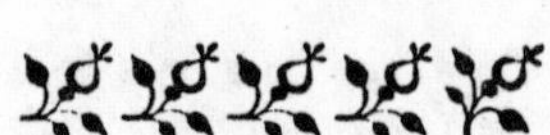

To Sweeten the Breath

Take two ounces of Terra Japonica, half an ounce of sugar candy, both in powder. Grind one drachm of the best ambergris with ten grains of pure musk; and dissolve a quarter of an ounce of clean gum tragacanth in two ounces of orange-flower water. Mix all together, so as to form a paste, which roll into pieces of the thickness of a straw. Cut these into pieces, and lay them in clean paper. This is an excellent perfume for those whose breath is disagreeable.

To Perfume Clothes

Take of oven-dried best cloves, cedar and rhubarb wood, each one ounce, beat them to a powder, and sprinkle them in a box or chest, where they will create a most beautiful scent, and preserve the apparel against moths.

Perfumed Bags for Drawers

Cut, slice, and mix well together, in the state of very gross powder, the following ingredients:

2 oz. of yellow saunders
2 oz. of coriander seeds
2 oz. of orris root
2 oz. of calamus aromaticus
2 oz. of cloves
2 oz. of cinnamon bark
2 oz. of dried rose leaves
2 oz. of lavender flowers, and
1 lb. of oak shavings.

When properly mixed, stuff the above into small linen bags, which place in drawers, wardrobes, &c., which are musty, or liable to become so.

Excellent Perfume for Gloves

Take of ambergris one drachm, civet the like quantity; add flour-butter a quarter of an ounce; and with these well mixed, rub the gloves over gently with fine cotton wool, and press the perfume into them.

A Perfume to Prevent Pestilential Airs, &c.

Take of benjamin, storax, and galbanum, each half an ounce, temper them, being bruised into powder, with the oil of myrrh, and burn them in a chafing-dish, or else take rosemary, balm, and bay leaves; heat them in wine and sugar, and let the moisture be consumed; likewise burn them by the heat of the pan, and they will produce a very fine scent.

Ambergris Hair-Powder

Take twelve pounds of fine starch-powder, add three pounds of the ambergris perfume: mix them well together, and run it twice through a fine hair sieve. Put it into a well closed box, or glass, for use.

Musk and Civet Hair-Powder

Mix twelve pounds of starch-powder, and three pounds of musk perfume. A second sort of this hair-powder may be made by using half the quantity of perfume.

SIMPLE DISTILLED WATERS

PRESERVATION OF FLOWERS FOR DISTILLATION

Rub three pounds of rose-leaves for three minutes with a pound of common salt. The flowers being bruised by the friction of the grains of salt, form a paste, which is to be put into an earthen jar, or into a watertight barrel. The same process is to be repeated until the vessel is filled, so that all the roses may be equally salted. The vessel is then to be shut up and kept in a cool place until wanted.

For distillation, this aromatic paste is, at any season, to be put into the body of the still with twice its weight of water; and when heat is applied, the oil, or essential water, is to be obtained in the common way. Both the oil and water are in this way produced in greater quantity than by using the leaves without the salt: besides, the preserved paste will keep its flavour and strength unimpaired for several years.

Other flowers, capable of affording essential oils may also be treated in the above-mentioned way, with economy and advantage; as there is thereby no occasion to carry on a hurried process in the heat of summer, when these are in perfection.

GENERAL RULES FOR THE DISTILLATION OF SIMPLE WATERS

1. Plants and their parts ought to be fresh gathered. When they are directed fresh, such only must be employed; but some are allowed to be used dry, as being easily procurable in this state at all times of the year, though rather more elegant waters might be obtained from them whilst green.

2. Having bruised the subjects a little, pour thereon thrice their quantity of spring water. This quantity is to be diminished or increased, according as the plants are more or less juicy than ordinary.

When fresh and juicy herbs are to be distilled, thrice their weight of water will be fully sufficient, but dry ones require a much larger quantity.

In general, there should be so much water, that after all intended to be distilled has come over, there may be liquor enough to prevent the matter from burning to the still.

3. Formerly, some vegetables were slightly fermented with the addition of yeast, previous to their distillation.

4. If any drops of oil swim on the surface of the water, they are to be carefully taken off.

5. That the waters may be kept the better, about one-twentieth part of their weight of proof spirit may be added to each after they are distilled.

STILLS FOR SIMPLE WATERS

The instruments chiefly used in the distillation of simple waters are of two kinds, commonly called the hot still, or alembic, and the cold still. The waters drawn by the cold still from plants are much more fragrant, and more fully impregnated with their virtues, than those drawn by the hot still or alembic.

The method is this:—A pewter body is suspended in the body of the alembic, and the head of the still fitted to the pewter body; into this body the ingredients to be distilled are put, the alembic filled with water, the still-head luted to the pewter body, and the nose luted to the worm of the refrigeratory or worm. The same intention will be answered by putting the ingredients into a glass alembic, and placing it in a bath-heat, or balneum mariae.

The cold still is much the best adapted to draw off the virtues of simples, which are valued for their fine flavour when green, which is subject to be lost in drying; for when we want to extract a spirit from plants so light and volatile, as not to subsist in open air any longer than while the plant continues in its growth, it is certainly the best method to remove the plant from its native soil, into some proper instrument, where, as it dies, these volatile parts may be collected and preserved. And such an instrument is what we call the cold still, where the drying of the plant, or flower, is only forwarded by a moderate warmth, and all that rises is collected and preserved.

Expeditious Mode of Distilling Simple Waters

Tie a piece of muslin or gauze over a glazed earthen pot, whose mouth is just large enough to receive the bottom of a warming-pan; on this cloth lay the herb, clipped; then place upon them the warming-pan, with live coals in it, to cause heat just enough to prevent burning, by which means a steam issuing out of the herb cannot mount upwards, by reason of the bottom of the pan just fitting the brim of the vessel below it, it must necessarily descend, and collect into water at the bottom of the receiver, and that strongly impregnated with the essential oil, and the salt of the vegetable thus distilled; which, if wanted to make spirituous or compound water, is easily done, by simply adding some good spirits, or French brandy to it, which will keep good for a long time, and be much better than if the spirits had passed through a still, which must, of necessity, waste some of their strength. Care should be taken not to let the fire be too strong, lest it scorch the plants; and to be made of charcoal, for continuance and better regulation, which must be managed by lifting up and laying down the lid, as wanted to increase or decrease the degrees of heat. The deeper the earthen pan, the cooler the season, and the less fire at first (afterwards to be gradually raised), in the greater perfection will the distilled water be obtained.

As the more moveable, or volatile parts of vegetables, are the aqueous, the oily, the gummy, the resinous, and the saline, these are to be expected in the waters of this process; the heat here employed being so great as to burst the vessels of the plants, some of which contain so large a quantity of oil, that it may be seen swimming on the surface of the water.

Although a small quantity only of distilled waters can be obtained at a time by this confined operation, yet it compensates in strength what is deficient in quantity. Such liquors, if well corked up from the air, will keep good a long time, especially if about a twentieth part of any spirits be added, in order to preserve the same more effectually.

Simple Pennyroyal Water

Take of pennyroyal leaves, dry, a pound and a half; water, as much as will prevent burning. Draw off by distillation 1 gallon.

Simple Spearmint Water

Take of spearmint leaves, fresh, any quantity; water, three times as much. Distil as long as the liquor which comes over has a considerable taste or smell of the mint.

Or, take spearmint leaves, dried, 1½ lbs, water as much as is sufficient to prevent burning. Draw off by distillation 1 gallon.

Cinnamon Water

Take of bruised cinnamon, 1 lb., water, 2 gallons. Simmer in a still for half an hour, put what comes over into the still again; when cold, strain through flannel.

COMPOUND DISTILLED WATERS

GENERAL RULES FOR THE DISTILLATION OF SPIRITUOUS WATERS

1. The plants and their parts ought to be moderately and newly dried, except such as are ordered to be fresh gathered.

2. After the ingredients have been steeped in the spirit for the time prescribed, add as much water as is sufficient to prevent a burnt flavour, or rather more.

3. The liquor which comes over first in distillation is by some kept by itself, under the title of spirit; and the other runnings, which prove milky, are fined down by art. But it is preferable to mix all the runnings together, without fining them, that the waters may possess the virtues of the plant entire.

4. In the distillation of these waters, the genuine brandy obtained from wine is directed.

Where this is not to be procured, take, instead of that proof spirit, half its quantity of a well rectified spirit, prepared from any other fermented liquors. In this steep the ingredients, and then add spring water enough, both to make up the quantity ordered to be drawn off, and to prevent burning.

Bergamot Water

Take of fine old French brandy, 2 gallons, or 1 gallon of highly rectified spirit of wine, and 1 gallon of spring water. Put to the brandy, or diluted spirits, ½ an ounce, or more, of true Roman oil of bergamot, whose parts have been previously well divided by trituration with lump sugar, in a glass mortar. Now distil by a water heat, and draw off six quarts only. By this operation, a most excellent bergamot water will be produced, which will remain good for twenty years.

Original Receipt for Hungary Water

The original receipt for preparing this invaluable lotion, is written in letters of gold in the hand-writing of Elizabeth, Queen of Hungary.

Take of aqua vitae, four times distilled, 3 parts, the tops and flowers of rosemary, 2 parts. To be put together in a close-stopped vessel, and allowed to stand in a warm place, during fifty hours, then to be distilled in an alembic, and of this, once every week, 1 drachm to be taken in the morning, either in the food or drink, and every morning the face and the deceased limb to be washed with it.

Lavender Spirit

Take 14 pounds of lavender flowers, 10½ gallons of rectified spirit of wine, and one gallon of water; draw off 10 gallons by a gentle fire; or, which is much better, by a sand bath heat.

Lemon Water

The peel of the lemon, the part used in making this water, is a very grateful bitter aromatic, and, on that account, very serviceable in repairing and strengthening the stomach. Take of dried lemon-peel, 4 lbs., proof spirit, 10½ gallons, and 1 gallon of water. Draw off ten gallons by a gentle fire.

Spirit of Peppermint

Take of the herb of peppermint, dried, 1½ lbs, proof spirit, 1 gallon, water, sufficient to prevent burning. Distil off a gallon.

SAL-VOLATILE

Compound Gentian Water

Take of gentian root, sliced, 3 lbs; leaves and flowers of the lesser centaury, each 8 ounces; infuse the whole in 6 quarts of proof spirit, and 1 quart of water; and draw off the water till the feints begin to rise.

Antiscorbutic Water

Take of the leaves of water-cresses, garden and sea scurvy-grass, and brook-lime, each 20 handsful; of pine-tops, germander, horehound, and the lesser centaury, each 16 handsful; of the roots of bryony and sharp pointed dock, each 6 pounds; of mustard-seed, 1½ pounds. Digest the whole in 10 gallons of proof spirit, and 2 gallons of water, and draw off by a gentle fire.

Lavender Water

Take 30 gallons of the best wine spirit; pour it into a copper still, placed in a hot-water bath, over a clear but steady fire; put to it 6 pounds of the largest and freshest lavender flowers, after having separated them from all stalks and green leaves, which give the lavender water a woody and faint smell. Put no water into the still; close all the junctures well, and let the spirits and flowers stand in a state of digestion for 24 hours; and then, with a gentle fire, draw off 25, or, at most, 26 gallons only, which, as soon as distilled, are to be poured into a copper vessel, for keeping. Wooden vessels and cans are to be avoided, as the best parts of the oil, and of the spirits, will be absorbed by them and consequently lost.

When the distillation is over, draw out, or quench the fire, and let the remaining spirits and flowers continue in the still until the next day.

When the above quantity of 25 or 26 gallons has stood for 4 or 5 days, put it to ten ounces of true English oil of lavender. Mix the whole well in the jar, by drawing out one or two gallons, and then returning them. Repeat this ten or twelve times, then stop the vessel up close, and do not disturb it for a month, at least.

ACID LIQUORS

Vinegar is used chiefly as a sauce, and to preserve vegetable substances; but it is employed externally when an over dose of strong wine, spirit, opium, or other narcotic poison has been taken. A false strength is give to it by adding oil of vitriol, or some acrid vegetable, as pellitory of Spain, capsicum, &c. It is rendered colourless by adding fresh burned bone black, 6 ounces to a gallon, and letting it stand for two or three days to clear.

To Make Vinegar

Mix cider and honey, in the proportion of 1 lb. of honey to a gallon of cider, and let it stand in a vessel for some months, and vinegar will be produced so powerful, that water must be mixed with it for common use.

Wine Vinegar

Take any sort of wine that has gone through fermentation, and put it into a cask that has had vinegar in it; then take some of the fruit or stalks of which the wine has been made, and put them wet into an open-headed cask in the sun, with a coarse cloth over the top of it, for six days—after which put them in the vinegar, and stir it well about—then put it in a warm place, if in winter, or if in summer, put it in a yard in the sun, with a slate over the bung. When the vinegar is sour enough and fine, rack it off into a clean sour cask, and bung it up; then put it in the cellar for use. Those wines that contain the most mucilage are fittest for the purpose.

The lees of pricked wine are also a very proper ingredient in vinegar.

Sugar Vinegar

To each gallon of water add 2 lbs of brown sugar, and a little yeast; leave it exposed to the sun for six months, in a vessel slightly stopped.

Gooseberry Vinegar

Bruise the gooseberries, when ripe, and to every quart put three quarts of water; stir them well together, and let the whole stand for 24 hours, then strain it through a canvas bag.

To every gallon of liquor add 1 lb. of brown sugar, and stir them well together before they are put into the cask. Proceed in all other respects as before. This vinegar possesses a pleasant taste and smell; but raspberry vinegar, which may be made on the same plan, is far superior in these respects. The raspberries are not required to be of the best sort, still, they should be ripe and well flavoured.

Currant Vinegar

This is made in the same way as that from gooseberries, only pick off the currants from the stalks.

Primrose Vinegar

To 15 quarts of water put 6 lbs of brown sugar; let it boil ten minutes, and take off the scum: pour on it half a peck of primroses; before it is quite cold, put in a little fresh yeast, and let it work in a warm place all night; put it in a barrel in the kitchen, and when done working, close the barrel, still keeping it in a warm place.

Raisin Vinegar

After making raisin wine, lay the pressed raisins in a heap to heat, then to each cwt. put 15 gallons of water, and a little yeast.

Cider Vinegar

The poorest sort of cider will serve for vinegar, in managing which proceed thus:—First draw off the cider into a cask that has had vinegar in it before; then put some of the apples that have been pressed into it, set the whole in the sun, and in a week or nine days it may be drawn off into another cask.—This is a good table vinegar.

Vinegar from the Refuse of Fruits

Take the skins of raisins after they have been used in making wine, and pour three times their own quantity of boiling water on them; stir them well about, and then set the cask in a warm place, close covered, and the liquor, in a week, when drawn off from its sediment, put into another cask, and well bunged down, will be a good vinegar for the table.

Vinegar from the Refuse of Bee-Hives

When honey is extracted from the combs, by means of pressure, take the whole mass, break and separate it, and into each tub or vessel, put one part of combs and two of water; place them in the sun, or in a warm place, and cover them with cloths. Fermentation takes place in a few days, and continues from 8 to 12 days, according to the higher or lower temperature of the situation in which the operation is carried on. During the fermentation, stir the matter from time to time, and press it down with the hands, that it may be perfectly soaked. When the fermentation is over, put the matter to drain upon sieves or strainers. At the bottom of the vessels will be found a yellow liquor, which must be thrown away, because it would soon contract a disagreeable smell, which it would communicate to the vinegar. Then wash the tubs, put into them the water separated from the other matter; it immediately begins to turn sour; when the tubs must be again covered with cloths, and kept moderately warm. A pellicle, or skin, is formed on their surface, beneath which the vinegar acquires strength; in a month's time it begins to be sharp; it must be left standing a little longer, and then put into a cask, of which the bung-hole is left open. It may then be used like any other vinegar.

To strengthen Vinegar

Suffer it to be repeatedly frozen, and separate the upper cake of ice, or water, from it.

All vinegars owe their principal strength to the acetic acid they contain; but the vinegar of wine contains also tartar, a small portion of the malic acid, alcohol, and colouring matter; that of cider contains merely the malic acid, little or no alcohol, and a yellowish colouring matter.

Vinegars from Orange and Elder Flowers, Clove-Gilliflowers, Musk-Roses, &c.

Dry an ounce of either of the above flowers (except the orange flowers, which will not bear drying,) for two days in the sun; then put them into a bottle, pour on them a pint of vinegar, closely stop the bottle, and infuse 15 days in moderate heat of the sun. Vinegars of any other flowers, as tarragon, &c. may be made in a similar manner.

Distilled Vinegar

This is obtained from vinegar by distillation, rejecting the 4th or 8th part that comes over first, and avoiding its acquiring a burnt flavour.

Distilled vinegar is weaker than the common, but is used sometimes in pickles, where its want of colour is an advantage.

Honey Water for the Hair

Take of honey, 4 lbs, very dry sand, 2 lbs. Mix and put into a vessel that will hold five times as much; distil with a gentle heat a yellowish acid water: this acid greatly encourages the growth of hair.

MISCELLANEOUS BEVERAGES

To Make Ginger Beer

Take of good Jamaica ginger, 2½ oz.
moist sugar, 3 lbs
cream of tartar, 1 oz.
the juice and peel of 2 middling sized lemons,
brandy, ½ pint,
good solid ale yeast, ¼ pint,
water, 3½ gallons.

This will produce 4½ dozen of excellent ginger beer, which will keep twelve months. Bruise the ginger and sugar, and boil them for 20 or 25 minutes in the water, slice the lemon and put it and the cream of tartar into a large pan; pour the boiling liquor upon them, stir it well round, and when milk warm, add the yeast; cover it over, let it remain two or three days to work, skimming it frequently; then strain it through a jelly-bag into a cask, add the brandy, bung down very close, and at the end of a fortnight or three weeks, draw it off and bottle, and cork very tight; tie the cork down with twine or wire. If it does not work well at first, add a little more yeast, but be careful of adding too much, lest it taste of it.

Spruce Beer

Take, if white is intended, 6 lbs of sugar; if brown, as much treacle, and a pot of spruce, and ten gallons of water. This is also managed in the same way as ginger beer, except that it should be bottled as soon as it has done working.

Seltzer Water

Take of water any quantity. Impregnate it with about ten times its volume of carbonic acid gas, by means of a forcing pump.

Liquid Magnesia

Take of water 1 gallon, carbonate of magnesia, 3 drachms, and impregnate it as above.

Potash Water

Take one ounce of subcarbonate of potash, and impregnate as above.

Soda Water

Take 2 ounces of subcarbonate of soda, and impregnate as above.

Portable Lemonade

Take of tartaric acid, ½ oz., loaf sugar, 3 oz., essence of lemon, ½ drachm.

Powder the tartaric acid and the sugar very fine, in a marble or wedgewood mortar (observe never to use a metal one), mix them together, and pour the essence of lemon upon them, by a few drops at a time, stirring the mixture after each addition, till the whole is added, then mix them thoroughly, and divide it into twelve equal parts, wrapping each up separately in a piece of white paper. When wanted for use, it is only necessary to dissolve it in a tumbler of cold water, and fine lemonade will be obtained, containing the flavour of the juice and peel of the lemon, and ready sweetened.

To make Chocolate

To make good chocolate, put the milk and water on to boil; then scrape the chocolate fine, from one to two squares to a pint, to suit the stomach: when the milk and water boils, take it off the fire; throw in the chocolate; mill it well, and serve it up with the froth; which process will not take 5 minutes. The sugar may either be put in with

the scraped chocolate or added afterwards.
It should never be made before it is wanted; because heating again injures the flavour, destroys the froth, and separates the body of the chocolate; the oil of the nut being observed, after a few minutes' boiling, or even standing long by the fire, to rise to the top, which is the only cause this chocolate can offend the most delicate stomach.

TEA AND COFFEE DUTIES.

To make Coffee

To have coffee in perfection, it should be made from the best production, carefully roasted, and after cooling for a few minutes, reduced to powder, and immediately infused; the tincture will then be of a superior description. But for common use, the coffee of our own plantations is, in general, of very good quality.

In England, too little powder of the berry is commonly given. It requires about one small cup of coffee-powder to make four cups of tincture for the table. This is at the rate of an ounce of good powder to four common coffee-cups. When the powder is put in the bag, as many cups of boiling water is poured over it as may be wanted.

Pour a pint of boiling water on an ounce of coffee; let it boil five or six minutes, then pour out a cupful two or three times, and return it again; put two or three isinglass slips into it; or a lump or two of fine sugar; boil it five minutes longer, set the pot by the fire to keep hot for ten minutes, and the coffee will be beautifully clear. A hot cream should always be served with coffee. For foreigners, or those who like it extremely strong, make only eight dishes from three ounces. If not fresh roasted, lay it before a fire till hot and dry; or put the smallest bit of fresh butter into a preserving-pan, when hot throw the coffee into it, and toss it about till it be freshened.

THE STORE-ROOM AND STILL-ROOM

These rooms are entirely under the management of the housekeeper. The STORE-ROOM is appropriated as a depository for such imperishable articles of household consumption as are in continual request, and may be laid up, when purchased in quantities,—at times when cheapest,—most in season, or best—to be ready at hand when wanted.

◊◊ *Let every thing, not only here, but all over the house, be kept in its **proper place**, applied to its **proper use**, and **replaced** when worn out or destroyed.*
N.B. To save the trouble of referring to different places, for the several methods of storing or preserving many articles which are proper to be kept, we shall insert under this head every thing of this description that may occur to us.

SOAP will be the better for keeping—indeed, it should not be used when newly made. The cakes should be cut with a wire or string, into oblong squares, and laid up, on a dry shelf, a little distance apart, and across each other, so as to admit the air betwixt them, to harden it.

CANDLES and SOAP made in cold weather, are best; and when the price of these articles are likely to be high, a reasonable stock of both should be laid in.

STARCH should be bought when flour is cheap, and may be kept in a dry warm place, if closely covered, as long as may be necessary.

LOAF SUGARS should be kept tied up in paper, and hung up in a dry place. Brown sugars should be kept covered up, and in a moderately dry place.

SWEETMEATS, PRESERVES, &c. must be carefully kept from the air, and in a very dry place.

TEAS, COFFEE, CHOCOLATE, DRIED FRUITS, and generally, all kinds of grocery and condiments require to be kept dry and free from air.

The various kinds of SEEDS and RICE, PEARL-BARLEY, OATMEAL, &c. must be kept in a dry place, and be *covered close*, to preserve them from insects.

BREAD is best kept in an earthern pan with a cover.

WRITING and other PAPERS, that are constantly wanted, should be bought by the ream or bundle, and kept in a dry place.

APPLES should be spread, separately, on clean dry straw, on a dry upper floor, and care must be taken to preserve them from frost.

PEARS should be hung up, singly, by the stalk in a dry place.

GRAPES should be gathered before they are ripe, and may also be preserved hung up in single bunches the same way.

ORANGES and LEMONS, if bought when cheapest, may be preserved a long time, packed in fine, dried sand, with their stems upwards, and kept from the influence of the air.

FRESH MEAT, POULTRY, FISH, &c. should be kept in a cool, airy place.

All SALTED and DRIED MEATS, hams, tongues, &c. should be tied up in strong paper, and must be kept in a cold, dry place.

GREEN VEGETABLES should be kept on a damp stone floor, and excluded from the air by a damp cloth thrown over them.

CARROTS, PARSNIPS, and BEETROOTS, must be kept in layers of dry sand for winter use. Neither these nor potatoes should be washed till wanted.

POTATOES must be carefully covered, to protect them from frost, in winter.

ONIONS should be tied in traces, and hung up in a cold dry place.

THE STILL-ROOM MAID

The business of this servant is to wait on and assist the housekeeper; not only in the distillation of aromatic waters, spirits, and oils,—in the making of essences, perfumery, &c. but also, in the making of pickles, preserves, pastry, and confectionary; in making coffee, &c. to go up stairs; in washing up the china; in the management and arrangement of the STORE-ROOM; and whatever else she may have to employ her in.

[Wages from eight to twelve guineas per annum.]

THE COOK

THE KITCHEN-MAID
OR
UNDER COOK

THE SCULLION
OR
SCULLERY-MAID

ORDERED TO LIE ON THE TABLE.

THE COOK

On her first going into a family the Cook will do well to inform herself of the rules and regulations of the house,—the customs of the kitchen,—the peculiarities of her master and mistress,—and above all, she must study, most sedulously, to acquire a perfect knowledge of their TASTE; which, when attained, will most probably lead to her permanent establishment in the sovereignty of the kitchen.

She will enter into all the economical plans of her employers, and endeavur to make the most of every thing, as well for the sake of her own character as for their interest. Not forgetting that "wilful waste makes woeful want."

She will consider the encomiums of her master and mistress as her highest praise, and will accept even their admonitions as pleasing proofs of their desire to make her useful to themselves, and to enhance her own confidence and consequence.

The presidency of the kitchen being a situation of great trust and responsibility, she will best evince her sense of the confidence reposed in her by her anxiety to please, and a sedulous regard to the health and comforts of the family, which are, necessarily, in her keeping; governing her whole conduct by that most excellent moral maxim "Do unto others as you would they should do unto you."

To be well qualified for every situation, the Cook must not only understand the business of the kitchen, but must be a good judge of provisions, as in many families, where there is no housekeeper, she will be required to go to market. She must also be able to keep an account of the current expenses of the family; and to examine, check, and pay the tradesmen's bills, which she will have to settle with her mistress weekly, or when required.

The Cook should give directions to her assistants to *rise early*, particularly when a great dinner is to be dressed, so that every thing may be got quite ready in the kitchen to begin business as early in the morning as possible; else, nine times out of ten, the dinner will be too late: and it must always be recollected that "things done in a hurry are never well done," and that, "an hour lost in the morning may be run after the whole day, but never overtaken." Besides, to have every thing properly dressed, and to be punctual, as to time, with the dinner, will afford great satisfaction to her employers, and do credit both to them and to herself. Having learnt the precise time of dinner, she must not fail to be *punctual*.

Cleanliness, in every branch of domestic concerns cannot be too forcibly inculcated, and in the business of a Cook, particularly, it becomes a CARDINAL VIRTUE. Cleanliness and neatness of person and dress are not less important in her than the arrangement of the kitchen and larder, and all her operations.

Boiling

The boilers, saucepans, and other vessels, to be used for culinary purposes, must be kept perfectly clean and well tinned. BLOCK TIN sauce pans, &c. are safest, and perhaps best for these purposes.—When washed they should be dried by the fire, before they are put away; and they should always be wiped out again, with a clean dry cloth, immediately before they are used. This is to be done chiefly to prevent rust, and its baleful effects.

Poultry, and every kind of meat, both fresh and salted, should be washed and wiped dry, and then dredged well with flour, before it be put into the boiler, or pot; this will prevent its being soiled in the water, and will, also, prevent its looking greasy, when taken up.

Meat must always be put into *cold* water, with *just enough water to cover it*; say, about a quart of water to a pound of meat,—and it must be kept *so covered*, during the whole process of dressing, by adding boiling water occasionally.—By this method the inside will always be heated thoroughly, and be properly swollen, before the outside becomes hard; and the whole will be regularly done. This will, also, occasion the meat to look plump; and veal and poultry, in particular, will be the whiter and the better for it.

Beef loses about one-fourth, and mutton about one-fifth, in boiling.

A moderate fire must be kept up under the pot, increasing the heat *gradually*, till it boils, when it must be drawn back, kept close covered, and *constantly simmering, quite gently*, but by no means boiling fast. A tea-spoonful of salt thrown into the water, before it boils, will cause the scum to rise the better, which must be very carefully skimmed clean off, immediately; and if, afterwards, a little cold water be thrown in, more scum will be cast up, which must frequently be taken off, *as it rises*, as on this alone depends the good appearance of all boiled articles.

Remember—that water cannot possibly be made *hotter* than it is when it first boils; it is, therefore, a waste of firing, and very detrimental to the meat to make it boil *fast*, as it is thereby rendered hard, and its juices and finest flavour are evaporated in steam.

Generally, beef, mutton, and lamb, unless the joints are very thin, or small, require boiling from a quarter of an hour to eighteen minutes to a pound; lamb, veal, and pork, and *thick* joints also, of whatever kind, require somewhat longer, especially in *cold* weather, or when *fresh* killed. A large leg of pork, for instance, will take a little more time;—always reckoning from the time of its first coming to boil, and taking into the account that the pot must *always be kept gently simmering;—the slower the better, so that it be kept boiling*. If you suffer boiled meats to remain in the pot after they are done, they become soddened and lose their flavour.

Greens must be carefully picked, neatly trimmed, washed *quite clean* from vermin, and laid on a cullender to drain. Then, having ready a well-tinned saucepan, with plenty of clean, soft, boiling water, into which some salt has been thrown, and the scum taken off, plunge them into it, boil them *quickly*, watch them, and keep continually pressing them under the water with a fork as they rise; and when they begin to sink of themselves, they are done, and must be taken up instantly, and drained dry; for if over done, they will lose not only their crispness and beautiful appearance, but their flavour also. Cabbages, savoys, and turnip-tops, require that the water should be changed when *half done,* the second water should be boiling, and if managed as above directed, they will eat much the milder and sweeter for it. *This is the whole art of dressing vegetables to look green and eat well.* We therefore deprecate the use of those factitious and filthy expedients recommended by some, and practised by many, to give, as they pretend, a *good colour,* to boiled vegetables. *This is the best way;*—and all artificial means ought to be avoided, as unnecessary and pernicious.

Esculent *roots* of all kinds may be set on to boil in cold water.

Elements of Roasting

CLEANLINESS must ever be the *maxim* for the kitchen.

Before the spit is drawn from the meat, let it be wiped clean, and when done with, let it be rubbed with a little sand and water.

A good brisk fire, due time, proper distance, and frequent basting, are the chief points to be attended to in roasting.

Much depends on the fire;—it should always be *brisk* and glowing, clear at the bottom, and suited to the article to be roasted.

Beef and mutton lose about one-third in roasting.

The ashes should be taken up, and the hearth made quite clean, before you begin to roast. If the fire require to be stirred during the operation, the dripping-pan must be drawn back, so that then, and at all times, it may be kept clean from cinders and dust.—Hot cinders, or live coals, dropping into the pan, make the dripping rank, and spoil it for basting.

Beef requires a strong, steady fire, which should be made up a little time previous to its being wanted. If the meat has been hung up some time, the dry outside parts must be pared off, and it must be basted, first, with a little salt and water, then well dredged with flour, and afterwards basted, continually, with the dripping; but, if the meat be frozen, it must be brought into the kitchen several hours before it is dressed.—Large joints should be kept at a good distance from the fire at first, and gradually brought nearer and nearer;—the average distance for a large joint, at a good fire, may be about ten or twelve inches, an inch or two more or less, according to circumstances: when kitchen paper, dipped in the dripping, must be tied, not skewered, over the fat parts, to prevent their being scorched. When nearly ready, the smoke will draw from the meat towards the fire; at which time the paper must be taken off, and the meat must be put nearer to the fire to *brown* it; it must also be sprinkled with a little salt, and well dredged again, with flour, to froth it.

It is as necessary to *roast slowly* as to *boil slowly;*—and the *General Rule* is to *allow a full quarter of an hour to a pound for roasting* with a proper fire, under ordinary circumstances, and with frequent basting. But neither beef nor mutton require to be so well done as pork, lamb, and veal.—Pork, in particular, requires to be thoroughly done. It must be basted with salt and water; and the skin or rind of the leg, loin, and sparerib, must be scored, with a sharp knife, after it has been some time at the fire, to make it eat the better. Geese, pigs, and young pork, require a brisk fire, and should be turned quickly.

Great care should be taken in spitting the meat, that the prime part of the joint be not injured:—to balance it on the spit, cook-holds and loaded skewers are very handy.

A BOTTLE JACK is an excellent substitute for a spit, *in small families*, and for want of that, ten or a dozen yards of worsted, folded to a proper length, will answer the purpose very well. Meat if *hung* to be roasted, should have its ends changed when about half done. A good meat screen, lined with tin, should always be set before the fire when roasting; it keeps off the cold air, renders the heat more equable, and saves coals.

After all, the above *General Rule* is liable to many exceptions. If the meat be *fresh killed*, or the weather be *cold*, a good joint will require half an hour longer than if the meat be *tender* and the weather *temperate* or *warm*.

Baking

We do not much approve of baking butcher's meat, as a substitute for roasting it, though it cannot be denied that some articles may be baked to answer nearly as well as if roasted; and when a great dinner is to be prepared it may be convenient to send a dish or two to the oven, but over these the cook can have no control, and must, therefore, depend entirely on the baker. The following are articles that may with most advantage be baked, provided the meat be good and fat, and the baker be very attentive:—A sucking-pig, goose, some joints of beef, leg and shoulder of mutton, leg and loin of pork, fillet of veal, ham, hare, sprats, and other small kinds of fish in pans or jugs. To poor families, however, the oven affords great convenience as well as a considerable saving of expense and trouble.

Beef loses about one third of its weight by baking.

Broiling

For this operation let the fire be *brisk* and *clear*. The bars of the gridiron must be bright at top and clean betwixt; wipe the gridiron quite clean with a cloth, make its bars hot, and rub them with nice mutton suet, before you lay on the meat. Set the gridiron slanting over the fire, to prevent the fat dropping into it so as to occasion a smoke, which must be prevented.

Frying

Frying is, in fact, *boiling in fat*. Before you begin to fry, rub the inside of the frying-pan with a little fat, warm it and wipe it out with a cloth, quite clean.—To fry fish, half fill the pan with fat, olive oil, nice fresh lard, clarified drippings, or beef or mutton suet;—but whatever fat be used let it be perfectly sweet, free from salt, and nice and clean. Keep a *brisk* fire, and make the fat *very hot*, which may be known by its having done hissing. When ready, carefully drain it quite dry before the fire.

We give the following as an example of *the best method of Frying* SOLES, *and most other kinds of fish*:

Let them be quite fresh, and some time before you dress them, wash them thoroughly, and wipe them with a clean cloth, quite dry.—If to be fried with bread-crumbs, beat up an egg, the white and yolk together, quite well, dip the fish in the egg, and cover them completely with grated crumbs, and if you wish the fish to look still better, do them twice over with egg. The fish, if large, may be cut into pieces, the proper size for the table, otherwise they may be fried whole; when cut they must be dished up as if whole. Let the fat in the pan be sufficient to cover the fish, and when it *quite boils*, and begins to smoke, put in the fish; it will be nicely browned in about five minutes, when it should be turned, and fried just as long on the other side. When done lay them on a soft cloth, before the fire, and turn them every two or three minutes, till they are perfectly dry on both sides. The fat in which any thing is fried will serve to fry the same kind of thing several times.

ONE OF THE FRY.

Broths, Soups, Stock, &c.

Cleanliness in this, as in every department of kitchen business, must ever be held as the *leading principle*, and will contribute most to the satisfaction of all parties.

An economical Cook, when she boils animal food, will make a rule to convert the liquor, or broth, into some sort of *soup* or *stock*, which may be done at her leisure, and by which means she will always have *a rich kitchen*, as it is technically called, and will be able to make an *extra dish*, or an additional tureen of soup, at a short notice, and at a trifling expense. The fragments of meat left after dinner, with the trimmings of undressed meat and game, the heads, necks, gizzards, and feet of fowls, &c. when picked and washed clean, will help to enrich *soups*, or make *stock*, and save much expense in gravy meat. The *broths*, if saved in separate pans, will assist in making white or brown soups, and the gravies left in the dishes after dinner, will be good in *hashes*, or, with some trifling ingredients added, will make sauce for fish, goose, &c.

The liquor of a knuckle of veal may be converted into GLAZE, if boiled with a knuckle of ham, till reduced to a fourth or a third part, with the necessary herbs and spices added.

To prepare Soups, &c.—the first care of the Cook will be to see that the stew-pan to be used is well tinned, scalded, and wiped out perfectly clean and dry. She will put some butter or marrow into the bottom of the pan, then lay in a leg or shin of beef with the bones well broken, and the meat cut to pieces; or the skirts of beef, the kidney or melt, or the shank bones of mutton, well cleaned, with the fragments and trimmings of meat and other articles, as above mentioned;—these she will cover close and keep over a *slow fire* an hour, stirring it up, occasionally, from the bottom, and taking great care that it does not burn.—When all the virtues of the meats are extracted, and the juices are again absorbed by them, she will add water enough to cover them, which will be in the proportion of about a quart of water to a pound of meat, for soup, and to two pounds, for gravies; the scum must then be carefully taken off, *quite clean*, as it rises, after it has boiled; for the more soups and broths are skimmed, the better, and more transparent they will be: and this transparency, combined with their uniformity of taste, constitutes their chief excellence. It is important that the soup be kept *gently simmering* five or six or more hours, and that then be added a scraped carrot, a head of celery, a couple of onions, two turnips, and a few sweet herbs;—when ready, let it be strained carefully through a clean tamis, previously dipped in cold water, into stone or unglazed earthen pans, and let the fat remain upon it, to preserve it, till wanted.

Soups and broths when done, ought not to be covered, nor put away with vegetables in them.

Use *soft* water to boil white peas, and let the peas be whole; but *pump* water will make green peas-soup of a better colour.

A good tureen of peas-soup may be made from the liquor of pork, mutton, or beef.

The lean of hams or gammon of bacon should be used when stock is made; but if the former, first give it a boil in water, before you put it in, else it will turn the soup red.

The *sediment* of gravies, &c. that have stood to be cold, should never be used.

A clear jelly of cow-heels makes a great improvement to gravies and soups.

A lump of clarified butter, thoroughly mixed with flour and boiled with the soup will give it a richness and a greater consistency, if required.—A little tarragon added, just before it is served up, will give it an agreeable flavour.

All soups should be sent to table quite hot.

CULLIS, or *brown gravy*, is made with lean veal and ham or gammon, and sweet herbs, &c.

BECHAMEL, or *white sauce*, is made in the same way, but is not browned; it must be improved by the addition of equal quantities of good broth and thick cream simmered with it half an hour, before it is strained off.

The articles used in thickening, seasoning, and flavouring broths and soups, are chiefly bread, flour, oatmeal, peas, rice, Scotch and pearl-barley, isinglass, maccaroni, turnips, beet, carrots, mushrooms, garlic, onions, shallots, cress, parsley, thyme, sage, mint, and other sweet and savoury herbs; also allspice, cinnamon, cloves, mace, nutmeg, ginger, pepper, lemon-juice, essence of anchovies, &c. These combined with wine and mushroom catsup, form an endless variety for flavouring and seasoning broths and soups.

Basil, savoury, and knotted-marjoram, are very pungent, and should be used cautiously.

No Cook can support the credit of her kitchen without having plenty of gravy, cullis, and stock always at hand, as these are the bases of all soups and high-seasoned dishes.

Sauces and Gravies

These are simple, and easily made.

Gravy for Roast Meat

Almost every joint will afford trimmings enough to make plain gravy for itself, which may be heightened with a little browning.

Or, half an hour before the meat is done, mix a little salt and boiling water, and drop it on the brown parts of the meat, which catch in something under, and set it by to cool; when the meat is ready, remove the fat, warm the gravy, and pour it into the dish.

Or, the brown bits of roasted or broiled meat, infused a night in boiling water, and the next day just boiled up, and strained off, will make a good gravy.

Gravy for Boiled Meat

Make it of the trimmings and paring of the meat. Or pour as much of the liquor as may be necessary into the dish, and pierce the meat, on the under part, with a skewer.

Lemon Sauce

Pare a lemon, cut it into thick slices, and divide these into small squares or dice, which mix with a quarter of a pint of melted butter.

Parsley and Butter

Wash and pick the parsley, very carefully, boil it ten minutes with a tea-spoonful of salt, in a little water, drain it, and bruise it to a pulp, then mix it by degrees with about half a pint of melted butter.

N.B. Sauces of fennel, chervil, basil, tarragon, burnet, cress, &c. may be made in the same way.

Anchovy Sauce

Pound three anchovies in a mortar with a bit of butter, rub it through a hair-sieve, with the back of a wooden spoon, and stir it into half a pint of melted butter.

Caper Sauce for Mutton

To a quarter of a pint of melted butter put a table-spoonful of capers, and nearly as much vinegar.

Garlic Sauce

Pound two cloves of garlic and proceed as with the anchovy sauce.

Shallot Sauce

Is made with three or four shallots pounded, and done in the same way.

Browning

Is nothing more than pounded white sugar, melted over a slow fire, with a little butter and water, till it begins to smoke and turn brown, then diluted with more water, till about the consistence of soy, and afterwards boiled, skimmed, strained, and preserved in well corked bottles.

ALL PLAIN SAUCES should taste only of the articles from which they take their names.

In COMPOUND SAUCES The several ingredients should be so nicely proportioned that no particular flavour should predominate.

Soy, walnut-peels, burnt treacle, or sugar, cayenne pepper, or capsicums, chillies, vinegar, pickled herrings, anchovies, sardines, or sprats, are the bases of almost all the sauces to be found in the shops.

Never season too highly your sauces, gravies, or soups.

Cloves and allspice,—mace and nutmeg,—marjoram, thyme, and savory,—leeks, onions, shallots, and garlic,—need not be mixed together in the same preparation, when either of them will supply the place of the others.

In short, Cooks now know, by experience, that a much less number of ingredients are sufficient to give a finer flavour to sauces, &c. than was formerly used; because, in this age of refined taste, we have learnt to combine the simply elegant with the purely nutritious.

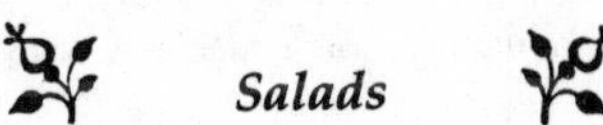

Salads

These may be eaten at all seasons of the year; but they are most wholesome in the spring, when green herbs, of all kinds, are in the greatest perfection. They are, then, most efficacious, in cleansing, sweetening, and purifying the blood. But, though Salads in the winter act not so powerful as in the spring, yet, such as are to be had, retain all the properties or qualities of their nature, and the warmer kinds, in particular, being gentle, salutary, and most excellent stimulants, are well calculated to warm the stomach, and exhilarate the spirits.

The following are the principal herbs, or vegetables, used in English salads; viz.

Beetroot	Mint	Small Salading which are
Celery	Onions	Turnip
Chervil	Parsley	Rape
Chives	Radish Common	Salad Radish
Corn Salad	Radish Turnip	Mustard
Cucumber	Shallots	Garden Cress
Garlic	Sorrel	
Lettuce	Water Cresses	

Balm, Dandelion, Nettle Tops, Sage, Spinach Tops, and Tarragon, are sometimes used.

Besides these, the French use many other articles as Salads, most of which being warm, exhilarating, and anti-scorbutic, contribute greatly to their health and cheerfulness; viz.

Balm	Pennyroyal Tops	Dandelion
Sage	Tarragon	Spinach Tops
	Nettle Tops	

Salad herbs should be used fresh from the gardens; but if grown stale, they must be refreshed in cold water. They must be carefully picked, and washed clean, and then shaken in a clean cloth to dry.

The ingredients generally used in mixing Salads are eggs boiled hard, and rubbed fine, oil, vinegar, mustard, pepper, and salt.

Kitchen Utensils

The adulteration of articles of provision is now so common, that the Cook will do well to be guarded against such impositions, by dealing with respectable tradesmen only.—The articles most frequently adulterated are bread, tea, brown sugars, coffee, mustard, pepper, and all other things that are to pass through the mill.

The Cook should take care to be amply provided with proper instruments, and kitchen utensils of all kinds, without which she can do nothing as it ought to be done. It will be necessary to have graduated glass measures, such as the apothecaries use, divided into teaspoonsful and table-spoonsful,—a common tea-spoon will be about a dram, 4 tea-spoonsful, a table-spoonful, and 4 of the latter will be about a common wine-glassful,—and also graduated on their sides, according to the following figures, in order to measure quantities of fluids with accuracy.

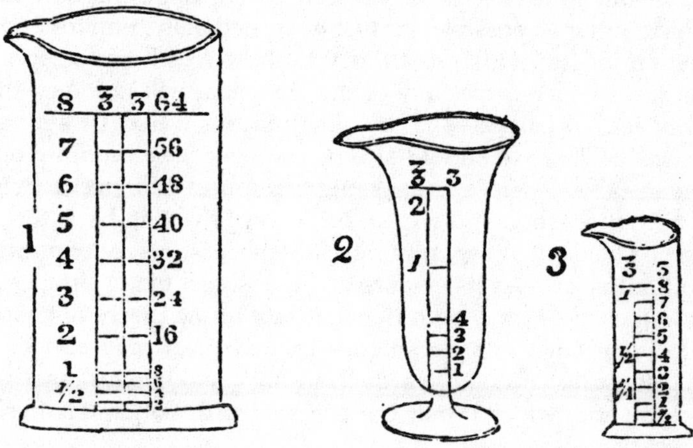

1. Represents a glass, calculated to measure any quantity from two drachms to eight ounces.
2. From one drachm to two ounces.
3. From half a drachm to one ounce.

Note.—Sixty drops or minims make one drachm.

Scales and weights should also be kept at hand, not only for weighing heavy articles, such as butcher's-meat, grocery, &c. but also such as will weigh small quantities with accuracy.

Before breakfast, or as soon as possible after, the Cook having seen that her assistants in the kitchen are getting forward all things preparatory to the principal dinner, and having also given the kitchen-maid directions for the servants' dinner, her attention will next be directed to

The Larder

The situation of the Larder should be dry, airy, and shady; it should be well ventilated, and kept perfectly clean, cool, and free from smells of all kinds.

The freezing point, or about 32° of Fahrenheit's Thermometer, is the most perfect temperature of the atmosphere for preserving animal food.

Moist and close weather is very bad for keeping meat, poultry, &c. A southerly wind is also unfavourable;—and lightning will quickly destroy it.

MEAT

A large Safe, pierced with holes on every side, to be hung up in an airy situation, would be a very valuable appendage to every Larder.

GENERAL BUSINESS OF THE LARDER

Joints of meat, game, &c. should be hung where there is a current of dry air, till they are tender. If they be not kept long enough, they will be hard and tough;—if too long, they lose their flavour. Much loss is sustained by the spoiling of meat in warm weather; to prevent which, as far as possible, it must be turned daily, end for end, and wiped every morning and night, with a clean, dry cloth, to free it and keep it from damp and moisture. If it be feared that any of the ripe meat will not keep till wanted, it should be parboiled, or part-roasted, by which means it may be kept a day or two the longer. Pieces of charcoal should also be put over meat, and a plug of charcoal put into the vents of fowls, &c. a string being tied round their necks. Before dressing meat it must be well washed and wiped dry; except roasting-beef, the dry outsides of which must be pared off. When meat indicates the least degree of putridity it should be dressed without delay, else it becomes unwholesome. In the latter case, however, even fish, as well as meat, may be reclaimed, by putting pieces of charcoal into the water with it, when boiled or parboiled.—Tainted meat may also be restored by washing it in cold water, and afterwards in strong camomile tea, and rubbing it dry with a clean cloth; after which it may be sprinkled with salt, and suffered to remain till the next day, if necessary.

In frosty weather all meat should be brought into the kitchen over night, or at least several hours before it is to be dressed.

Early in the morning remove the cold meat into clean dishes; change also, all the broths, soups, gravies, stock, cullis, &c. that require it, into clean scalded stone-pans; and never leave any eatables in copper or brass vessels, for if touched with salt or vinegar, or any acid, and left wet, they will corrode and gather poison.

Turn and rub the meat that is in salt; after which let the Larder be well scoured and cleaned out.

Dried meats, hams, tongues, bacon, &c. must be hung up in a cool, dry place, otherwise they will become rusty.

Bread should be kept in an earthen pan, with a cover, to exclude the air;—it should not be cut till it is a day old.

The vigilant Cook, having attended to the minutiae of the LARDER, and directed that the shelves and floor be well scoured and washed, and every part made perfectly free from smells, will next, if it be in her department, prepare to go to market, and consult her mistress or the housekeeper accordingly.

Having seen that all the marketing is properly disposed of,—the parlour lunch, nursery and servants' dinners getting forward, or got out of the way, then commences the *principal* preparations for the day.

HARE DRESSING.

In families where great dinners are seldom given, it will be better, when it can be conveniently done, to make an arrangement, as to the principal dishes, a day or two, or more, beforehand. The Cook should never quit her post, on such an occasion, as it requires not only great skill but the utmost attention and exertion to send up the whole of a great dinner, with all its accompaniments, in perfect order.

When there is an opportunity of getting forward the soups, sauces, and made dishes, on the preceding day, it should, by all means, be done; but if not, the soups, &c. should be forwarded early in the morning, and while these are preparing, the joints of meat, cutlets, and other articles should be trimmed, the poultry and game, &c. trussed and made ready for dressing; the vegetables picked quite clean, trimmed, and *well* washed, and laid separate, in dishes or cullenders. The shallots, onions, sweet-herbs, spices, &c. should also be prepared, and laid quite at hand.

The *Bill of Fare* being made out, and the hour of active operation approaching, the clock must be consulted, and the different articles prepared and laid to the fire, in succession, according to the times they will take, that all may be ready in due time.—A scene of activity now commences, in which you must necessarily be cool, collected, and attentive.—Have an eye to the roast meat, and an ear to the boils,—and let your thoughts contiually recur to the rudiments of your art, which at this moment must be called into practical requisition. You will endeavour that every kind of vegetable, and of sauce, be made to keep pace with the dishes to which they respectively belong—so that all may go up stairs *smoking hot* together, and in due order.

Let a clean cloth be laid on the kitchen-table, and with the *bill of fare* for your guide, if neither housekeeper nor the butler be present, let the dishes, intended to be used, be placed on this table, exactly as they are meant to stand on the table in the dining-room, and let every article be taken off the table in the kitchen, by the footman, and proper assistants, in regular order, by which means the butler cannot fail to set them in their proper places above stairs.

In some families, the soups are sent up first; and next, after a few minutes, the fish, then the removes, vegetables, sauces, and the whole of the first course:—mean time the *entremets*, or second course, will be dished and sent up, precisely in the same way. This would be done in all families, at all times, were it not deemed necessary frequently to sacrifice convenience, comfort, and every other consideration, at the shrine of fashion and elegance of appearance.

When the dinner things are brought down, the meat must be removed into clean common dishes; and as many things, such as fricandeaus, stews, &c. may remain untouched, or can be made to do again, when tossed up afresh, in different ways; they must be taken out of the gravies, the garnish, &c. picked clean off them, and the meat put by in clean dishes, and covered with thin slices of bacon. These gravies, and those from the roast meats of different kinds, must all be saved in separate stone pans, as all things of this kind serve to make a *rich kitchen*, and may be converted or applied to various useful purposes. The soups that are left should be strained through sieves to take out the bread and other vegetable matters, which, if left in, would turn them sour.

What sweets are left, such as Blancmange, Jellies, &c. may be melted and run into smaller moulds or shapes, and made to do again. Such management as this is highly commendable in all families, as thereby you are at all times provided for *extra visitors*.

Potted Meats, Collared articles, Anchovies, Oysters, and other shell-fish, mock Brawn, cold Hams, Tongue, Stewed Peas, Black Caps, Sweets of various kinds, and some sorts of Tarts, should also be kept ready for suppers and *extra occasions*.

The kitchen fire being reduced, and made up for ordinary occasions,—the dishes and every other article that has been used in the course of the day, and particularly the *pots, kettles, sauce-pans,* and other *culinary utensils*, being all scoured, and made perfectly clean, dried, wiped out, and put in their proper places;—the dressers and tables scoured down, and the whole kitchen made quite clean and put into perfect order, the principal business of the day may be considered at an end, as little more, of consequence, will seldom be required on the part of the Cook, except what further attention the LARDER, in hot weather, may demand, before she retires.

Useful Hints

With the utmost attention of the Cook, she can gain no credit, if she send up more than one dish, with all its accompaniments, at a time, and that as quickly as possible.

Old meats do not require so much dressing as young, because they may be eaten with the gravy in them.

Pickled pork requires longer dressing, in proportion, than any other meat.

Hashes and minces should be only simmered; if boiled, they become hard.

Meat hastily boiled or roasted is, thereby, made the more indigestible, and its juices are wastefully extracted.

To keep meat hot, when done, take it up, set the dish over a pan of boiling water, put a deep cover over it, and throw a clean cloth over that.

Broiled beef steaks, mutton-chops, &c. should always be sent to the table hot.

Whole peas are better than split peas for soup, in winter. It is a good practice to steep them an hour or more in cold water, before they are boiled.

Wines and spices should not be put into soups, stews, &c. too early, as the heat evaporates both the spirit and the flavour.

Vermicelli, when used in soups, &c. should not be suffered to remain in it more than fifteen minutes, as it will become a paste.

Dripping will do as well as butter to baste anything.

A small quantity of cream is better than flour and water, in melting butter.

Much butter is not to be recommended on all occasions.

When the palate is become dull by frequent tasting, wash the mouth with milk;—or eat an apple.

A bit of bread stuck upon the point of the knife with which you peel or cut onions, will prevent their disagreeable effect on the eyes.

A kettle of water kept boiling, over a charcoal fire, will effectually prevent its deleterious effects in the room.

Coals. Judicious Cooks will perform their culinary operations with much less coal than those who erroneously conceive that the greater the fire, the greater the dispatch. Time, rather than a fierce fire, answers best both for roasting and boiling meats.—Round coals are best for use, and small coal should never be thrown on a weak fire, as it will stop the progress of the air through the fire; and perhaps extinguish it. But small coal, or culm, a little wetted, and thrown at the back of a good fire, will become cinders or coke, and greatly improve it.

All the ashes of the kitchen and other grates should be sifted, and the cinders saved, to be used under the boilers in brewing and washing, or in the ironing stove.

A simple and excellent contrivance for sifting cinders may be purchased at the Ironmongers.

Omelettes should be made to eat full and thick at the mouth. They should be sent up quite hot, after dinner, and are wholesome, and great favourites in most countries.

A little sugar much improves the taste of green peas.

Potted meats make excellent sandwiches.

Sandwiches should be neatly cut in mouthfuls, so as to be taken up with a fork.

Maxims

Do every thing in the proper time.

Keep every thing in its proper place.

Use every thing for its proper use.

Never use any boiling or stewing utensil, pot or pan, spit, cookhold, spoon, ladle, or skewer, sieve, tammy or pudding cloth, jelly bag, net, tape, or other kitchen article, that have not been well scalded or washed with boiling water, and thoroughly dried.

The Cook's Catechism

Browning	A preparation of white sugar, browned over the fire, and then diluted to the consistency of soy, for the purpose of colouring soups, gravies, &c.
Bechamel	A simple white gravy or sauce
To Braize	To stew over a slow fire
Consommé	A rich soup or gravy consumed over the fire to the consistency of a jelly, to be diluted and converted, when wanted, into soup
Cullis	A rich brown gravy, made in various ways, according to the purpose for which it is intended
Entrées	Dishes for a first course
Entremets	Dishes for a second course
Esculents or Edibles	Animal or Vegetable food—any article that may be eaten
Fricandeau	A sort of Scotch collops
Fricassee	Fowls, rabbits, or other things cut to pieces and dressed with a strong white sauce
Garnishes	Articles laid round a dish by way of ornament, and generally, but not always, intended to be eaten therewith
Glaze	A very rich sauce or gravy boiled to a thick substance, and preserved in pots, to be laid on with a long-haired brush, over high-seasoned dishes
To Glaze	To cover the outsides of hams, tongues, and all stewed dishes, with glaze or braize, to give them a rich appearance
Haricot	Veal, mutton, &c. stewed with vegetables
Hot-Bath	A pan or other vessel filled with water, and placed in a pot, which is kept boiling over the fire, for the purpose of scalding fruits, or preparing meats
Maigre	Soup, or any other dish, made without meat or gravy
To Pass	To dress a thing partially, by setting on, or shaking it over the fire for a short time
Ragoût	Or stewing or boiling meat or other articles, to preserve their juices
To Sheet	To line the inside of a dish with paste
Stock	A preparation from gravy meats, &c. always to be kept at hand, for the purpose of making soup or gravy

We have now initiated our honest candidate for culinary fame, by regular and easy gradations, into the whole *arcana* of the profession,—taught her to judge of the natures and qualities of provisions, and their comparative values;—the best seasons and methods of purchasing, and of managing undressed animal and vegetable food; and the general economy of the LARDER. The best methods of making soups, gravies, sauces, and salads: and, lastly, the modern mode of preparing a good dinner, with all its most approved accompaniments.

Above all things, a cook should avoid all cruelty, and no custom or usage should be an excuse for any practices, by which living and sensitive creatures are to be put to wanton and unnecessary torture.

LIKELY TO ANSWER.

THE KITCHEN MAID
OR
UNDER COOK

Cleanliness must be considered as the *first and leading principle* of the kitchen-maid, as well as of the head cook and all other persons in any way employed in the business of the kitchen.

This servant has, in many families, the hardest place in the house. It is her business, under the superintendance of the cook, to take nearly the whole management of roasting, boiling, and otherwise dressing all plain joints and dishes, and all the fish and vegetables.—She is also, if there be no *scullion*, to keep the *kitchen, larder, scullery,* all the *kitchen utensils,* and every thing belonging to it perfectly clean,—in the best possible condition, and always fit for use. On the due performance of this important part of her business mainly depends the credit and character, not of herself only, but of the cook also; it therefore behoves the cook to see it properly done.

The kitchen-maid must always rise betimes, light the kitchen fire, and set on water to be heated for all the purposes of the family, the first thing she does.—She next scours the dressers and shelves, and the kitchen tables, with soap and sand, and hot water; and cleans up the kitchen; she then clears out and cleans the housekeeper's room, the hall and passages, the front door, and area steps, the larder, and the butler's pantry; in doing which, the scullion (if there be one kept) takes the dirtiest and most laborious part. She then prepares the breakfasts in the housekeeper's room, and the servants'-hall. These things, if she be active, she will have accomplished before the cook begins to require her attention and attendance in the larder, in the furtherance of the culinary preparations; to which, however, she must have an eye, even from her earliest rising, particularly to the soups and other things, that require a long time to prepare.

After breakfast, if not before, the cook will require her assistance in the larder, and afterwards for the remainder of the day she will be occupied in the kitchen, under the direction of the cook; first, in preparing for the servants' dinner, the dinner in the nursery, or elsewhere, and the lunch in the parlour; next in helping to get ready the family dinner; then in washing up and clearing away every thing, and cleaning up the kitchen; and lastly, in setting out and preparing the supper, either hot or cold, for the servants.

As the kitchen-maid generally fills her situation with the view of becoming a cook, at a future day, it behoves her to read with attention the foregoing *Directions to the Cook*, which contain the rudiments of the art, and which, if she attentively study, and practically apply, will enable her to attain such a proficiency in her business, as will render her a valuable acquisition to her future employers. [Wages from 12 to 14 guineas per year.]

THE SCULLION, OR SCULLERY-MAID

It is the business of this servant to light the fires in the kitchen range, and under the copper or boilers, and stew-holes—to wash up all the plates and dishes—scour and clean all the sauce-pans, stew-pans, kettles, pots, and all other kitchen utensils; and to take care that all the latter are *always kept clean, dry*, and *fit for use*. She is to assist the kitchen-maid in picking, trimming, washing and boiling the vegetables, cleaning the kitchen and offices, the servants'-hall, housekeeper's room, and steward's room; and to clean the steps of the front door and the area. She makes the beds for the stable men—and generally fetches, carries, and clears away for the cook and kitchen-maid, and otherwise assists in all the laborious parts of the kitchen business. [Wages from 8 to 12 guineas a year.]

To Clean Block-Tin Dish-Covers, Pewter Pots, &c.

Mix a little of the finest whiting, free from sand, with the smallest drop of sweet oil; rub the outside well and wipe it clean, with clean, dry soft linen rags.—Do the same to the inside, but wet with water, not oil:—always wiping these articles dry immediately after using them, and drying them by the fire, prevents their rusting, and saves much trouble in cleaning them.

THE LADY'S MAID

AND

YOUNG LADIES' MAID

SLAP DASH.

THE LADY'S MAID

The business of the lady's-maid is extremely simple, and but little varied. She is generally to be near the person of her lady; and to be properly qualified for her situation, her education should be superior to that of the ordinary class of females, particularly in needlework, and the useful and ornamental branches of female acquirements. To be peculiarly neat and clean in her person and dress, is better than to be tawdry or attractive, as intrinsic merit is a much greater recommendation than extrinsic appearance. In her temper she should be cheerful and submissive, studying her lady's disposition, and conforming to it with alacrity. A soft and courteous demeanour will best entitle her to esteem and respect. In fine, her character should be remarkable for industry and moderation,—her manners and deportment, for modesty and humility—and her dress, for neatness, simplicity, and frugality.

It will be her business to *dress, re-dress,* and *undress* her lady; and, in this, she should learn to be perfectly *au fait* and expeditious, ever studying, so far as it depends on herself, to manifest good taste, by suiting the ornaments and decoration of her dress to the complexion, habits, age, and general appearance of her person. Thus will she evince her own good sense, best serve her lady, and gratify all those who are most interested in her welfare and happiness. She should always be punctual in her attendance, and assiduous in her attention. Her's will be the care of her lady's *wardrobe,* and she should make that her *particular* care; appropriating to each article of dress its proper place, where it always may be found when wanted. It will be her business carefully to examine every part of her dress, when taken off, and if they have sustained an injury, or acquired any spots or stains, immediately to clean and repair them; then fold them up neatly, and put them away.

Her first business, in the morning, will be to see that the house-maid has made the fire, and properly prepared her lady's dressing-room:—she then calls her mistress, informs her of the hour, and having laid out all her clothes, and carried her *hot water,* to wash, she retires to her breakfast with the housekeeper and other principal servants. When her lady's bell rings, she attends her in her dressing-room,—combs her hair for the morning, and waits on her till dressed; after which, she folds and puts away her night-clothes, cleans her combs and brushes, and adjusts her toilet-table:—she then retires to her workroom, to be ready if wanted, and employs herself in making and altering dresses, millinery, &c. About one o'clock the family generally take their lunch, and the servants their dinner.—After this, she is again summoned to attend her lady's toilet whilst dressing to go abroad. When gone, she again adjusts her clothes, and every thing in the room, and lays out and prepares the several articles that may be required for her dinner, or evening dress, and afterwards employs herself at needle-work in her own room, or in her other avocations, till her mistress returns to dress for dinner, perhaps about five, when she attends her for that purpose; and having done this, it may happen that no further attendance on her mistress' person will be required till she retires to bed: meanwhile she employs herself at needle-work, as in the morning*—or else in the various occupations of getting up the fine linen, gauzes, muslins, cambrics, laces, &c. washing silk stockings, taking the spots or stains out of silks, &c. &c.

It is her business to see that the house-maid, or chamber-maid, empties the slops, keeps up the fires, both in this and the bed-room (if wanted), and keeps the rooms in perfect order.—Previous to her mistress' retiring for the night, she will have looked out her night-clothes, and aired them well; and she will, not only now, but at all times when she goes to dress, carry up *hot water*, for washing, &c. and when she is gone to bed, she will carefully examine all her clothes, and do all that is necessary to be done to them, before she folds them away. If her lady be elderly, infirm, or unwell, she will sometimes be required to bring her work, and sit with her, to administer her medicines, and sometimes to read to her. To qualify herself for this latter purpose, and to acquit herself with propriety, she will, at her leisure, practise reading aloud, from the best authors; as it is important to acquire a proper style and manner of reading, in all the varieties of poetry or prose, ode or epistle, comedy, or sermon; avoiding, alike, the dull monotony of the school girl, and the formal affectation of the pedant; but following nature as her guide, in all that appertains to emphasis, modulation, and delivery.

If acquainted with the superior branches of needle-work, she might afford her lady much gratification, in presenting her, occasionally, with such trifles as will be acceptable, and suitable ornaments for her person.—This will evince her disposition to be grateful and to oblige; and this, combined with a feminine sweetness of temper, and suavity of manners, cannot fail to be her sure recommendation to the esteem of her superiors and others, through all the various circumstances of life. [Wages, from 18 to 25 guineas per annum, with tea and washing.]

*In the absence of the housekeeper, she will be required to make tea and coffee for the drawing-room company.

THE YOUNG LADIES' MAID

In large families, where there are young ladies who require attendance, a maid is appointed to wait on all, or perhaps each lady has a maid. The duties of these are in all respects the same as the ladies'-maid; we therefore refer them to the directions given to her, for the necessary instructions. As this situation is considered merely initiatory to a better, and is occupied, generally, by an upper house-maid, or a young woman on her outset in life, the salary is somewhat less than that of a well qualified servant; and the perquisites, including that of her mistress' left-off clothes, are also reckoned at the same rate.

HEAD NURSE

UNDER NURSE

NURSERY MAID

THE GOVERNESS
OR
GOUVERNANTE

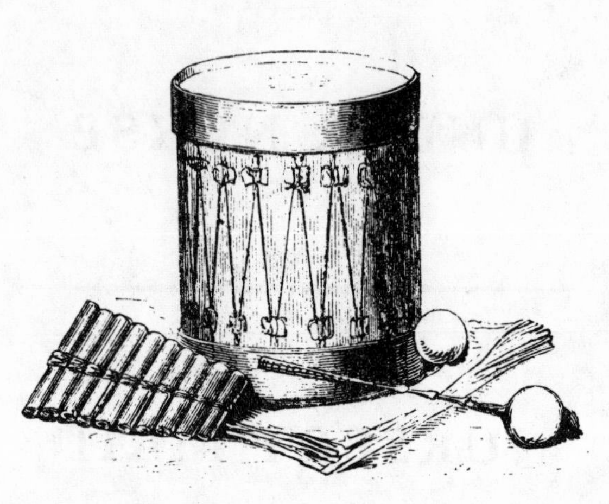

THE HEAD NURSE

As the hopes of families, and the comfort and happiness of parents are confided to the charge of females who superintend nurseries of children, no duties are more important, and none require more incessant and unremitting care and anxiety. Every symptom of approaching disease should be watched and reported to the parents or medical attendant of the family, and in this respect, nothing should be concealed or deferred till remedies are too late. In the daily washings, the state of the skin should be examined and noticed, as well as the tongue and the appetite, and spirits; and above all things, all chances of accident or juvenile mischief should be guarded against and removed. Windows should be fenced with bars, or the lower sashes nailed down; knives and sharp instruments should be kept out of reach; scalding water and dangerous ingredients secured from access; ponds and rivers fenced in; ladders removed; and fireplaces guarded by well-fastened wire fenders.

This important Servant ought to be of a lively and cheerful disposition, perfectly good tempered, and clean and neat in her habits and person. She ought also to have been accustomed to the care and management of young children, as all the junior branches of the family are entrusted to her care and superintendence, confiding in her skill, experience, and attention. She usually takes the sole charge of the infant from its birth, when the parent suckles it: to assist her in the management of this and the other children in the nursery, she has under nurses assigned her, who are entirely under her control.

The youngest nurse, or nursery maid, usually rises about six o'clock to light the fire, and do the household work of the nursery before the children are up, perhaps about seven o'clock, at which time the head nurse is dressed, and ready to bathe and wash them all over with a sponge and warm water; after which they are rubbed quite dry and dressed. This process, when there are several children, usually occupies the nurses an hour, or an hour and a half, when their breakfast is got ready, and the children are placed at their meal in the most peaceable and orderly manner. After breakfast, if the weather be favourable, the children are taken out by the assistant nurse, or nursery maid, for air and exercise, an hour or perhaps two, but not so long as to fatigue either of them. On their return, their hands and feet are washed, if damp or dirty, after which they attend to their lessons till dinner time. After dinner, if it be fine weather, the children are again taken abroad for air and exercise, and on their return again, after having their hands and feet washed, if necessary, they are in due time, about eight o'clock, dressed and put to bed. The Head Nurse finds ample employment during the whole day, in paying due attention to her infant charge, in giving directions, and in seeing that the whole business of the nursery is properly executed.

The sleeping room of the Nursery should be spacious, lofty, dry, airy, and not suffered to be inhabited in the day time. No servants should sleep in the same room, nor ought any thing to be done there that may contaminate the air, in which so great a portion of infantine life is to be spent. The consequences of vitiated air in bed-rooms are often fatal. Feather-beds and bed-curtains ought to be proscribed, as tending to debility; neither ought the beds to be placed too low, as the most pernicious stratum of air is that nearest the floor.

The air of the sleeping room ought to be changed immediately on the children's leaving the room, by opening the windows and doors; the beds ought, also, to be shaken up and left to cool; the slops cleared away; and every thing made and kept perfectly clean. In damp or bad weather, a fire must be made in the room to purify the air.

The management of infant children, has a more important influence on the health and happiness of man, than is generally imagined; as, at this period of existence, the foundation is laid either for irremediable debility, or for *mental* and *bodily* vigour. An Infant, consequently, requires considerable care, and indefatigable personal attention.

Its management for the first two months, cannot be too gentle, kind, or tender. Nothing should be done at first that can give it uneasiness; therefore, next to its health and well-being, regard should be had to its disposition, and the regulation of its temper; with this view also, the most rational way is to let the infant enjoy all the liberty it possibly can, without being restrained by its clothing, or starved by system. To set a child upright before the end of the first month is hurtful: afterwards the nurse may begin to set it up and dance it by degrees. It must be kept as dry as possible.

The clothing should be very light, and not too long, so that the legs may be got at with ease, in order to have them often rubbed in the day, with a warm hand, or flannel, and particularly the inside of them. Rubbing the child all over takes off scurf, and promotes the circulation of the blood.

A nurse ought to keep a child as little in her arms as possible, lest the legs should be cramped, and the toes turned inwards. Let her always keep the child's legs loose. The oftener the posture is changed, the better.

For the first fortnight or three weeks it should be always laid on a bed, except when taken up to supply its wants, which will give it habits of cleanliness at a very early age.

It may be very comfortably laid on a cushion, where it can be in no danger of falling, nor of any thing falling on it. Some one should sit by it, and divert and cheer it, if necessary, and take it up instantly, when it expresses the least dissatisfaction. A nurse should make it a strict rule, that the child should be in her own view, in whatever she may be employed.

By slow degrees, the infant may be accustomed to exercise, both within doors and in the open air: but it never should be moved about immediately after sucking or feeding, as that will be apt to sicken it. Exercise should be given it by carrying it about, and gently dandling it in the arms; tossing an infant about, and exercising it in the open air, in fine weather, is of the greatest service to it, in preventing distortion. In cities, children ought not to be kept in hot rooms, but to have as much air as possible; want of exercise being the cause of rickets, large heads, weak joints, a contracted breast, and diseased lungs, besides a numerous train of evils.

Endeavour to harden the body, but without resorting to violent means. A child is constitutionally weak and irritable to a high degree; hence we should endeavour to diminish this irritability, in order to procure it the greatest happiness of life, a firm body, whence may result a sound mind.

Such management is highly advantageous, as it will enable children to support every species of fatigue and hardship, when they become adults.

The plan of hardening children may, however, be carried to excess. An extravagant attempt to strengthen youth, deprives them of all their natural susceptibility of excitement, renders them insensible, and produces many bad effects, while they only acquire temporary energy, which decreases as they advance in years, and is attended with an early loss of their primitive vigour.

All attempts to render children hardy must, therefore, be made by gradual advances: for nature admits of no sudden transition. When children have once been accustomed to a hardy system of education, such a plan must be strictly adhered to.

The child's skin is to be kept perfectly clean by washing its limbs morning and evening, and likewise its neck and ears; beginning with warm water, till, by degrees, it will not only bear, but like to be washed with cold.

After it is a month old, if it has no cough, fever, nor eruption, the bath should be colder and colder (if the season be mild) and by degrees it may be used as it comes from the spring. After carefully drying the whole body, head, and limbs, a second dry soft cloth, somewhat warmed, should be gently used, to take all the damp from the wrinkles or soft parts of the body. Then rub the limbs; but when the body is rubbed, take special care not to press upon the stomach or belly. On these parts, the hand should move in a circle, because the bowels lie in that direction. If the skin be chafed, hair-powder is to be used. The utmost tenderness is necessary in drying the head; and a small, soft brush, lightly applied, is safer than a comb.

Clean cloths, every morning and evening, will tend greatly to a child's health and comfort.

The dress of the child by day should be light and loose, and for the night, it may be a shirt, a blanket to tie on, and a thin gown to tie over the blanket.

The unnecessary haste in which some nurses are accustomed to dress children, cannot be too strongly reprehended. In addition to this hurried dressing, its clothes

L 's for Mrs. Lilly, who
was once a nurse of mine.

are often injuriously tight. Pins should never be used in an infant's clothes; and every string should be so loosely tied, that two fingers may be introduced under it. Bandages round the head should be strictly forbidden, for to this error many instances of idiotism, fits, and deformity, may be traced.

Never allow the infant to be held opposite to open doors and windows. The air is beneficial, when it is in motion, and the weather is moderate, but it should always have some covering besides that which it wears in the house, when taken out; and it must not be laid on the cold ground, nor allowed to step on it, when it begins to use its feet. The intense heat of a summer day should likewise be avoided; excessive heat or cold being equally injurious.

The wisest maxim in treating infants with respect to food and drink, is to follow the simple dictates of nature; yet some nurses give them wine, spirits, spices, sugar, &c. which the stomach of a grown person would reject. At all times the utmost care will be necessary to avoid hurting its gums when feeding it. Its food should be gradually cooled in a saucer, and it should be given to it in a small spoon, only half filled, which will save its clothes from being soiled, and keep its bosom dry. Let it swallow one small portion, before another is offered, and raise its head, that it may pass the gullet easily. Never entice or press it to take more, if it once refuses, for it knows best when it has had enough.

As long as it has its mother's milk, no other sustenance will be wanting, if she be a good nurse. If there should be the least doubt of her having milk enough, the child may have cow's milk, mixed with two-third's soft boiled water, presented to its lips very frequently; but it never should be urged to accept it.

ONE IN HAND, TWO IN CRIB.

Rising early in the morning is good for all children, provided they awake of themselves, which they generally do; but they ought never to be waked out of their sleep. As soon as possible, however, they should be brought to regular sleep in the day.

Children, till they are two or three years' old, must never be suffered to walk so long at a time as to be weary.

In laying a child to sleep, it should be placed on the right side oftener than on the left. Laying it on its back when it is awake, is enough of that posture, in which alone it can move its legs and arms with freedom.

Infants cannot sleep too long; and it is a favourable symptom when they enjoy calm and continued rest, of which they should by no means be deprived, as this is the greatest support granted to them by nature. Sleep promotes a more calm and uniform circulation of the blood, and it facilitates assimilation of the nutriment received.

The horizontal posture, likewise, is the most favourable to the growth and bodily development of the infant.

Sleep ought to be in proportion to the age of the infant, and this salutary refreshment should fill up the greater part of a child's existence. After the age of six months, the periods of sleep, as well as all other animal functions, may, in some degree, be regulated; yet, even then, a child should be suffered to sleep the whole night and several hours both in the morning and afternoon. Nurses should endeavour to accustom infants, from the time of their birth, to sleep in the night in preference to the day, and for this purpose they will remove all external impressions which may disturb their rest, but especially they ought to avoid obeying every call for taking them up, and giving food at improper times.

To awaken children from their sleep with a noise, or in an impetuous manner, is certainly injudicious and hurtful; nor is it proper to carry them from a dark room immediately into a glaring light, against a dazzling wall; for the sudden impression of light debilitates the organs of vision, and causes weak eyes from early infancy.

Infants are sometimes very restless at night, which is generally owing either to their eating a heavy supper, to their tight night-clothes, or their being over-heated by too many blankets. [Wages £18 to £25. Perquisites at christenings.]

THE UNDER NURSE

Is chiefly engaged in attending to the senior children, and is entirely under the control of the head nurse. She assists in getting them up in the morning, washing and dressing them; attends them at their meals and takes them out for air and exercise, and performs or assists in the performance of all the duties of the nursery, while the head nurse is chiefly engaged with the infant child. [Wages 10 to 12 guineas.]

THE NURSERY MAID

The Nursery Maid is generally a girl who does the household work of the nursery, and attends the children when they go out for the air, &c. carrying such of them as may be required. [Wages 6 to 10 guineas.]

THE GOVERNESS, OR GOUVERNANTE

As many mothers have an aversion to public education for their daughters, the system of PRIVATE INSTRUCTION, by a respectable and well-educated female, is very generally adopted, in many families of moderate fortune, and in all of rank and opulence. Hence there is a constant demand for females of genteel manners, and finished education, at salaries which vary according to qualifications, and number and age of pupils, between £25 and £120 per annum, and often improved, on certain great length of service, by some provision for life.

Teachers in seminaries, half-boarders, educated for the purpose, and the unsettled daughters of respectable families of moderate fortune, who have received a finished education, are usually selected for this important duty; and the engagement is made either through an advertisement in the newspapers, or by agents who arrange between the parties for a moderate fee. But, in general, families apply to the governesses of public seminaries, who have young women in training for these employments.

The qualifications, of course, are various, and may vary with the age of the pupils. Good temper, and good manners, with a genteel exterior, are indispensable: for more is leant by example than precept. Besides, the governess who desires to be on a footing with the family, ought to be able to conduct herself in such manner, as never to render an apology necessary for her presence at family parties.

In addition to a thorough knowledge of the ENGLISH LANGUAGE, and to the power of being able to write a letter in a graceful and accurate style, the governess ought to be moderately acquainted with the FRENCH LANGUAGE; and it would be an advantage if she knew something of ITALIAN, as the language of music. She ought also to be able to play on the PIANOFORTE, so as to give the first lessons, and to superintend the practice directed in the lessons of a master; and in cases where great perfection is not desired, to render a master unnecessary. If she can perform on the harp or guitar, these instruments will qualify her to accommodate her instructions to various tastes. It will be also expected that she shall be able to teach the elements of DANCING, at least, the steps and ordinary figures of fashionable practice. Nor ought she to be ignorant of the useful art of ARITHMETIC, the constant exercise of which, will so much improve the reasoning powers of her pupils. NEEDLE-WORK of various descriptions, from the plain to the ornamental, will, as matter of course, be expected; and there can be no reason why she should omit to introduce to her pupils the geographical copy books, and other elementary books of GEOGRAPHY, by Goldsmith; and the familiar keys to the POPULAR SCIENCES, published by Blair and Barrow, such as the Universal Preceptor, the Class Book, the Grammar of Natural Philosophy, the Key to General Knowledge, by Barrow, and other superior works of the same kind, the selection of which, will distinguish her good sense: while the answering of questions, and filling up the copy books on the admirable Interrogative System, will be the means of incalculable advantage to her pupils, and a source of infinite gratification to their parents. The branches of ELEGANT LITERATURE are also within her reach, in such books as Aikin's Poetry for Children, and Pratt's Selection of Classical Poetry; and if she chooses to expand their intelligence, she can provide them with Blair's Belles Lettres, Shaw's Nature Displayed (a book which ought to be found in every family), and with a pair of globes, a microscope, and a telescope. DRAWING is also so essential an accomplishment, that its constant exercise should be kept up by means of Hamilton's Elementary Examples, or those of Chalons and Calvert.

THE SPELLS OF CHILDHOOD.

No young persons who are born to the enjoyment of fortune, and destined to fill any stations in society with credit and advantage, ought to have these accomplishments and sources of knowledge withheld from them; and the governess who contents herself with mere personal attainments, without at the same time addressing instruction to the MIND of her pupils, and who lays before them old-fashioned books, and obsolete systems of knowledge, compromises her own character, and sacrifices through their lives, the interests, welfare, and reputation, of her pupils.

In the sub-division of time, prolonged application is wearisome, and too frequent renewals are irksome. The best time for learning is in the morning before breakfast, and one hour and a half, or two hours, between seven and nine, will always be worth the three hours, which should be industriously passed, between eleven and two. The rest of the day should be devoted, in fine weather, to EXERCISE and AMUSEMENTS in the open air; and in bad weather to such amusements as induce exercise, of which, dancing, the skipping-rope, and dumb-bells, should form a part, and certain games which are practised in genteel society, as chess and cards, may be advantageously introduced in winter evenings.

Religion, morals, and temper, should be specially studied, and the essays of Mrs. Chapone, and Mrs. Hannah More, Barrow's Questions, his School Bible, and School Sermons, with Blair's or Enfield's Sermons, are suitable auxiliaries. Bad habits should be watched and corrected, and graceful ones, cleanliness and neatness of person, be stimulated. Blair's Governess's Register of Study and Conduct, will prove an excellent auxiliary. Superstitions, and vulgar faith in dreams, signs, omens, fortune-telling, and other weaknesses of mind, should be constantly exposed.

A governess, influenced by these practices and principles, will entitle herself to live on a footing with a family, when there are no special parties; and she must possess good sense enough not to intrude on that domestic privacy, and personal independence, which, without offence, is often desirable. Her own apartment, or that of her pupils, ought to be at once the scene of her pleasure and amusement, and if she mingles with the parties of the families, she must, of course, not make herself too familiar with the domestic servants.

Thus conducting herself with propriety, and identifying herself with the growing minds and affections of her pupils, she may secure their personal friendship to the end of their mutual lives, and if their moral feelings are not blunted, she may calculate on their gratitude in her old age, or if she survive them, in their last will.

THE UPPER HOUSE MAID

THE SERVANT OF ALL WORK

THE LAUNDRY MAID

THE DAIRY MAID

THE CHAMBER NURSE

AN INDIGNANT HOUSEMAID.

THE UPPER HOUSE MAID

In large families, where there is much work, two or more house maids are kept, but as the Upper House Maid has generally the superintendence and responsibility of all, we shall include their principal labours under one general head.

The Upper House Maid should be fully competent to undertake the management of all the household business of a gentleman's family; and to be perfectly qualified for her situation, she ought to have been previously initiated in the capacity of *Under House Maid*.

In most families she has the care of all the household linen, bed and table linen, napkins, towels, &c. which she also makes and keeps in repair, and besides cleaning the house and furniture, and making the beds, she washes her own clothes, and has sometimes to assist the laundry-maid in getting up the fine linen, washing silk stockings, &c. instead of the lady's maid; but these latter are considered as rather *extra* labours, and are not, in all families, deemed a necessary part of the house maid's business. She also cleans all the coal scuttles in use above stairs, and all the kettles used for warming water in the dressing-rooms, &c. When there are dinner parties the house maid washes up the plate and china.

The house maid, in a regular family, will find it necessary to rise about five o'clock, and her first business will be to open the shutters of the usual family sitting-rooms; as the breakfast-room and library, whence she clears away all the superfluous articles that may have been left there, and prepares for cleaning the stoves, fireplaces, and hearths, by rolling up the hearth rugs, carefully carrying them out to be shaken, and then laying down a piece of canvas, or coarse cloth, to keep the place clean, while she rakes out the ashes, takes them up, and brushes up the fireplace. She then rubs the bright bars of the stoves, and the fire-irons, first with oil, and afterwards with emery-paper, No. 3, or with brick-dust, till clean and bright—and, finally, with scouring-paper; and this should be done in the summer time, particularly when the stoves may have acquired spots for want of constant use.

The backs and sides of the fireplaces are next to be brushed over with black-lead, and then rubbed dry and bright with a hard brush kept for the purpose.

The fires are next lighted, and the marble hearths washed with flannel, dipped in a strong hot lather of soap and water, which must be cleaned off and wiped dry with a linen cloth;—the marble chimney pieces need not be thus cleaned above one or twice a week.

Common free-stone hearths may be scoured with soap and sand and cold water, and afterwards rubbed dry with a clean house cloth.

By this time the footman will have done all his work in the pantry, and have rubbed all the tables, chairs, cellerets, and other mahogany furniture, and cleaned the brass and other ornaments, the mirrors, looking-glasses, &c. in these rooms, when the carpets are to be swept, on ordinary occasions, with a carpet mop to take off the flue, lint, and dust; or more thoroughly, once a week with a long hair-brush or carpet-broom, first having strewed them over with damp tea-leaves (see receipt for scouring and cleaning carpets). The sides of the carpet are then turned up all round the room, and the dust on the floor swept away, or, occasionally, the floor scoured with soap and water. The carpet is then turned back again; the chairs and other furniture dusted singly, and removed from the middle of the room, where they were cleaned, to their proper places.

The window curtains and hangings may not require to be shaken and dusted every day, but the dust on the windows should be removed with a long hair-broom, and the cobwebs or any dirt on the ceiling, and in the corners of the room, must be sought for and removed.

Every thing being adjusted in the rooms for the reception of the family, the house maid next opens the shutters of the dining-room, and drawing-room, where she and the footman regularly proceed with their respective business in the manner above mentioned. The house maid with the fires and fireplace, floors, carpets, &c. scouring, washing, brushing, and dusting them; and the footman, rubbing and cleaning the mahogany furniture, looking-glasses, and other articles in his department, till all is made quite clean, and the rooms are fit for the reception of the family.

At an appointed time she repairs to the dressing-rooms of the master and mistress, and others in use, empties the slops, replenishes the ewers and water-carafes with fresh spring and soft water, and fills the kettles for warm water—cleans up the fireplaces, lights the fires, brushes the carpets, sweeps the rooms, dusts the furniture, and puts the rooms in order before the lady's maid and valet come to make their arrangements previous to the rising of their superiors.—Having done these, she sweeps down the principal staircase and goes to her breakfast.

As soon as the best bedrooms and dressing-rooms are at liberty, she repairs thither, puts out the fires, or not, according as the weather is,—throws open the windows (or the doors only, in unfavourable weather), to air the rooms, and the beds; opens all the beds, throws the bed-clothes off, on the backs of chairs, placed at the foot of the bed, shakes up each bed, and then proceeds to her other business in the rooms, in order to give as much time as can be spared for airing the beds. Meanwhile, she cleans up the fire-places, again, lays the fires to be ready when wanted, and having washed her hands and put on a clean apron, she makes the beds. (In this business she is usually assisted by the under house maid, as it requires two persons to make a bed well.) This done, she mops or brushes the carpets, to clean off the flue or feathers and dust,—sweeps out the rooms, rubs and dusts the furniture, supplies the ewers and carafes with clean water, and then retires; leaving the rooms properly arranged against the coming of the lady's maid and valet to prepare for their master's and mistress's dressing, previous to their going out.

She next proceeds to the other bedrooms—opens the windows and makes the beds—empties the slops—cleans out the rooms, rubs and dusts the furniture, and puts them in proper order.

Having finished all the bedrooms, the staircases, landings, and passages, will next claim her attention, which are also to be swept, the carpets brushed or swept, and the floor-cloths rubbed over with a clean wet flannel, and wiped dry with a clean house-cloth. On the appointed general cleaning days, the floor-cloths must be scoured with warm soap suds, and afterwards wiped dry, with a clean linen cloth.

On the general cleaning days also, which are usually Tuesdays and Saturdays, every branch of the household work must be thoroughly done, in the best manner;—the rooms are then to be scoured instead of being merely wiped or swept;—the carpets are to be well brushed or taken up to be beaten or shaken;—the stoves and fireplaces brightened and cleaned with particular care;—the marble hearths and chimney-pieces scoured;—the mahogany furniture and the brass or other ornaments in the best rooms, and the mirrors and looking-glasses cleaned, with more than ordinary attention;—the bed-furniture, window curtains and hangings well shaken, whisked and brushed: in short, the best practical methods for thoroughly cleaning the whole house, must be resorted to on that day.

If the house maid rise in good time, and employ herself busily, she will get every thing done above stairs in time to clean and make herself comfortable for dinner, about one o'clock; after which she will attend to her needle work, under the direction of the housekeeper. About four, in the winter, the fires in the dressing-rooms are to be lighted—the slops emptied—clean water supplied (hot and cold), and the dressing-rooms again dusted and cleaned, preparatory to the lady and gentleman dressing for dinner. While the family is at dinner, the dressing-rooms must be again prepared; and in the evening the shutters of the bedrooms and dressing-rooms must be fastened—the curtains let down—the beds turned down—the fires lighted, and the rooms put into proper condition for the night. [Wages from 12 to 16 guineas a year.]

NO FOLLOWERS ALLOWED.

To Scour Carpets, Hearth-Rugs, &c.

Rub a piece of soap on every spot of grease or dirt; then take a hard brush dipped in boiling water, and rub the spots well. If very dirty, a solution of soap must be put into a tub, with hot water, and the carpet well beat in it, rinsing it in several clean waters, and putting in the last water a table-spoonful of oil of vitriol, to brighten the colours.

To Dust Carpets and Floors

Carpets should not be swept with a whisk-brush more than once a week; at other times sprinkle tea-leaves on them, and sweep carefully with a hair-broom, after which they should be gently brushed on the knees with a clothes'-brush.

To Clean all sorts of Metal

Mix half a pint of refined neats'-foot oil, and half a gill of spirits of turpentine; wet a woollen rag therewith, dip it into a little scraped rotten-stone, and rub the metal well. Wipe it off with a soft cloth, polish with dry leather, and use more of the powder. If steel is very rusty, use a little powder of pumice with liquid, on a separate woollen rag, first.

To Restore Hangings, Carpets, Chairs, &c.

Beat the dust out of them as clean as possible, then rub them over with a dry brush, and make a good lather with Castille soap, and rub them well over with a hard brush, then take clean water and with it wash off the froth; make a water with alum, and wash them over with it, and when dry, most of the colours will be restored in a short time; and those that are yet too faint, must be touched up with a pencil dipped in suitable colours; it may be run all over in the same manner with water colours mixed well with gum water, and it will look at a distance like new.

To Clean Paper Hangings

Cut into eight half quarters a stale quartern loaf: with one of these pieces, after having blown off all the dust from the paper, to be cleaned by means of a good pair of bellows, begin at the top of the room, holding the crust in the hand, and wiping lightly downwards with the crumb, about half a yard at each stroke, till the upper part of the hangings is completely cleaned all round; then go again round with the like sweeping stroke downwards, always commencing each successive course a little higher than the upper stroke had extended, till the bottom be finished. This operation, if carefully performed, will frequently make very old paper look almost equal to new. Great caution must be used not be any means to rub the paper hard, nor to attempt cleaning it the cross or horizontal way. The dirty part of the bread too must be each time cut away, and the pieces renewed as soon as necessary.

To Whitewash

Put some lumps of quick-lime into a bucket of cold water, and stir it about till dissolved and mixed, after which a brush with a large head, and a long handle to reach the ceiling of the room, is used to spread it thinly on the walls, &c. When dry it is beautifully white, but its known cheapness has induced the plasterers to substitute a mixture of glue size and whiting for the houses of their opulent customers; and this, when once used, precludes the employment of lime-washing ever after; for the latter, when laid on whiting becomes yellow.

Whitewashing is an admirable manner of rendering the dwellings of the poor clean and wholesome.

To Preserve Polished Irons from Rust

Polished iron-work may be preserved from rust by a mixture not very expensive, consisting of copal varnish intimately mixed with as much olive oil as will give it a degree of greasiness, adding thereto nearly as much spirit of turpentine as of varnish. The cast iron-work is best preserved by rubbing it with black-lead.

But where rust has begun to make its appearance on grates or fire-irons, apply a mixture of tripoli with half its quantity of sulphur, intimately mingled on a marble slab, and laid on with a piece of soft leather: or emery and oil may be applied with excellent effect, laid on with a spongy piece of the fig-tree fully saturated with the mixture. This will not only clean but polish, and render the use of whiting unnecessary.

To Clean Marble

Take verdigris and pumice-stone, well powdered, with lime newly slacked. Mix with soap lees, to the consistence of putty. Put it in a woollen rag, and rub the stains well one way. Wash off with soap and water. Repeat, if not removed.

To Clean Floor-Cloths

Sweep them and wipe them with a damp flannel, after which wet them all over with milk, and rub them till bright with a dry cloth.

N.B. Floor-cloths should be chosen that are painted on fine cloth, well covered with colour and perfectly dry. The durability of the cloth depends greatly on these points, and particularly on its having had time for the paint to get quite dry. Old carpets answer extremely well, if painted and hung up to season some time, before they are laid down for use.

To Clean Looking-Glasses

Remove fly stains or any other soil from the glass with a damp cloth, then polish with a woollen cloth and powder-blue.

To Take Spots of Grease or Oil out of Boards

Drop a few drops of oil of turpentine on the spots and rub it hard with your finger; this will dissolve the grease, and make it mix with the soap (or suds) and water when the room is washed.

To Extract Lamp Oil, &c. out of Stone or Marble Halls, &c.

Mix well together a pint of strong soap lees, some fuller's earth, well dried, and a little pipe-clay, powdered fine; lay it on the part which is oiled, then put a hot iron upon it till dry. If all the oil come not out the first time, repeat it, and rub it well in. By doing it two or three times it will come out.

THE UNDER HOUSE MAIDS

Are entirely under the direction of the Upper House Maid, and are chiefly employed in cleaning and scouring the stoves and grates, scouring the coal scuttles, kettles, and fire-irons, beating and cleaning the carpets—scouring the floors, stairs, and passages;—washing the dishes when there is company, &c. &c.; besides assisting to make the beds, and carrying up the coals and water. In the afternoon, evening, or at leisure time, they are engaged with the *Upper House Maid* at their needle-work, in making and mending the household, bed and table linen,—mending stockings—washing and mending their own linen, and occasionally, assisting in the laundry. When there is no still-room maid, the Under House Maid has to wait at table in the housekeeper's room. [Wages £10 to £12 per year.]

THE HOUSEMAID'S BEST FRIEND.

THE SERVANT OF ALL WORK

In small families where only one female servant is kept, the servant of all work will be required to do all the work of the house, which in large establishments is very properly divided into several departments.

This description of servants is usually taken from the industrious and labouring classes of the community, who are bred up with a view to the situation, having no other prospect or dependence; and are taught, from their earliest age, to assist in the management of the house, the care of the younger children, preparing the meals, making the beds, scouring, washing, and in every other branch of domestic business:— In short, no girl ought to undertake, or can be qualified, for such a situation, who has not been thus bred up. And if, in addition to these preparatory qualifications, she comes from a sober, well-disposed family, and is of a tractable disposition, there can be but little doubt of her acquiring the good-will of her master and mistress, of qualifying herself for a superior service, and of finally succeeding in her sphere of life.

She will receive her first instructions from her mistress, or probably from the former servant, as to the peculiarities of the house, and will very soon, with attention, become versed in all.

Industry and cleanliness, with a determination to be useful, and to please, will speedily overcome all difficulties.

To rise early is indispensably necessary. ''Those who would thrive, must rise by five.'' And, recollect, that ''the servant who begins her work late, will have to run after it all the day, but will never overtake it.''

Every morning, the first business will be to light the kitchen fire, brush up and clean around the grate and fireplace, take up the ashes, sweep the floor and hearth, and having made all quite clean, rinse out the tea-kettle, and set it on the fire, with clean spring water, preparatory to the family breakfast; and also another kettle to heat water for household purposes. She next takes the tray, carpet-broom, hair-broom, hearth-rug, a clean dry duster, and the basket or box, containing the brushes, rags, leathers, brick-dust, scouring-paper, and other things for cleaning the grate and fireplace, and proceeds to the parlour, or sitting-room, to get that in order, before the family comes down to breakfast. She begins there by clearing away the candlesticks, dirty glasses, and such other things as may have been left there the preceding night. She then rolls up the hearth-rug, so that no dirt or dust may drop from it, as it is carried out to be shaken; she next turns back the carpet, with the drugget, baize, or other covering, if any, and lays down a piece of canvas, or coarse cloth, to keep the place clean; after which she rakes out the ashes from the grate, takes them up, and brushes up the dust and dirt; then rubs the bright bars of the grate, and the fire-irons, with emery paper, No. 3, or brick-dust; or if there be very fine steel stoves, fenders, &c they should be first rubbed with oil, then with emery, till clear and bright, and afterwards with scouring paper, which is an excellent article to use every second or third day in summer-time, when stoves are not in constant use, as it will take off all the spots they may have acquired.

After the stove and fire-irons are cleaned, and the back and sides of the hearth are washed over with black-lead mixed with water, and rubbed dry and bright with a hard brush, light the fire, and proceed to wash the marble hearth.

For this purpose, take a piece of flannel dipped in a strong, hot, lather of soap and water, and having washed off the dirt, wipe it dry with a clean linen cloth. The jambs and chimney-piece need only be cleaned thus, once or twice a week, or as the custom of the family may be. Soap and sand, with cold water, will answer for washing free-stone hearths, &c. which must be afterwards wiped dry with a clean house-cloth. The next business will be to clean the brass locks, finger-plates, and other brass furniture; for which see the receipt.—If the locks are stiff, or hang, put a very little sweet oil on the bolts with a feather; the same ought to be done occasionally to the hinges, latches, bolts, and locks of every door in the house. A few minutes thus employed, when necessary, will prevent most of the disagreeable noises of creaking hinges, rusty bolts, and useless locks.

For the finger-plates, and other brass ornaments about the room, you must have pieces of pasteboard, with holes cut in them of the size of the respective articles, to prevent soiling or rubbing the door or furniture to which they are fixed.

The carpet next requires attention; this must generally be swept with the carpet-mop, to clean off the lint and dust, but, occasionally with the carpet-broom, or long hair-broom, first strewing it over with a few damp tea-leaves (which should always be saved for the purpose, when the tea-things are washed up). Then remove the chairs, and other furniture, to the middle of the room, turn up the sides of the carpet, and sweep up all the dust and flue round the sides of the room before replacing the carpet.

Always rub and dust the chairs, tables, and other mahogany furniture, in the middle of the room, and return them to their places, one by one, as you finish them; this will prevent your scratching or soiling the walls or the wainscot. The window-curtains and hangings may not require to be shaken and brushed every day, but the windows should be brushed with the long hair-broom, and cobwebs and other filth, on the ceiling, and upper corners of the room, should be occasionally sought for, and removed. When she has swept the room, and rubbed and dusted the furniture, she must dust the window-frames, ledges of the wainscot, and doors, chimney-pieces, glass, china, and other ornaments, and having seen that every article is in its proper place, stir the fire, and taking all her brushes, &c. leave the room perfectly clean, and fit for the reception of the family at breakfast. She next proceeds (if the parlour be upstairs) to sweep the dust the stairs, which she does one by one, sweeping the dust from each into the dust-pan, and afterwards dusting the windows and balustrade as carefully as she had done the room.

She should also sweep the passage in the same way. The floor-cloth in the passage, for the daily cleaning, need only to be swept and rubbed with a damp flannel first, and afterwards with a dry one. The steps, at the front door, should be cleaned every morning, after the passage is swept out, and the street-door and the knocker, &c. must be cleaned or polished. The kitchen stairs also, and the steps at the back-door, if any, are to be cleaned. Above all, the kitchen must now be put in order.

YOU'VE MISS'D YOUR TIP.

She then washes her hands and face, and puts on a clean apron, &c. so as to be cleanly before the parlour bell rings for breakfast. Directions for setting out the breakfast table will be found in the Instructions to the Footman, as well as for dinner, lunch, tea, &c.

As soon as the family is seated at breakfast, she throws open the bed-room doors and windows, and uncovers the beds to be aired, and placing the bed-clothes across a chair at the foot of the bed, leaves them in that state till breakfast is finished, when she proceeds to make the bed.

On going down, she takes the slop-pails, night-candlesticks, and the water-ewer and carafes to be filled with fresh water, and brought up again immediately, lest they should be wanted. When she goes up after breakfast, if there have been fires, the fireplaces must be swept up, the fires laid, and before she makes the beds, she should wash her hands and put on a clean apron. Every bed should be well shaken daily, and the mattresses turned, at least once a week. The head of the bed, the curtains, vallance, &c. will often require attention; when they should be brushed with a whisk-brush, and well shaken, the bed-side carpets having been first taken up. After she has made the beds, and before the carpets are laid down again, the chairs, glasses, and other articles of furniture in each room are to be properly rubbed and dusted, and the floors swept clean. The sleeping rooms being thus prepared, and the stairs swept down, she will scarcely have occasion to go up again till evening, when she turns down the beds, lets down, or draws the curtains, and puts the rooms in order for the night.

At intervals, she will, perhaps, be called to bring coals for the parlour fire, in the winter time; (see directions to the footman;) but, in addition to this, little will occur to take her from the regular routine of the morning's work, till the preparation for dinner requires her attention. She will find ample instructions for the care of the kitchen and larder, and for dressing dinners, under the directions to the cook.

If she is required to wait at table, she will find instructions for the purpose in the directions to the footman. After the dishes, &c. and the cloth and table-cover are removed, when there is no company present, her mistress will, perhaps, require her to bring a piece of cloth, with bees'-wax on it, and a hard furniture brush, to rub the dining-table, and take out the stains of the hot dishes.

When all things are set right in the parlour, as her mistress may direct, she will get her own dinner, (which she will contrive to keep as warm as circumstances allow;) meanwhile the water must be heating to wash the dishes, and all the kitchen utensils, which being washed, and the several articles (particularly the tinned ones) wiped out clean and dry, they are to be put away, always in their proper places, in the cleanest and nicest order, and fit for immediate use.

This done, she is to make up the fire (having due regard to the very expensive article of coals), and put on the kettle for tea. The kitchen is next to be set to rights, and every article in and about it is to be made quite clean, and disposed in perfect order. In fact, the cleanly and orderly state of the kitchen ought, at all times, to claim her utmost attention, as it is there that all the food of the family is prepared, and nothing does, nor, indeed, can, more deservedly contribute to the good character of a servant, than the well-regulated state and cleanly appearance of her kitchen.

The situation of a servant of this denomination is, as we have seen, one continued round of activity, but industry becomes habitual, and she will reap the benefit of it throughout life. To be content is the main thing, and others, seeing her good tempered, and disposed to be happy, will study to make her so; while experience and habit will greatly contribute towards it, by daily rendering the routine of the service more familiar, and consequently, more easy.

There are times, however, when the regular course of business will be interrupted. Once a week is the appointed day for a thorough scouring and cleaning, viz. Saturday. But even this day is rendered less formidable by an attentive servant, and by a little charitable consideration in the mistress (which is generally the case), who will contrive that there shall be less of the ordinary business of the family to be done on that day than on any other. The maid will, perhaps, manage to get the bedrooms thoroughly scoured on Friday. This should be done as early in the day as possible, and in the winter, fires should be made in the rooms, in order that they may be quite dry and safe by bed-time. For cleaning calico and other bed-furniture, and for scouring rooms, see Head House Maid. The sitting-room, and the spare rooms, if any, instead of the usual everyday cleaning, should now be thoroughly cleaned, the floors scoured, the grates, hearths, chimney-pieces, carpets, curtains, and furniture rubbed, scrubbed, dusted, and otherwise cleaned in the best manner; the kitchen, it is presumed, is already clean—*always clean*; the pots, pans, kettles, and every other culinary utensil being *always cleaned as soon as done with;—scoured, wiped out dry, and put away in their proper places, fit for use at a moment's notice*. However laborious the work of the Saturday may appear, it is but getting up an hour or two earlier, and setting about it with a good heart, and all the extra business of the house, in every part, is completely finished, and you sit down in the evening, to tea, rejoicing that all is comfortable, and in order.

Another, and more laborious deviation from the regular routine of family business is—the appointed "Washing-Day", which is, indeed, a day of bustle and activity;

perhaps the only one that can be called a hard day's work, from one washing-day to another. But, here also, if the intervals between the washings be long, a washer-woman will be hired, and the mistress will probably lend her aid, in sorting the clothes, getting up the small linen, ironing, &c.

In proportion to the arduous and active duties of a situation, is the satisfaction to be enjoyed from a regular and attentive discharge of those services: hence no servant has it in her power to render herself and her employers more comfortable, than the maid of all work. By a methodical division of her time, she is enabled to keep in order every apartment in the house, from the kitchen to the attic, all of which may be accomplished without any extraordinary effort on her part: and while she thus promotes the comforts of her master and mistress by her industry and regularity, they will not be backward in rewarding those meritorious qualities. [Wages from 8 to 12 guineas.]

To Light and Manage a Parlour Fire

There is more art, perhaps, and more economy than is considered necessary in making well, and managing a fire.

First rake out all the ashes, quite clean, leaving in the bottom of the grate a few light cinders, through which the air, from beneath, may pass freely; upon these lay shavings, or waste paper, and then the wood, the smaller pieces under, of course, and the whole crossing each other promiscuously, and in all directions; throw cinders behind, and some at the sides, to fill out the grate, and in the front, betwixt the bars, put small knobs of fresh coals, with some larger knobs at top, and a little small coal behind, but not so much at first as to prevent a draft of air through the grate at the top. The fire, thus prepared, may be lighted with a match, and will kindle well of itself, whilst the ashes are taken up, and the fireplace cleaned. When it is found necessary to blow a fire, do not thrust the nose of the bellows between the bars, but keep it at an easy distance from the fire, and rather below the centre of the fire, that so, the air may be dispersed around to a considerable distance in front of the fire. When you stir a fire, always put the poker between the second and third bars.—After you have stirred the fire, rake out the ashes at the bottom of the grate, and sweep up the hearth.

THE LAUNDRY MAID

This Servant washes all the household and other linen belonging to her employers, and is assisted, generally, by the house maids; or the house maids, kitchen maids, and scullery maids wash for themselves. All the men servants find their own washing, except the footmen's aprons and jackets.

The foul linen is given out to her on Monday morning, and returned clean, on Friday night or Saturday morning. [Wages £8 to £15 a year.]

Two ounces of pearl-ash, to a pound and a half of soap, will make a considerable saving. Soda, by softening the water, saves a great deal of soap. It should be dissolved in a large jug of water, some of which should be poured into the tubs and boiler, and when the lather becomes weak, add more.

The use of soft soap, saves nearly half in washing.

Good new hard soap contains full half of oil, one-third water, and the rest soda.

To Make Town-Washed Linen White

In large towns, where linen cannot be exposed to the air and sun upon the grass, let it be steeped, for some time before it is washed, in a solution of oxymuriate of lime. Let it then be boiled in an alkaline ley. Linen or cotton thus treated will not become yellow by age.

To Take Out Iron Moulds from Linen

Hold the iron mould on the cover of a tankard of boiling water, and rub on the spot a little juice of sorrel and salt, and when the cloth has thoroughly imbibed the juice, wash it in ley.

To Scour Thick Cotton Counterpanes

Cut a pound of mottled soap into thin slices; and put it into a pan with a quarter of an ounce of potash. Pour a pail of boiling water on it, and let it stand till dissolved. Then pour hot and cold water into a scouring tub, with a bowl of the solution. Put in the counterpane, beat it well, turn it often, give it a second liquor as before, and then rinse it in cold water. Then put three teaspoonsful of liquid blue into a thin liquor; stir it, and put in the counterpane: beat it about five minutes, and dry it in the air.

To Scour Flannels or Woollens

Cut ½ a pound of the best yellow soap into thin slices, and pour such a quantity of boiling river water on it as will dissolve the soap, and make it of the consistence of oil. Cover the articles about two inches with water, such as the hand can bear, and add a lump of American pearl ash, and about a third of the soap solution. Beat them till no head or lather rises on the water; throw away the dirty water, and proceed as before with hotter water without pearl ash.

To Take Mildew out of Linen

Rub it well with soap: then scrape some fine chalk, and rub that also in the linen; lay it on the grass; as it dries, wet it a little, and it will come out after twice doing.

To Take out Spots of Ink

As soon as the accident happens, wet the place with juice of sorrel or lemon, or with vinegar, and the best hard white soap.

THE DAIRY MAID

Manages the dairy, milks the cows, makes the butter, cheese, wheys, syllabubs, &c. attends the poultry, picks and prepares them for trussing, makes bread and fresh butter for the parlour every morning, and bakes all the bread of the family.

The greatest possible attention must be paid to the Dairy. Cleanliness being the primary object, all the utensils, shelves, and the floor, should be kept perfectly neat, and cold water should be frequently thrown over it.—There should be shutters to the Dairy to keep out the sun and hot air.

The cows should be milked at a regular and early hour, and their udders should be *perfectly emptied*, else the quantity given will be diminished. When you go to the cow, take with you, *cold water* and a sponge, and wash each cow's udder; bathe it well with cold water, both in winter and summer, as that braces them and repels heat. But, if any cow has sore teats, let them be soaked in warm water twice a day, and either dressed with soft ointment, or bathed with spirits and water. In either case, the milk should be given to the pigs.

When the milk is brought into the Dairy, it should be strained and emptied into clean pans, immediately, in winter, but not till cool, in summer. Suffer no one to milk the cows but yourself, as much depends on their being *dripped quite clean*, particularly after a calf is taken away.

The quantity of milk given by cows, will be different according to their breed, health, pasturage, the length of time from calving, and other circumstances. Change of pasturage will tend to increase the quantity.

In good pastures, the average of each cow will be about three gallons a day from Lady-day to Michaelmas; and thence to Christmas, one gallon a day.

Cows will be profitable yielders of milk, to fourteen or fifteen years of age, if of a good breed. They should be fed well two or three weeks before calving, which will increase the quantity of milk. In gentlemen's Dairies, more attention is paid to the beauty and size of cows, than to their produce.

It is absolutely necessary that the cows should be kept feeding whilst you are milking them.

It should be contrived that cows kept for a gentleman's family, should calve at different seasons, and, particularly, that one or two should calve in August or September, to insure a supply of milk in winter.

When there is not a great demand for cream in the family, the Dairy-maid will take that opportunity to provide for the winter store. She should keep a regular weekly account of the quantity of milk given by each cow, and the quantity of butter she pots. The average of a good fair Dairy cow, during several months after calving, will be seven pounds of butter a week, and from three to five gallons of milk per day; afterwards a weekly average of three or four pounds of butter, from barely half that quantity of milk. On an average, three gallons of good milk, will yield one pound of butter. The annual consumption of a good cow, turned to grass, is from an acre to an acre and a half in the summer, and from a ton to a ton and a half of hay, in the winter. Each cow should be allowed two pecks of carrots per day. The grass, if cut and carried to the cows green, will economize full one-third.

Alderney cows yield rich milk, upon less food, than larger cows, but are seldom large milkers, and are particularly scanty of produce in the winter.

[Wages from £8 to £12 a year.—Perquisites, 1d. per pound for butter; 1½d. for each chicken, or fowl killed; 2d. each, for ducks, geese, and turkeys; and 3d. a score for eggs.]

To Preserve Milk

Provide bottles which must be perfectly clean, sweet, and dry; draw the milk from the cow into the bottles, and as they are filled, immediately cork them well up, and fasten the corks with pack-thread or wire. Then spread a little straw on the bottom of a boiler, on which place the bottles with straw between them, until the boiler contains a sufficient quantity. Fill it up with cold water; heat the water, and as soon as it begins to boil, draw the fire, and let the whole gradually cool. When quite cold take out the bottles, and pack them with straw or sawdust in hampers, and stow them in the coolest part of the house. Milk preserved in this manner, although eighteen months in the bottles, will be as sweet as when first milked from the cow.

To Fatten Poultry

An experiment has lately been tried of feeding geese with turnips, cut in small pieces like dice, but less in size, and put into a trough of water; with this food alone, the effect was, that six geese, each when lean weighed only 9 lbs, actually gained 20 lbs each in about three weeks fattening.

Malt is excellent food for geese and turkeys; grains are preferred for the sake of economy, unless for immediate and rapid fattening; the grains should be boiled afresh.

Other cheap articles for fattening, are oatmeal and treacle; barley-meal and milk; boiled oats, and ground malt.

Corn before being given to fowls should always be crushed and soaked in water. The food will thus go further, and it will help digestion. Hens fed thus have been known to lay during the whole of the winter months.

GETTING UNDER WHEY.

To Determine the Economy of a Cow

The Annual Product of a good fair dairy cow, during several months after calving, either in summer or winter, if duly fed and kept in the latter season, will be an average of seven pounds of butter per week, and from five to three gallons of milk per day. Afterwards, a weekly average of three or four pounds of butter from barely half the quantity of milk. It depends on the constitution of the cow, how nearly she may be milked to the time of her calving, some giving good milk until within a week or two of that period, others requiring to be dried 8 or 9 weeks previously. I have heard (says Mr. Lawrence) of 20 lbs of butter, and even 22 lbs made from the milk of one long-horned cow in seven days; but I have never been fortunate enough to obtain one that would produce more than 12 lbs per week, although I have had a Yorkshire cow which milked 7 gallons per day, yet never made 5 lbs of butter in one week. On the average 3 gallons of good milk will make 1 lb of butter.

To Make Salt Butter Fresh

To every pound of salt butter put a quart of new milk, and a little arnotto. Churn it an hour, then take it out and treat it as fresh butter, by washing it with water, and add the usual quantity of salt. The butter gains about three ounces in the pound.

Substitute for Milk and Cream

Beat up the whole of a fresh egg, in a basin, then pour boiling tea over it gradually, to prevent its curdling. It is difficult, from the taste, to distinguish the composition from rich cream.

To Preserve Eggs

Apply with a brush a solution of gum-arabic to the shells, or immerse the eggs therein; let them dry, and afterwards pack them in dry charcoal dust. This prevents their being affected by any alterations of temperature.

To Test the Purity of Flour

Grasp a handful briskly, and squeeze it half a minute: if genuine, it will preserve the form of the cavity of the hand, even though rudely placed on a table; if adulterated, it will almost immediately fall down.

To Produce One-Third more Bread from a Given Quantity of Corn

Boil 5 lbs of the coarsest bran in four gallons and half of water, keep stirring it, that it may not stick to the bottom, till reduced to four gallons, then pour it off into a trough, or tub full of holes, over which lay a coarse cloth or sieve. On the top of the whole put a wooden cover, with a weight sufficiently heavy to press out the liquor from the bran, which will sink to the bottom of the tub in a thick pulp. This liquor will contain the essential oil of the corn, and when kneaded in with half a hundred weight of flour, and the usual quantity of salt and yeast, it will yield one-third more bread than the same quantity of flour would, made with water in the usual way. Divide into middle sized loaves and bake two hours and a half.

When ten days old put it into the oven for twenty minutes and it will appear quite new.

To Make Flour Paste

Paste is made principally of wheaten flour boiled in water till it be of a glutinous or viscid consistence. It may be thus prepared simply for common purposes; but when it is required for paper hangings to rooms, it is usual to mix a fourth, fifth, or sixth of the weight of the flour of powdered resin; and where it is wanted still more tenacious, gum arabic, or any kind of size may be added.

THE CHAMBER NURSE

Every experienced person, and every liberal physician and medical man, is sensible of the value of a careful, skilful, and kind-hearted nurse, and that the alleviation of sickness and the actual cure of diseases, depend as much on the anxious attention of the nurse, as on the efficacy of medicine itself. Good temper, patience, watchfulness, and sobriety, are the cardinal virtues of every good nurse, and when possessed by one who unites skill with those personal qualities, she is a treasure above all price.

Although the chamber nurse forms no part of the establishment of healthy families, yet as in every family she is a necessary auxiliary for longer or shorter periods, a brief notice of her qualifications and duties, will confer completeness on such a volume as the present.

The chamber or sick nurse should be qualified for her duty by some experience; and if her experience has been considerable, and she is a woman of good understanding, she will prove herself quite as important in the nursery of the sick, as medical practitioners, or all the drugs in an apothecary's shop. She ought to be past the middle age, and if a married woman or widow, so much the better. She ought to be clean in her person, and neat in her dress, and free from habits of drinking or snuff-taking. She ought also to be a woman of cheerful and equable temper, and, above all things, free from superstition, or belief in charms, omens, signs, dreams, and other follies of gross ignorance.

The sick room should be clean, well aired, and free from noisome smells; and, on the contrary, the air should be purified by sprinkling vinegar or eau de cologne, and occasionally burning a little vinegar in a heated shovel.

Quietness, in every respect, is of the first consequence. Fire irons should be avoided: creaking doors and locks should be oiled; and list shoes constantly worn. Talking loud and whispering, so as to excite the suspicion of the patient, should be equally avoided; and a long feather should be pushed through the key-hole, as a signal on the outside, when the patient is asleep. The nurse should only sleep when the patient sleeps, as one means of preventing the patient being awoke by her frivolous activity.

In cases of contagion, whatever is sent out of the room, should be immersed in water, and the nurse should be careful not to receive the breath of the patient, nor to sit on the bed. She should also carry about her person a bag of camphor, and during such diseases, frequently fumigate the room with vinegar and indulge occasionally in half a glass of brandy.

The sick chamber should be provided with a lamp and appurtenances, for heating whatever may be wanted; with a tea kettle, two or three saucepans, empty bottles for hot water (to put to the feet), some sal volatile and spirits, a bottle of salts, and of eau de cologne; some lambs-wool gloves to rub the patient, a bed-pan, a foot-bath, or a large tin bath; some lemonade, barley-water, and toast and water: oranges, lemons, and empty medicine bottles, which occasion smells that infect the air, should be kept in an adjoining room. There should also be a supply of flannel, old linen, and napkins, for every purpose. Different medicines should be carefully kept apart; lest pernicious ones be given, or proper ones, at improper times. A thermometer in the room is the only means of keeping an equal temperature, or increasing or diminishing it, as the medical attendants may direct.

The reports of the nurse to the physician, and the observations of the physician, should always be made in an adjoining room, and the mind of the patient not be distracted by details of symptoms, and of the nurse's business. Changes which take place after the visit of the medical attendant, should be immediately reported, and in all that regards the administration of the medicines, and the general system of treatment, the nurse should scrupulously obey the instructions of the medical advisers, not only as the most likely means of promoting the speedy recovery of the patient, but to remove from herself all responsibility and blame. At the same time, she should not withhold her opinion, in regard to the effect of the medicines administered, and in her conferences with the medical advisers, should suggest whatever appears likely to be useful.

Nurses, according to the length of a disease, are paid by the day, week, or month; and as boarders in the family, they ought not to take advantage of the sympathy which induces the relatives of the sick to afford them every indulgence, so as to involve unnecessary or wanton expenses; but consider the interest of the family, whose affliction requires their attendance, as their own. The usual payment of a nurse in London, is from 10s 6d. to 15s. per week, according to the circumstances of the parties, and of the case.

Nurses who have to compound and administer Family Medicines must be prepared with proper scales and weights; and with graduated glass measures, such as are used by Apothecaries; according to the following

TABLES OF WEIGHTS AND MEASURES

Measure of Fluids

1 gal. measure	contains 8 pints
1 pint	contains 16 ounces
1 ounce	contains 8 drams
1 dram	contains 60 minims

Weights of Dry Substances

1 pound	contains 12 ounces
1 ounce	contains 8 drams
1 dram	contains 60 grains
1 scruple	contains 20 grains, or ⅓ of a dram

It is customary to distinguish quantities of fluid from dry substances, by prefixing the letter f. (fluid) when an ounce or dram is mentioned in medical works.

*The following table of the gradations of doses of medicines for **different ages**, will in general be found pretty correct, and ought never to be deviated from, except by professional advice.*

*If at the age of **maturity** the dose be **one dram**, the proportion will be at*

From 14 to 21 years, 2 scruples
7 to 14 years, half a dram
4 to 7 years, 1 scruple
4 years, 15 grains
3 years, half a scruple
2 years, 8 grains
1 year, 5 grains
6 months, 3 grains
3 months, 2 grains
1 month, 1 grain

To make a Warm Bath

Water for a warm bath should be rather more than a blood heat, or from 90 to 100 of the thermometer, and if a portable tin bath is not at command, and a warm bath is suddenly wanted, the quickest mode of making one, is to knock in the head of a beer or wine cask, according to the size of the patient, and every neighbourhood will supply these, as well as sufficient quantities of hot water, clean or dirty.

To Restore Suspended Animation

In cases of substances being stopped between the mouth and the stomach, where they cannot be extracted by the fingers or otherwise, the person should swallow a piece of meat or tow tied to a thread, which should be immediately drawn up again. Emetics are sometimes serviceable, and injections of warm milk and water frequently remove the obstructions. When animation is suspended by noxious vapours, the usual methods in fainting should be employed, and lemonade or vinegar and water given to the patient as soon as he can swallow.

When it proceeds from extreme cold, the part affected should be immersed in cold water, or rubbed with snow till they recover their natural warmth.

To Relieve an Apoplectic Fit

Every method should be taken to lessen the circulation of blood towards the head; the patient should be kept easy and cool, the head raised high, and the feet suffered to hang down. The clothes should be loosened and fresh air admitted into the room, and medical assistance procured immediately for bleeding. Apoplexy is preceded by giddiness, pain, and swimming of the head, loss of memory, &c. and on the symptoms appearing, bleeding, slender diet, and opening medicines are advisable, and often act as preventives.

To Ease or Cure Headaches

Most headaches arise from imperfect digestion, either from acidity, or from accumulations of bile. The first cause may be removed by half a teaspoonful of carbonate of soda, or by a dessert spoonful of magnesia, in a small tumbler of water. But if the cause is bilious, then two or three antibilious pills, or a pill of from two to five grains of calomel, is the best remedy, and this may be assisted in its operation by half an ounce of salts in a large tumbler of water, in the morning. Washing the head with cold water, is always salutary in habitual headaches, particularly at rising in the mornings.

For Cancer

One part of red lead, in fine powder, and two parts of hog's-lard.—Spread on lint, and dress the sore twice a day.

For the Gravel

Three drams of prepared natron (which may be obtained for three pence) in a quart of soft cold water, and take half of it in the course of the day; continue it for a few days, and the complaint will subside. It may be taken at any hour, but it is best after a meal.

For a Cold and Cough

A large tea-cupful of linseed, two pennyworth of stick-liquorice, and a quarter of a pound of sun raisins, put to two quarts of soft water, and simmered over a slow fire, till reduced one third or more; add thereto a quarter of a pound of sugar-candy pounded, a table-spoonful of old rum, and a table-spoonful of white wine vinegar, or lemon-juice. Note—the rum and vinegar should be added only to the quantity which is about to be taken immediately. Drink half a pint at going to bed, or a small quantity at any time when the cough is troublesome.

For a Sore Throat

Inhale the steam of hot vinegar, through the spout of a teapot, or a funnel, for about half an hour just before you go to bed:—also two or three times in the course of the day, and keep at home. A piece of flannel dipped in harts-horn will be serviceable, applied when going to bed. In a relaxed sore throat, a few lumps of sugar dipped in brandy, and gradually dissolved in the mouth, will be very efficacious.

Warts

Cut an apple, and rub it for a few minutes over the wart; the juice of the apple will loosen the wart, and in a few days it will drop off. Any strong acid, either vegetable or mineral, has the same tendency.

Corns

Mr. Cooper, in his Dictionary of Surgery, gives the following recipe as infallible for the cure of corns:—Take two ounces of gum ammoniac, two ounces of yellow wax, six drams of verdigris, melt them together, and spread the composition on a piece of soft leather or linen; cut away as much of the corn as you can with a knife before you apply the plaster, which must be renewed in a fortnight, if the corn is not by that time gone.

For Burns or Scalds

When the blisters are open, dress them with a simple white ointment spread thinly on the smooth side of lint, the first day, and every day after sprinkle a little powder of prepared chalk, and dress it as before. To alleviate the immediate pain, apply any quick evaporating fluid, as ether, spirits of wine, or brandy; or better than all, if at hand, spirits of turpentine, or rags dipped in vinegar and water, and often renewed.

To Extinguish Fire which may have Caught the Clothes

The mischief which arises from this accident is owing to the party standing in an erect position, because flame ascends, and feeds and accumulates in intensity during its ascent. The first remedy is, therefore, to lay the child or other person on the floor, in which position the flames will not only make no progress, but will do little or no harm to the person. The fatal consequences of this accident arise from the ascent of the flame to the throat, head, and sensitive organs, an effect which cannot take place if the body is instantly placed in an horizontal position. Sir Richard Phillips, who first promulgated this treatment, proved its efficacy by taking two strips of muslin, a yard long, and one of them, which was set on fire at the end, and held perpendicularly, burnt out with an intense flame in less than half a minute; but the other piece, laid hollow and horizontally, on being set on fire at the end, burnt even with difficulty, and twenty minutes elapsed before it was entirely consumed; the flame at the same time being inconsiderable and harmless.

After the person on fire has been laid horizontally, the best method of extinguishing the fire, is an immediate covering of any kind, and when every spark has been extinguished, spirits and water, or vinegar and water, should be applied to affected parts till the pain is removed. Adult females, whose clothes take fire, should have the presence of mind instantly to throw themselves on the floor, and in that case, no serious injury can ever arise, and if this precaution were generally known, many families would have been relieved from the unavailing affliction of the loss of dear connections, and from the heart-rending scenes which, under other circumstances, they have been fated to witness.

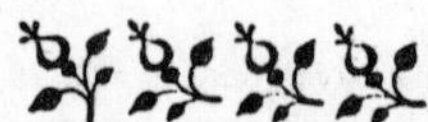

For a Bruised Eye

Take conserve of red roses and rotten apple in equal quantities, wrap them in a fold of thin cambric, or old linen, and apply it to the eye; it will relieve the bruise and remove the blackness.

For a Sprained Ankle or Wrist

Foment it with warm vinegar for five minutes every four hours, wet it afterwards with rectified spirit of wine, and rub it gently. Sit with the foot on a low stool, and occasionally rest upon the ankle, and move it gently backwards and forwards.

Oxalic Acid

A heaped table-spoonful of magnesia, mixed in a middling sized tumbler of water, and drank immediately after oxalic acid has been swallowed, will save life.

For the Bite of a Mad Dog

Take a spoonful of common salt, add as much water as will make it damp; apply it like a poultice every six hours, and it will be sure to stop the hydrophobia.

Remedy for a Wasp's Sting

Over the spot where the sting has entered, apply the pipe of a key, press it for a minute or two, and the pain and swelling will disappear.

To Avoid Injury from Bees

A wasp or bee swallowed, may be killed before it can do harm, by taking a tea-spoonful of common salt dissolved in water. It kills the insect and cures the sting. Salt, at all times, is the best cure for external stings; sweet oil, pounded mallows, or onions, or powdered chalk made into a paste with water, are also efficacious.

If bees swarm upon the head, smoke tobacco, and hold an empty hive over the head, and they will go into it.

For the Poison of the Adder

Olive oil is an absolute specific for the bite (or sting, as it is erroneously called) of the adder; the oil should be well rubbed upon the part bitten: in case of violent symptoms a glass or two should be taken inwardly. If olive oil is not at hand, common sweet oil will answer the purpose.

Bathing the Feet and Legs in Warm Water at Night

This is an excellent remedy in all cases of cold, coughs, hoarseness, pains and headaches; for in the above-mentioned complaints, inflammation, or undue determination of blood to the part affected, is present. After this operation the patient should instantly go to bed.

To Clean the Teeth and Gums, and make the Flesh Grow Close to the Root of the Enamel

One ounce of myrrh, in fine powder, two spoonsful of the best honey, and a little sage, in fine powder, mixed together, with which rub the teeth and gums night and morning.

A Preservative from the Toothache

After having washed your mouth with water, rinse the mouth with a tea-spoonful of lavender water mixed with an equal quantity of warm or cold water, to diminish its activity.

Method of Restoring Life to the Apparently Drowned

Avoid all rough usage. Do not hold up the body by the feet, or roll it on casks, or rub it with salt, or spirits, or apply tobacco. Lose not a moment, carry the body, the head and shoulders raised, to the nearest house. Place it in a warm room. Let it be instantly stripped, dried, and wrapped in hot blankets, which are to be renewed when necessary. Keep the mouth, nostrils, and the throat free and clean. Apply warm substances to the back, spine, pit of the stomach, arm-pits, and soles of the feet. Rub the body with heated flannel, or warm hands.—Attempt to restore breathing, by gently blowing with bellows into one nostril, closing the mouth and the other nostril. Keep up the application of heat. Press down the breast carefully with both hands, and then let it rise again, and thus imitate natural breathing. Continue the rubbing, and increase it when life appears, and then give a tea-spoonful of warm water, or of very weak wine or spirits and warm water. Persevere for six hours. Send quickly for medical assistance.

THE LAND STEWARD

AND

BAILIFF

THE HOUSE STEWARD

AND

STEWARD'S ROOM BOY

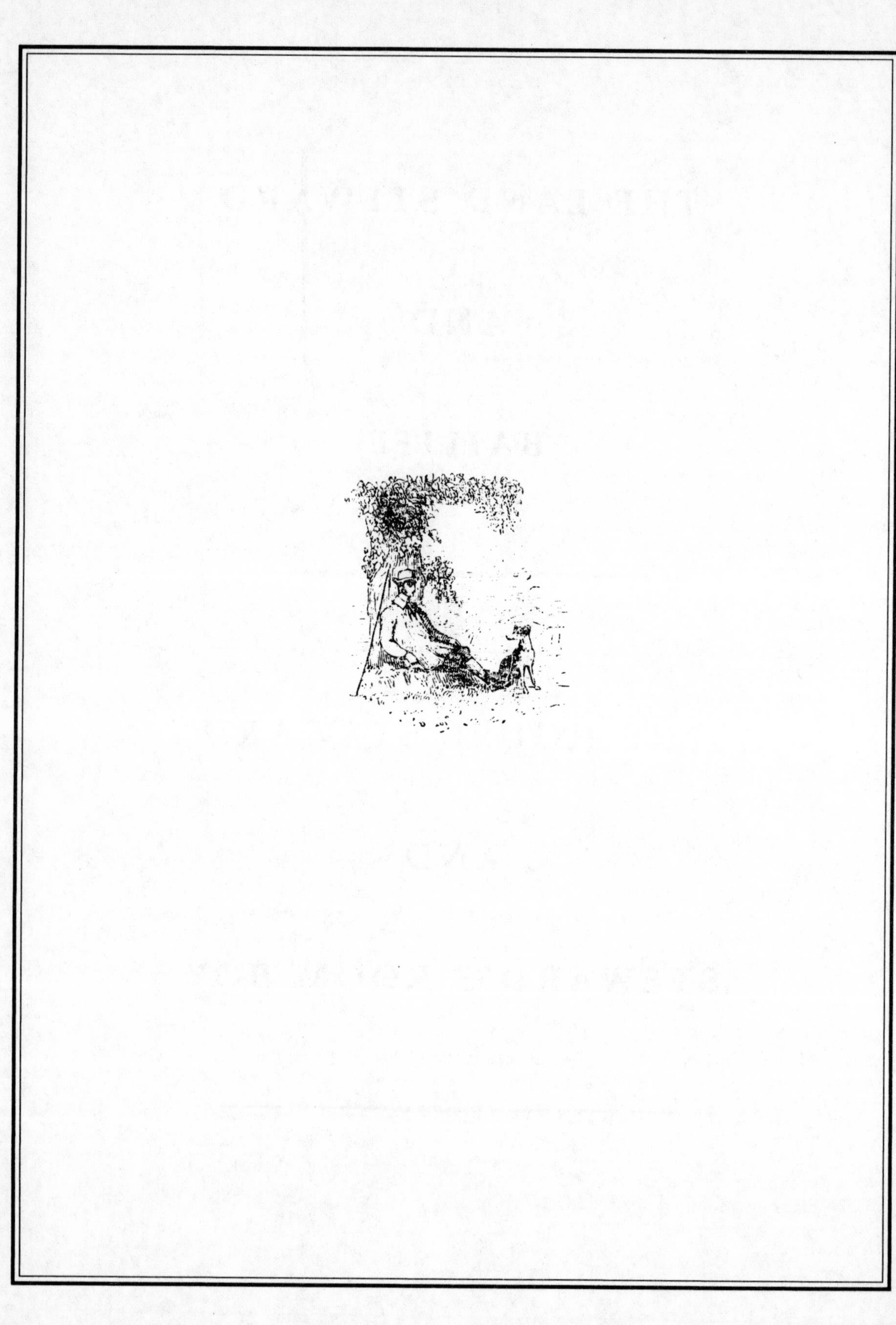

THE LAND STEWARD AND BAILIFF

To form a complete LAND STEWARD, it is requisite that theory and practice should be combined. By consulting books we profit by the experience of other men, enlarge our own sphere of thinking, and add more, perhaps, to our stock of knowledge in a short space of time, than could be acquired by long and laborious practice. No land steward or even ordinary farmer should be without *Young's Farmer's Calendar*, the last edition of which, improved by Middleton, contains a body of valuable information; but Mr. Lawrence on this subject, with great propriety, recommends the reading of Tull and Miller, as the great originals on tillage; Ellis on sheep and other livestock; and the Surveys of the several Counties of the Kingdom, made, and published by the Board of Agriculture.

To these, for a further knowledge in the treatment of livestock, may be recommended a perusal of our best veterinary treatises. We must also recommend Sir John Sinclair's Code of Agriculture, as a companion to Middleton's edition of Young's Calendar, and these, with Mackenzie's Receipt Book, ought to be the standing literary furniture of every steward's room.

The land steward should never undertake more business than he can faithfully and properly execute, and therefore should have no other occupation or profession to attend; the mere collecting of rents and giving discharges being the least considerable part of his duty.

On his first entering into office, he should make a general survey of all the estates and property entrusted to his care:—he should also form an inventory, and open a set of books on a clear and perspicuous plan, if not already done by his predecessor, taking care to enter in them a correct list of all the books, writings, deeds, schedules, court-rolls, &c. From this survey, whether left by his predecessor, or taken by himself, regular memorandums should be made in a book, of every thing necessary to be remarked or executed, of the places where deficiencies are found, or improvements may be made; of buildings and repairs necessary; insurances, dates of leases, rates, nuisances, trespasses, live and dead stock, game, timber, fencing, draining, paths, and roads, culture, commons, rivers, and sea coasts, and of every other specific article relative to his trust, which deserves attention, and therefore ought not to be committed to loose papers, or left to memory.

He should endeavour to gain a practical knowledge of the characters and conduct of inferior servants, taking nothing upon trust; but observing with his own eyes their performances early and late. A faithful steward will lose no time in detecting the peculations, and counteracting the combinations among those servants who are under his control, which may be prejudicial to the estate of his principal; and of replacing them with servants of fair character, to whom ample wages should be allowed; and the job work, or more profitable kinds of labour, should be impartially dealt out to them, that so, all may be equally benefited, and equally satisfied.

Every farm, when surveyed, should be correctly described in a map, of which the tenant should have a copy. A Terrier should also be kept of the commonfield-lands, for the satisfaction of the tenant as well as the lord, and where the bounds of any parcel of land are dubious, they should be fixed, and properly marked out, by a jury impannelled at the manor court. The boundaries of the parish and precincts should also be ascertained, and the particular property of the lord kept entire, by the annual custom of perambulation on Holy Thursday, and its concomitant ceremonies. The steward should frequently ride round and make an eye survey of the estates, in order to obviate any disputes,—to prevent encroachments, and to afford timely advice and assistance if necessary. He should see that all repairs are duly and substantially performed according to convenant, ditches cast and scoured, water courses kept free, common rights fairly enjoyed, according to the custom of the manor, the commons not overstocked by one, in prejudice to others, observe that the underwood be cut at the stated periods, that the trees are properly lopped and topped without damage to the lord, that the wood-wards do watch and report all trespasses by cattle and otherwise, and to discourage poaching and the destruction of game, by all fair, moderate, and rational means.

The tenants should not be suffered to let their lands be over-run by moles—nor the commons and woodlands by swine unrung.

The strictest caution should be used to prevent all the produce of the estates, that is fit for manure or other useful purposes, from being alienated or carried off.

An eye ought always to be kept on the surveyor of the highways of the neighbouring parishes, to see that no nuisance exists, or bridge or highway be neglected.

Trespasses from stray cattle ought to be prevented, and if necessary punished, as well as the depredations of dogs, which often do much injury to the farmer.

It behoves the steward to support, and cause to be recognized, all the ancient manorial rights and privileges that are usually respected.

Heriots accruing from copyhold estates, ought not to be taken in kind, but a moderate fine should be levied in lieu thereof.

Encouragement should be given to improvements in cultivation. The best heads of cattle should be introduced, and any successful mode of culture recommended among the tenantry. They should also be stimulated to plant fruit-trees, as means of adding to the produce without encumbering the land.

The transactions of the steward should always be pure, incorruptible, and free even from suspicion. He ought not to sell preference, either for money or for any indirect consideration, such concession to him being in effect a robbery on the tenant, or on his employer, who is entitled to all the advantages which can accrue from his estate. If a sum of money is covertly given for preference in a lease, then the lease is worth so much more, and the proprietor is defrauded of the difference. Nothing can be more pernicious to an estate than such underhand transactions. Modest industry and merit are thereby subverted by the audacity of knaves, and the steward from the moment he has thus sold himself becomes a dependent on the honour of the parties. Preference given to kin ought also to be avoided, and every nobleman and gentleman is justified in being jealous of the introduction of his steward's kindred upon his estate, often to the great prejudice of his old and attached tenants.

Many stewards become the tyrants of their vicinity by an impertinent interference with the domestic economy of the families of the tenants, presuming to prescribe in regard to their dress, habits, and amusements, seeming thereby to consider them as vassals, instead of freemen, to whose industry their landlord is indebted for his ease and luxury. With these affairs the steward has no concern, and every farmer and his family should be left to their own discretion in such particulars, if they pay with regularity the average rent of their vicinity, and do not manifestly deteriorate the estate; they are, and ought to be, in all their domestic and personal concerns, and also in their opinions, religious and political, as independent of the steward, or of his employer, as these parties are of them. His interference has, in truth, tended to retard the civilization of the agricultural classes, and, in many districts, placed them one or two centuries behind the inhabitants of towns. The steward, therefore, who forbears to meddle with what does not properly concern him, will enjoy the love of tenantry, and that affection will always best promote the interest of his employers.

Whilst the steward is not unmindful of every possible improvement, he should keep in view every appearance of the existence of minerals or metals, that so the needful essays or experiments may be made under the superintendance of persons of experience and fidelity. Proximity to the sea coast, navigable rivers, canals, or great towns, will much enhance the value of such discoveries.

Every opportunity should be embraced of letting land on building leases, as a means of greatly improving the value of estates; the fitness by means of water and roads

for the establishment of a manufactory, or a village, or, by being near the sea coast, for a fishery, are objects too important to be overlooked by a faithful and intelligent agent.

It has already been remarked, that the land steward should not be engaged in any business that would detract from that attention which is required in the faithful discharge of the duties of his office; and even in performing those engagements, he should occasionally be assisted, in cases of importance, where he may consider his own knowledge not sufficient, by an able professional adviser. he will most require this aid in the making of leases, deeds, agreements, and other legal instruments.

The balance of cash, which may often be considerable, ought not be allowed to lie idle in the house. All money is part of the vital blood of society, and should be kept in circulation. This may be effected either by lodging it at a country bank, where moderate interest will be allowed for it, or by discounting the notes of respectable tenants, who, at certain turns of the season, are often in want of ready money, and their notes will, in many cases, serve as cash payments for other purposes, or they may be made to fall due at periods when cash will be wanted, while it will thus be accumulating at five per cent. No risk need be incurred in such transactions, while the accommodation would add much to the prosperity of the estate. If the steward reside in London, spare cash may, in like manner, be employed at a full rate of interest, by discounting such good bills as are always to be met with at the principal brokers in and about Lombard Street; and these bills will be received by the bankers as they arrive at maturity. By this means three or four per cent may always be added to the income of a nobleman or gentleman, or sufficient to pay the wages of all the servants.

In the business of accounts, the first objects are, arrangement, perspicuity, and security. In all accounts of property, there are certain general rules which must be attended to, the chief of which are the following: 1st. Trust as little as possible to memory, but make memorandums of payments, receipts, bargains, agreements, &c. on the instant. 2nd. Pay no money without receiving a proper discharge. 3rd. Give up no security, lease, agreement, or other valuable property, without taking in return a written acknowledgement. 4th. Let all contingent, undecided, or uncertain transactions be forthwith entered, with every necessary remark, voucher, and reference. 5th. Post all the various transactions under their proper heads as soon as possible. 6th. Fold, label, date, and class all papers, the most valuable of which are to be deposited at the end of every year, in a secure place, with the date on the outside. Perhaps the two principal books necessary to be kept, are a DAY-BOOK or JOURNAL, and a LEDGER, with two other books, to be called the MEMORANDUM-BOOK, and GENERAL INVENTORY. A portable POCKET MEMORANDUM-BOOK will also be found to be convenient. Every servant in trust under the land steward ought to be provided with an account book appropriately ruled: this book should be examined and passed monthly by the steward and an abstract of it transcribed into his journal.

THE HOUSE STEWARD

This is the most important officer in domestic establishments, and is seldom adopted except in the families of noblemen or gentlemen of great fortunes, by whom he is appointed as their *locum tenens,* not only to superintend such necessary business as, from their rank and condition, or other circumstances, they cannot undertake, but also to control and manage, generally, all the most important concerns of the household. It follows, therefore, that he ought to be a man of great experience in household affairs, steady and attentive in his conduct, and of approved principles and integrity. His character must be irreproachable and exemplary, that he may be regarded with confidence and satisfaction by his employers, and respected by those around him.

His chief business wil be to hire, manage, and direct, and discharge every servant of every denomination. To appropriate to every domestic his proper and express business, and to see that it be done accordingly. He ought to make it a point never to take a servant without strict enquiry as to his moral character, orderly conduct, and abilities for his situation, nor ought he to withhold a fair character from any servant he discharges.

The House Steward, by the suavity of his manners, and equable deportment, has it in his power to sustain the reputation of his master in high estimation, and to make his whole household comfortable and happy.

Ability to provide for the family in the best manner, is another qualification indispensably necessary in the House Steward. He is expected to be a competent judge of the nature and qualities of provisions, their comparative values, the best seasons for purchasing the several articles, and the cheapest and most economical markets or places to attend. The best way to go to market is with *ready money;* or to deal with tradesmen of probity, and to settle their accounts early and at regular and stated periods, but never to disappoint them, at the expected times, which makes his custom nearly equivalent to cash, and he will consequently be served with the best articles and on the lowest terms. A conscientious and honest discharge of his duty in this respect, will tend greatly to the satisfaction of his employers and rebound to his own credit.

The abilities of the House Steward, as an accountant, are not required to be very considerable. He is merely to keep an account of monies received by him, on one page, and of monies paid or disbursed by him, on the opposite page; and these two pages being cast up, and the amount of one side being deducted from the amount of the other, will, if the account has been correctly kept, shew at once the exact balance, belonging to his employer, remaining in his hands. It will be the business of the housekeeper to examine, weigh, and compare the several articles, as they are brought in, with the tickets sent with them by the respective tradesmen, and these tickets, so examined and signed, will enable the Steward to check the tradesmen's bills when brought in, previously to their being paid. An upright and trustworthy Steward will discharge this part of his duty, as well as every other, with zeal, fidelity, impartiality, and integrity; bearing for ever on his mind this pleasing truth, that, "every man's station is honourable or otherwise, as his own conduct makes it."

[Salary from £100 to £250 and upwards.]

THE STEWARD'S ROOM BOY

There is seldom a lad of this description kept, except in families where there is a house steward, or comptroller of the household, when the servant is appointed to attend on him, run on errands, carry messages, &c. He waits at table, or makes himself otherwise useful in the steward's-room; trims the lamps that are in use below stairs, and cleans the servants' boots and shoes.

[Wages from £8 to £12 per annum.]

THE BUTLER

AND

UNDER BUTLER

THE VALET

THE BUTLER

At first rising, it is the duty of the Butler, where no valet is kept, to manage and arrange his master's clothes, and carry them to his dressing-room, his boots and shoes being cleaned by the footman or under butler.

It is his proper business to see that the breakfast is duly set, the under butler or footman carrying up the tea urn, and the butler the eatables; he, or the under butler waiting during breakfast. The footman lays the green cloth on the table, then the table cloth, and sets the tea things, plates, knives and forks, the urn rug, &c. The Butler places the tea urn and such other things as may be ordered during breakfast, and takes all things off also; the footman bringing and carrying them away. On taking away, he removes the tea-tray, and the under butler or footman the urn, cloth, &c.

The breakfast things being taken away, and the plate, &c. cleaned and put away under his directions, the Butler then gets his own breakfast with the housekeeper, unless the servants all breakfast together at an earlier hour.

If no valet is kept, he then attends in his master's dressing-room, sets it in order, carries down his clothes to be brushed by the under butler or footman, and attends to everything connected with his master's clothes, linen, &c. or sees that what is wanted is done by others.

He now cleans himself to attend company or visitors at the door, which he is to answer, receive cards, deliver messages, &c.

At luncheon time, the cloth being laid by the under butler or footman, it is the duty of the Butler to carry in the tray, or arrange the table, and when there is company, he waits in the room assisted by the other servants.

If wine is wanted for the luncheon, it is his duty to fetch it from the cellar; and if ale, to draw or bring it up when wanted.

The keys of the wine and ale cellars are specially kept by him, and the management of the wine, the keeping the stock book, and also of ale in stock, or in brewing, are in his particular charge. This duty he generally performs in the morning before he is dressed to receive company, and he then brings out such wine as is wanted for the day's use. It is his duty to fine wine as it comes in the pipe, and to superintend the bottling, sealing it himself, and disposing it in bins so as to know its age and character. While these duties and those of brewing are in hand, he leaves the parlour and waiting duties to the under butler and footman.

Where no steward is kept, he pays all bills for wine, spirits, ale, malt, coals,and in general, all bills not in the housekeeper's or kitchen department. Sometimes, also, he pays the other male servants.

At dinner time, the under butler or footman lays the cloth, and carries up the articles wanted, under the direction of the Butler, who gives out the necessary plate, kept by him under lock, and generally in an iron chest.

He sets and displays the dinner on the table, carrying in the first dish, waits at the sideboard, hands wine round or when called for; removes every course, and sets and arranges every fresh course on the table according to his bill of fare, which is placed on the sideboard for reference; and does not leave the dinner room till the dessert and wine have been placed on the table by him or under his direction. Lose not a *moment of time* in placing the dinner on the table in proper order, and let not only every dish be as hot as possible, but every plate also, else the whole dinner will be spoiled. The cook's labour will be lost if the cloth be not laid in the parlour, and all the paraphernalia of the dinner table completely arranged an hour before dinner. An invitation to dinner at five generally means six—at five precisely, half past five—and not later than five, five o'clock exactly, so that the dinner may be served up a few minutes after.

It is then his business to see that the plate, glasses, &c. are carried to the pantry, cleaned, and wiped by the under butler and footman, and the whole carefully put in their proper places.

Having taken his own dinner with the other servants out of livery, generally at one o'clock, he gets his tea while the family in the parlour are taking their wine and dessert, and in the meantime, the under butler or footman prepares the tea things for the parlour.

If the bell rings during the dessert, the Butler answers, and does the same for the remainder of the evening.

The under butler is now engaged in cleaning the plate and arranging the pantry.

The tea-tray is carried up by the Butler, assisted by the footman; and in waiting at tea, the Butler hands round the cups on the tray, the footman assisting with the eatables. The Butler removes the tea-tray, and the footman the urn, &c. The footman carries in coals, but the Butler manages the candles.

When tea is made below, it is done by the housekeeper, but carried up and handed round by the Butler and footman.

If there is company, the refreshments, wine, ices, &c. are carried up by the Butler, assisted and followed by the footman.

When there is supper, the under Butler or Butler arranges the same, and it is managed like the dinner.

Slippers, dressing gown, night candles, &c. are carried up and disposed by the Butler.

After his master has gone to bed, he goes to his dressing-room, takes down such things as want cleaning or brushing, and gives them to the footman. He then looks over the plate, locks it up, sees that all the men servants are gone to bed, the doors locked, and windows fastened, and then retires to rest himself.

This business is strictly domestic, but he goes out to order things in his department, and he is sometimes employed abroad in any confidential business, to which the under servants are considered unequal.

The wages of regular Butlers, in large families, are from £50 to £80 per annum; but in smaller families, from £30 to £50. The perquisites, if he perform the duty of valet, are his master's cast off clothes; and as Butler, he gets the pieces of wax candles, the second hand cards, compliments on paying tradesman's bills, or Christmas boxes and wine for his own use. He finds his own clothes, washing, &c. and is expected to be genteel and clean in his person.

In all things connected with the establishment, he is supposed, when no steward is kept, to represent his master; and as various accounts are under his direction, he ought to be able to write a fair hand, and to be ready in the first rules of arithmetic. From this display of his duties, it will appear that his office is no sinecure; and as the good order and economy of an establishment depends much on the vigilance of the Butler, when no steward is kept, so a Butler who knows his duties, and performs them with zeal, integrity, and ability, cannot be too highly prized by judicious heads of families.

To manage foreign Wines

The principal object to be attended to in the mangement of foreign wine vaults, is to keep them of a temperate heat. Care must be taken, therefore, to close up every aperture or opening, that there may be no admission given to the external air. The floor of the vault should likewise be well covered with saw-dust, which must not be suffered to get too dry and dusty, but must receive now and then an addition of new, lest, when bottling or racking wine, some of the old dust should fly into it. At most vaults, in the winter, it is necessary to have a stove or chafing-dish, to keep up a proper degree of warmth. In the summer time it will be best to keep them as cool as possible.

MIXTURE AS BEFORE.

To Fit up a Cellar of Wines and Spirits

Provide a good rope and tackling, to let down the casks into the vault or cellar, and a slide, ladder, or pulley for the casks to slide or roll on.

A pair of strong slings

A pair of can hooks and a pair of crate hooks

A block of wood to put under the pipes when topping them over in a narrow passage, or in casing them

A small valinch to taste wine

A crane, and a small copper pump to rack off

Two or three gallon cans, made of wood

A large wooden funnel
Two or three copper funnels from a quart to a gallon each
Two racking cocks
Two wine bottling cocks
A brace and various bits
Two small tubs
A square basket to hold the corks
Two small tin funnels
A small strainer
Two corkscrews
Two or three baskets
A whisk to beat the finings
Three flannel or linen bags
A strong iron screw to raise the bungs
A pair of pliers
Bungs, corks, and vent pegs
Two frets or middle sized gimblets
Some sheet lead and tacks to put on broken staves
Brown paper to put round cocks and under the lead, when stopping leaks
A staff with a chain at one end to rumage the wines, &c.
Shots and lead canister, or bristle brush, and two cloths to wash bottles
Two large tubs
Some small racks that will hold six dozen each
A cooper's adze
An iron and a wooden driver to tighten hoops
Two dozen of wooden bungs of different sizes
A thermometer, which is to be kept in the vault, a stove or chafing-dish, to keep the heat of the vault to a known temperature
A few dozen of delf labels
A cupboard to hold all the tools
A spade, two good stiff birch brooms, and a rake to level the saw-dust.

To rack Foreign Wines

The vault of cellar should be of a temperate heat, and the casks sweet and clean. Should they have an acid or musty smell, it may be remedied by burning brimstone matches in them; and if not clean, rinse them well out with cold water, and after draining rinse with a quart of brandy, putting the brandy afterwards into the ullage cask. Then strain the lees or bottoms through a flannel or linen bag. But put the bottoms of port into the ullage cask without going through the filtering bag. In racking wine that is not on the stillage, a wine-pump is desirable.

To manage and improve poor Red Port

If wanting in body, colour and flavour, draw out thirty or forty gallons, and return the same quantity of young and rich wines. To a can of which put three gills of colouring, with a bottle of wine or brandy. Then whisk it well together, and put it into the cask stirring it well. If not bright in about a week or ten days, fine it for use; previous to which put in at different times a gallon of good brandy. If the wine is short of body, put a gallon or two of brandy in each pipe, by a quart or two at a time, as it feeds the wine better than putting it in all at once. But if the wines are in a bonded cellar, procure a funnel that will go to the bottom of the cask, that the brandy may be completely incorporated with the wine.

To manage Claret

Claret is not a wine of a strong body, though it requires to be of a good age before it is used, and, therefore, it should be well managed; the best method is to feed it every two or three weeks with a pint or two of French brandy. Taste it frequently, to know what state it is in, and use the brandy accordingly, but never put much in at a time, while a little incorporates with the wine, and feeds and mellows it.

If the claret is faint, rack it into a fresh-emptied hogshead, upon the lees of good claret; and bung it up, putting the bottom downwards for two or three days, that the lees may run through it.

To recover pricked Foreign Wines

Take a bottle of red port that is pricked, add to it half an ounce of tartarised spirit of wine, shake the liquor well together, and set it by for a few days, and it will be found much altered for the better. If this operation be dexterously performed, pricked wines may be absolutely recovered by it, and remain saleable for some time; and the same method may be used to malt liquors just turned sour.

To manage Hermitage and Burgundy

Red hermitage must be managed in the same way as claret, and the white likewise, except the colouring, which it does not require. Burgundy should be managed in the same manner as red hermitage.

To manage Lisbon Wine

If the Lisbon is dry, take out of the pipe thirty-five or forty gallons, and put in the same quantity of calcavella, stir it well about, and this will make a pipe of good mild Lisbon: or, if it be desired to convert mild into dry, take the same quantity out as above mentioned, before, and fill the pipe with Malaga sherry, stirring it about as the other. The same kind of fining used for Vidonia will answer for Lisbon wines; or it may be fined with the whites and shells of sixteen eggs, and a small handful of salt; beat it together to a froth, and mix it with a little of the wines; then pour it into the pipe, stir it about, and let it have vent for three days; after which bung it up, and in a few days it will be fine. Lisbon when bottled should be packed either in sawdust or leather in a temperate place.

To improve Sherry

If the sherry be new and hot, rack it off into a sweet cask, add five gallons of mellow Lisbon, which will take off the hot taste, then give it a head, take a quart of honey, mix it with a can of wine, and put it into the cask when racking. By this method, Sherry for present use will be greatly improved, having much the same effect upon it as age.

To improve White Wines

If the wine have an unpleasant taste, rack off one half; and to the remainder add a gallon of new milk, a handful of bay-salt, and as much rice; after which take a staff, beat them well together for half an hour, and fill up the cask, and when rolled well about, stillage it, and in a few days it will be much improved.

If the white wine is foul and has lost its colour, for a butt or pipe take a gallon of new milk, put it into the cask, and stir it well about with a staff; and when it has settled, put in three ounces of isinglass made into a jelly, with a quarter of a pound of loaf sugar scraped fine, and stir it well about. On the day following, bung it up, and in a few days it will be fine and have a good colour.

To fine a hogshead of Claret

Take the whites and shells of six fresh eggs, and proceed as with port finings. Claret requires to be kept warm in saw-dust when bottled.

To fine Port Wine

Take the whites and shells of eight fresh eggs, beat them in a wooden can or pail, with a whisk, till it becomes a thick froth; then add a little wine to it, and whisk it again. If the pipe is full take out four or five gallons of the wine to make room for the finings. If the weather be warmish, add a pint of fresh-water sand to the finings. Stir it well about; after which put in the finings, stirring it for five minutes; put in the can of wine, leaving the bung out for a few hours, that the froth may fall: then bung it up, and in eight or ten days it will be fine and fit for bottling.

To make and apply Finings

Put the finings into a can or pail, with a little of the liquor about to be fined, whisk them altogether till they are perfectly mixed, and then nearly fill the can with the liquor, whisking it well about again; after which, if the cask be full, take out four or five gallons to make room; then take the staff, and give it a good stirring; next whisk the finings up, and put them in; afterwards stir it with the staff for five minutes. Then drive the bung in, and bore a hole with a gimblet, that it may have vent for three or four days, after which drive in a vent peg.

To convert White Wine into Red

Put four ounces of turnesole rags into an earthen vessel, and pour upon them a pint of boiling water; cover the vessel close, and leave it to cool; strain off the liquor, which will be of a fine deep red inclining to purple. A small portion of this colours a large quantity of wine. This tincture may either be made in brandy, or mixed with it, or else made into a syrup, with sugar, for keeping.

In those countries which do not produce the tingeing grape which affords a blood-red juice, wherewith the wines of France are often stained, in defect of this, the juice of elderberries is used, and sometimes log-wood is used at Oporto.

To clean Wine Decanters

Cut some brown paper into very small bits, so as to go with ease into the decanters; then cut a few pieces of soap very small, and put some water, milk-warm, into the decanters, upon the soap and paper; put in also a little pearl ash; by well working this about in the decanters it will take off the crust of the wine, and give the glass a fine polish. Where the decanters have had wine left to stand in them a long time, take a small cane with a bit of sponge tied tight at one end; by putting this into the decanters any crust of the wine may be removed. When the decanters have been properly washed, let them be thoroughly dried, and turned down in a proper rack.

If the decanters have wine in them when put by, have some good corks always at hand to put in instead of stoppers; this will keep the wine much better.

To decant Wine

Be careful not to shake or disturb the crust when moving it about, or drawing the cork, particularly Port wine. Never decant wine without a wine-strainer, with some fine cambric in it, to prevent the crust, and bits of cork going into the decanter. In decanting Port wine do not drain it too near; there are generally two-thirds of a wine glass of thick dregs in each bottle, which ought not to be put in; but in white wine there is not much settling; pour it out however slowly, and raise the bottle up gradually: the wine should never be decanted in a hurry, therefore always do it before the family sit down to dinner. Do not jostle the decanters against each other when moving them about, as they easily break when full.

To mix a Salad

Always inquire before you mix a salad, how your master or mistress would like to have it done. If no particular method be pointed out to you, adopt the following, which has been much approved of. Let the salad be well washed and dried in a cloth before you cut it up; save a part of the celery with a little beetroot and endive for ornament in the middle of the dish; cut the rest small as well as the lettuce and mustard and cresses, and put to it the following mixture: take the yolk of an egg boiled hard, rub it quite smooth with a tablespoonful of oil and a little mustard; when they are well mixed together add six spoonsful of milk or cream, and when these are well mixed, put six or seven spoonsful of vinegar to the whole, and mix it all together with the salad. Never make the salad long before it is wanted, as it becomes flat with standing.

To make Punch

Put 40 grains of citric acid, 7 full drops of essence of lemon, 7 oz. of lump sugar, in a quart mug; pour over 1 pint of boiling water, when the sugar is melted, stir; then add ½ pint of rum, and ¼ pint of brandy.

To prepare Soda Water

Soda water is prepared (from powders) precisely in the same manner as ginger beer, except that, instead of the two powders there mentioned, the two following are used: for one glass, 30 grains of carbonate of soda; for the other, 25 grains of tartaric (or citric) acid.

Method of preserving Peas Green for Winter

Put into a kettle of hot water any quantity of fresh shelled green peas, and after just letting them boil up, pour them into a large thick cloth, cover them with another, make them quite dry, and set them once or twice in a cool oven to harden a little; after which put them into paper bags, and hang them up in the kitchen for use.—To prepare them when wanted, they are first to be soaked well for an hour or more, and then put into warm water, and boiled with a little butter.

To Mend Glass

The juice of garlic, pounded in a stone mortar, is said to be the strongest cement to mend broken glass.

LIGHT SPIRITS.

To convey Fresh Fish

To ensure the sweetness of fish conveyed by land carriage, the belly of the fish should be opened, and the internal parts sprinkled with powdered charcoal. The same material will restore impure or even putrescent water to a state of perfect freshness.

To purify Water by Charcoal

Nothing has been found so effectual for preserving water sweet as charring the insides of the casks well before they are filled. When the water becomes impure and offensive, from ignorance of the preservative effect produced on it by charring the casks previous to their being filled, it may be rendered perfectly sweet by putting a little fresh charcoal in powder into the cask, or by filtering it through fresh burnt and coarsely pulverized charcoal.

To extinguish a Recent Fire

A mop and a pail of water are generally the most efficacious remedies, but if it has gained head, then keep out the air, and remove all ascending or perpendicular combustibles, up which the fire creeps and increases in force as it rises.

To extinguish Fire in a Chimney

Shut the doors and windows, throw water on the fire in the grate, and then stop up the bottom of the chimney.

THE UNDER BUTLER

Is entirely under the control and direction of the Butler. He cleans all the plate—the parlour knives and forks—lays the cloths—sets out the side-board, and assists to wait at table. As he is supposed to be busily employed, after dinner, in the Butler's pantry, cleaning the plate, he is not usually expected to answer the bells at that period. He trims the lamps belonging to the dining and drawing-rooms, and is frequently required to assist the Butler in cleaning his master's clothes and shoes. The Under Butler, generally looking to the situation of Butler, and as even in his present station he will have occasion for more particular directions, he will do well frequently to refer to the hints to the Butler, where he will find the immediate duties of the Butler and himself more particularly given.

A chief part of his duty consists in assisting in the rough work of the butler, such as brewing, bottling, and cellar business in general, in all which he should be as expert as the butler himself.

[Wages 16 to 25 guineas.]

To clean China and Glass

The best material for cleaning either porcelain or glassware is Fuller's earth, but it must be beaten into a fine powder, and carefully cleared from all rough or hard particles, which might endanger the polish of the brilliant surface.

To clean Plate

Wash the plate in boiling water to free it from grease, and if it has wrought edges, brush it well before you begin to clean it. The leathers ought to be soft and very thick, and the sponges well soaked in water.

To clean Plated Articles

Take an ounce of killed quicksilver, which you may buy at the chemist's, and half a pound of the best whiting sifted; mix them with spirits of wine when used. Hartshorn-powder may be used instead of whiting; but whiting is quite as good, when dried and pounded.

To give Silver Plate a lustre

Dissolve alum in strong ley, skim it carefully, mix it with soap and wash your silver utensils with it, using a linen rag.

To take stains out of Silver Plate

Steep the plate in soap leys for the space of four hours; then cover it over with whiting wet with vinegar, so that it may stick thick upon it, and dry it by a fire; after which, rub off the whiting, and pass it over with dry bran, and the spots will not only disappear, but the plate will look exceedingly bright.

To make Plate look like new

Take of unslaked lime and alum, a pound each, of aqua vitae and vinegar, each a pint, and of beer grounds, two quarts; boil the plate in these, and they will set a beautiful gloss upon it.

To take Fruit Spots out of Cloth

Let the spotted part of the cloth imbibe a little water without dipping, and hold the part over a lighted common brimstone match at a proper distance. The sulphurous gas which is discharged, will soon cause the spot to disappear.

Plate Powder

Whiting properly purified from sand, applied wet, and rubbed till dry, is one of the easiest, safest, and, certainly the cheapest, of all plate powders.

THE VALET

The duties of this servant are not so various nor so important as those of the footman; indeed, they are very frequently, and particularly in small families, a part of the business of a footman. The particular province of the valet is to attend to the personal accommodation of his master. He waits on him when dressing and undressing, has the care of his wardrobe, brushes and keeps his clothes in good order and ready to put on when wanted. For this purpose every garment or other article of wearing apparel, should be carefully examined, cleaned or brushed on the first opportunity that offers, and then put away in its proper place.

He should choose the earliest part of the morning to clean the boots and shoes, unless it be otherwise arranged, and brush the clothes, and to do all such work, so as to be able to get to his master's dressing-room time enough to make the necessary arrangements there before he expects him to rise. He will see that the housemaid has lighted the fire, and cleaned out and dusted the rooms; will prepare the washing-stand, fill the ewer with clean soft water, and the carafe with fresh spring water.—The basin and towels, the hair, nail and tooth-brushes clean, and in their proper places; hot water, and all the necessary apparatus for shaving, quite ready; his dressing-gown and slippers airing before the fire; and his clean linen perfectly well aired by himself, before it be considered as fit to be put on. The coat, trousers, &c. intended to be worn must be taken out and placed at length across the backs of chairs, the sleeves and outsides turned inward, with a clean linen or brown Holland wrapper thrown over them, to save them from dust. Having once ascertained the way in which these things are to be done, he will find it easy in future, and will be sure to please. The best way to hang up a coat is, to fold it once at full length, with the inside outward, the sleeves put straight, and the two fronts together, and then hang it on a cloak-pin by the inside of the shoulder.

If the wardrobe be sufficiently large to hold each kind of garment separately, it will be so much the better, as the coats and other articles may then be laid in smoothly and at length, as soon as they are brushed and cleaned, and a brown Holland cloth may be spread over each drawer or shelf, to preserve them from the dust.

Gentlemen who shave themselves, usually strop their own razors immediately after the operation, whilst the metal is yet warm, which is the best way: but if it be left to the valet to do, the razor must be dipped in warm water and wiped dry with a clean cloth or rag; then laying it flat on the strop, draw it diagonally, from the heel to the point, the whole length of the strop, turning the elbow in and out every time the razor is turned; half a dozen or half a score strokes backwards and forwards, as often as it is used, will keep it in good order for a considerable time. Good razors are made concave, or hollow, between the back and the edge, on both sides, for the greater security in shaving, and for the purpose of giving them a better edge in setting or stropping.

Having attended his master while dressing, combed his hair, &c. the valet will take the first opportunity, after he is gone, to set the room in order, by looking over his things, folding away his night clothes, washing the brushes and combs occasionally, when necessary, with warm water and soap, wiping them clean, and drying them at an easy distance from the fire, and then putting them away in their places.— The dressing-stand must be wiped clean and dry, the basin washed and wiped, the ewer and carafe rinsed out and filled again with clean water, the towels taken away and replaced with clean ones, the fire stirred, the room dusted, and every thing put in order, as if immediately to be used again. This must always be done as soon as possible after his master is dressed or re-dressed, and every garment or other article that has been taken off, must be brushed, folded, and put away in its proper place.

In case of the master's coming home wet from a ride, or otherwise, an immediate change of warm dry clothes must be provided, and the wet or damp things taken away and dried at a proper distance from the fire; after having wiped the coat, or other woollen garments, with a sponge, the way of the nap, or, if only spotted, with a silk handkerchief, in the same manner, which will effectually smooth the grain of the cloth, and remove all the spots.

When preparing for a journey, care should be taken to ascertain the probable time of absence, that sufficient change of linen, &c. may be provided—nor must the shaving and dressing apparatus be forgotten. When arrived at an inn, or visiting place, all his master's things must be carried into his dressing-room, and set in order for dressing, or for the night, as nearly as possible in the same order as at home. If the footman be not there, the valet will have to attend to his master's accommodation below stairs also.

The valet is to be always in attendance, in case of his master's coming home unexpectedly—and he is to assist in waiting at table at all meal-times.

As the valet is much about his master's person, and has the opportunity of hearing his off-at-hand opinions on many subjects, he should endeavour to have as short a memory as possible, and, above all, keep his master's council; and he should be very cautious of mischief-making or tale-bearing, to the prejudice of other persons, as calculated to involve his master in disputes, and ruin himself, if by chance he is incorrect.

[The usual salary is from £30 to £60 per annum, but in some situations much more. Perquisites, his master's cast-off clothes.]

To clean Gold Lace

Rub it with a soft brush dipped in roche alum burnt, sifted to a very fine powder.

To remove stains from Mourning Dresses

Boil a good handful of fig-leaves in two quarts of water till reduced to a pint. Bombazine, crêpe, cloth, &c. need only be rubbed with a sponge dipped in the liquor, and the effect will be instantly produced.

New mode of Shaving

Mix up with the brush, in prepared lather, one tea-spoonful of finely pounded best lump whiting, without the smallest danger to the razor's edge or the surface of the chin. Perhaps the very best edge may be given to the razor also, by throwing a pinch of whiting on a moderately oiled or soaped strop.

To clean Gilt Buckles, Chains, &c.

Dip a soft brush in water, rub a little soap on it, and brush the article for a minute or two, then wash it clean, wipe it; place it near the fire till dry, and brush it with burnt bread finely powdered.

To manage Razor Strops

Keep them moderately moist with a drop or two of sweet oil: a little crocus martis and a few drops of sweet oil, rubbed well in with a glass bottle, will give the razor a fine edge; pass it afterwards on the inside of your hand when warm, and dip it in hot water just before using.

To scour Clothes, Coats, Pelisses, &c.

If a black, blue, or brown coat, dry 2 ounces of Fuller's earth, and pour on it sufficient boiling water to dissolve it, and plaster with it the spots of grease; take a penny-worth of bullock's gall, mix with it half a pint of stale urine, and a little boiling water; with a hard brush, dipped in this liquor, brush spotted places. Then dip the coat in a bucket of cold spring water. When nearly dry, lay the nap right, and pass a drop of oil of olives over the brush to finish it.

If grey, drab, fawns, or maroons, cut yellow soap into thin slices, and pour water upon it to moisten it. Rub the greasy and dirty spots of the coat. Let it dry a little, and then brush it with warm water, repeating, if necessary, as at first, and use water a little hotter; rinse several times, in warm water, and finish as before.

To clean Gloves without wetting

Lay the gloves upon a clean board, make a mixture of dried fulling-earth and powdered alum, and pass them over on each side with a common stiff brush: then sweep it off, and sprinkle them well with dry bran and whiting, and dust them well; this, if they be not exceedingly greasy, will render them quite clean; but if they are much soiled, take out the grease with crumbs of toasted bread, and powder of burnt bone: then pass them over with a woollen cloth, dipped in fulling-earth or alum powder; and in this manner they can be cleaned without wetting, which frequently shrinks and spoils them.

Fuller's purifier for woollen cloth

Dry, pulverize, and sift the following ingredients:

6 lbs of Fuller's earth, 1 lb of pipe-clay, and 4 oz. of French chalk.

Make a paste of the above with the following:

1 oz. of rectified oil of turpentine, 2 oz. of spirit of wine, and 1½ lbs of melted oil soap.

Make up the compound into cakes, which are to be kept in water, or in small wooden boxes.

To drive away, or prevent the approach of Moths

Wrap up yellow or turpentine soap in paper, or place an open bottle, containing spirits of turpentine within the wardrobe. But as the smell of the latter may be unpleasant, sprinkle bay leaves, lavender, or walnut-leaves, black pepper in grains, or Russia leather shavings.

To clean Gold Lace and Embroidery

For this purpose alkaline liquors are not to be used; for while they clean the gold they corrode the silk, and change or discharge its colour. Soap also alters the shade, and even the species of certain colours. But, spirit of wine may be used without any danger of its injuring either colour or quality; and, in many cases, proves as effectual for restoring the lustre of gold, as the corrosive detergents. But, though spirit of wine is the most innocent material employed for this purpose, it is not in all cases proper. The golden covering may be in some parts worn off; or the base metal, with which it has been alloyed, may be corroded by the air, so as to leave the particles of gold disunited; while the silver underneath, tarnished to a yellow hue, may continue a tolerable colour to the whole: so it is apparent that the removal of the tarnish would be prejudicial, and make the lace or embroidery less like gold than it was before.

To revive faded Black Cloth

Having cleaned it well, boil two or three ounces of logwood for half an hour. Dip it in warm water and squeeze it dry, then put it into the copper, and boil half an hour. Take it out and add a small piece of creen copperas, and boil it another half hour. Hang it in the air for an hour or two, then rinse it in two or three cold waters, dry it and let it be regularly brushed over with a soft brush, over which a drop or two of oil of olives has been rubbed.

To dry-clean Cloth

Drip a brush in warm gall, apply it to greasy places, and rinse it off in cold water; dry by the fire, then lay the coat flat, strew damp sand over it, and with a brush beat the sand into the cloth; then brush it out with a hard brush, and the same will bring away the dirt. Rub a drop of oil of olives over a soft brush, to brighten the colours.

To make Breeches Ball

Mix 1 pound of Bath brick, 2 pounds of pipe-clay, 4 ounces of pumice stone powder, and six ounces of ox gall; colour them with rose pink, yellow ochre, umber, Irish slate, &c. to the desired shade.

Clothes' Ball

Mix 2 pounds of pipe clay, 4 ounces of Fuller's earth, 4 ounces of whiting, and a quarter of a pint of ox galls.

To take grease out of Leather Breeches

The white of an egg applied to the injured part, and dried in the sun, will effectually answer this purpose.

Another Method

To two tablespoonsful of spirit of turpentine, put half an ounce of mealy potatoes, add some of the best Durham mustard, with a little vinegar; let them dry, and when well rubbed, the spots will be entirely removed.

To clean Leather

Take of French yellow ochre, 1 lb, sweet oil, a dessert spoonful. Mix well together, so that the oil may not be seen: then take of pipe clay, 1 lb, starch, ¼ lb. Mix with boiling water; when cold lay it on the leather; and rub and brush it well when dry.

To make Scouring Balls

Portable balls for removing spots from clothes, may be thus prepared. Fuller's earth perfectly dried (so that it crumbles into a powder), is to be moistened with the clear juice of lemons, and a small quantity of pure pearl-ashes is to be added. Knead the whole carefully, till it acquires the consistence of a thick elastic paste: form it into convenient small balls, and dry them in the sun. To be used, first moisten the spot on the clothes with water, then rub it with the ball, and let the spot dry in the sun; after having washed it with pure water, the spot will entirely disappear.

To take stains out of Scarlet Cloth

Take soap wort, bruise it, strain out the juice, and add to it a small quantity of black soap; wash the stains a few times with this liquor, suffering it to dry between whiles, and in a day or two they will disappear.

To take stains out of Black Cloth, Silk, Crêpe, &c.

Boil a large handful of fig-leaves in two quarts of water until reduced to a pint. Squeeze the leaves, and put the liquor into a bottle for use. The articles need only be rubbed with a sponge in the liquor, and the stains will instantly disappear.

THE MAN COOK

THE FOOTMAN

THE LADY'S FOOTMAN

THE UNDER FOOTMAN

THE HALL PORTER

CHICKEN HAZARD.

THE MAN COOK

The man Cook, now become a requisite member in the establishment of a man of fashion, is in all respects the same as that of a female Cook. He is generally a foreigner, or if an Englishman, possesses a peculiar tact in manufacturing many fashionable foreign delicacies, or of introducing certain seasonings and flavours in his dishes, which render them more inviting to the palate of his employer, than those produced by the simply healthful modes of modern English Cooks.

The man Cook has the entire superintendance of the kitchen, while his several female assistants are employed in roasting, boiling, and all the ordinary manual operations of the kitchen. His attention is chiefly directed to the stew-pan, in the manufacture of stews, fracassees, fricandeaux, &c. At the same time, his situation is one of great labour and fatigue, which, with the superior skill requisite for excellence in his art, procures him a liberal salary, frequently twice or thrice the sum given to the most experienced female English Cook.

As the scientific preparations of the man cook would themselves fill a large volume, and are not generally useful in English families, it is not deemed necessary to give place to them in this work; but the following useful receipts having, inadvertently, been omitted under the head Cook, they are inserted in this place rather than omitted altogether.

As the art of Cookery, or *gourmanderie,* is reduced to a regular science in France, where an egg may be cooked half a hundred ways, so those who can afford large families of servants, and give frequent entertainments, consider a man-cook as economical, because he produces an inexhaustible variety without any waste of materials, and that elegance and piquancy of flavours which are necessary to stimulate the appetites of the luxurious. In France, all culinary business is conducted by men, and there are, at least, as many men cooks as considerable kitchens; but in England, men cooks are kept only in about three or four hundred great and wealthy families, and in about forty or fifty London hotels. But it is usual in smaller establishments to engage a man cook for a day or two before an entertainment.

[It is understood that HRH the Duke of York pays Mons. Ude, his French Cook, £500 per annum.]

Method of preparing an East India Curry, with the articles used therein

Let the fowl, duck, rabbit, meat, fish, or vegetable, &c. be cut up into small pieces, sprinkling a little flour thereon, fried in butter (with two middle-sized onions sliced fine), or what is called drawn in a pan, then stewed in the gravy from a pound of beef (though water is as frequently used) over a brisk fire, for about twenty minutes, with two or three table-spoonsful of the mixture, as below, stirring the whole occasionally; or the powder may be rubbed well over the fowl, &c. and fried with it, adding two ounces of butter, the juice of a fine lemon, or half a wine glass of lemon juice, or lemon pickle,—two cloves of garlic, chopped very fine, and one tea-spoonful of salt. If any of the ingredients predominate too much, or an insufficiency prevail, subtract or add according to taste. For a larger quantity of meat than the weight of a large fowl, use more of the mixture in proportion. The curry will be much improved by the mixture being made into a thin paste with a few spoonsful of cream, and then rubbed over the meat, previously to its being put into the stew-pan.

Curry Powder

Thirteen ounces coriander seed, three ounces cumin seed, two ounces black pepper, four ounces China turmeric, or curcuma root, half an ounce Cayenne pepper, one quarter of an ounce powdered cassia, one quarter of an ounce powdered white ginger, also one half of an ounce of cardamums, one quarter of an ounce of cloves, and one quarter of an ounce of allspice. The above quantities are enough for twenty curries, but it should be kept dry in a tin canister. The curried fowl, &c. as above, will require three quarters of a pound of rice to be a sufficiency for curry eaters. The curry and the rice should be served in separate dishes, with covers, the dishes having heaters, or in hot water dishes, such as those used for beef-steaks.

N.B.—Two or three sour apples cut into quarters, as well as a few fresh mushrooms are great improvements to all curries; as are truffles. If the latter are used, the liquor in which they are boiled should be added to the curry.

Mode of preparing Mulga-tawney, as at Madras

Cut up a fowl, duck, rabbit, beef, or mutton, boil the same in two quarts of water for a quarter of an hour; then mix the under-mentioned therein, previously bruising the spices in a mortar, rejecting the husk. For a larger quantity of meat than the weight of a large fowl, use more of the mixture in proportion.

Two tablespoons over-filled of the curry powder or ingredients, answers the purpose, and better, adding the butter, onions, garlic, pease-flour, acid, &c.

One quarter of an ounce China turmeric, one sixth of an ounce Cayenne pepper, one ounce and a quarter coriander seed, one third of an ounce of powdered cassia, two drams two scruples black pepper.

One tablespoon of butter; juice from a fine lemon, or equal quantity of lemon pickle, three middle-sized onions cut fine, six cloves of garlic chopped very fine, six tea-spoons of pease-flour, high-dried or baked; then pour thereon half a pint of boiling water, strain the ingredients through a fine cloth or sieve, then put the same with fowl, &c. over the fire, adding at this time the butter and onions previously fried together, boil the same for half an hour, adding, in the last five minutes, the acid, when the Mulga-tawney will be ready for the table; which eaten as soup and bouilli, mixing rice therein, will prove not only palatable, but an excellent stomachic. The Mulga-tawney, or soup, when done, should be nearly the consistency of cream; if it should prove otherwise, when proceeding as above, more or less water should be used on the onset, but not afterwards added. The soup with the meat to be served in a tureen, and sent to table quite hot; the rice in a dish having hot water below and a cover.

A prejudice may exist against Curry and Mulga-tawney, but there can be no doubt of both being perfectly wholesome; as, to wit, throughout the East Indies, it is the daily food of millions of all ages.

Method of Boiling Rice

The following is different from that adopted generally in England, but was followed by an old Indian officer when here, and found to answer perfectly well: but the object to be accomplished is, that the rice should be well done, as white as possible, and perfectly free from water: the rice used should be Patna; the Carolina, though much whiter, is not so good either for Curry or Mulga-tawney.

Take a pound of Patna rice, have the same well washed, looking over each grain for small stones, husks, &c. then put the rice into a saucepan, and pour thereon boiling water, put on the cover, and let the saucepan remain off the fire about a quarter of an hour; in that time, if the water was full boiling, the rice will be sufficiently softened for use; pour the water off, and to dry the rice, set it over the fire for a couple of minutes, stirring it well during the time with a fork. Proceeding as above the rice will be as dry and as well cooked as that prepared by the natives in the East Indies; great care to be taken that it does not become hard by the heat.

Another way of boiling the rice is, to soak it an hour in cold water, then put it into a saucepan and cover it with hot water, adding one tea-spoonful of salt to every teacup full of rice. Place it over the fire, and when it has boiled about ten minutes, the water should be poured off. Then cover the saucepan close down, and let it stand by the fire for a few minutes, when the rice will become dry, and fit to serve up with your curry.

A DIFFICULT DISSECTION.

THE FOOTMAN

The business of the Footman is so multifarious and incessant, that in most families, if he be industrious, attentive, and disposed to make himself useful, he will find full employment in the affairs of the house, and the more useful he can make himself, in a general way, the more acceptable will be his services to the whole house, the greater will be his reward, and the more comfortable he will be himself.

In many genteel small families, the footman is the only man servant, in which case he is expected to make himself generally useful; but his particular departments are, the cleaning of the knives, shoes, plate, and furniture; answering the door, going on errands, waiting at table, and answering the parlour bell. The footman finds himself merely in linen, stockings, shoes, and washing; but if silk stockings, or any extra articles are expected to be worn, they are found by the family. On quitting service, every livery servant is expected to leave behind him any livery had within six months; the last new livery is usually reserved for Sundays and dress occasions.

For the better dispatch of his own particular business, it is indispensably necessary that the footman should *rise early*, and as every moment of his time will be appropriated, he must endeavour to get that part of his business, which depends upon himself, done before the family are stirring, as interruptions may then occur, and his necessary labours be unavoidably delayed, or made to interfere with other business, not less necessary.

The footman should endeavour to get the dirtiest part of his work done first; such as cleaning the shoes and boots, knives and forks, brushing and cleaning clothes, hats and gloves, and cleaning the furniture, &c. &c. For these purposes, his working dress should be generally a pair of overalls, a waistcoat and fustian jacket, and a leather apron, with a white apron to put on occasionally, when called from these duties. Good families generally allow the footman a proper dress of this sort, exclusive of his liveries, as it is equally creditable to both master and servant, that the livery he is to appear in, when attending his ordinary avocations, should be kept clean, and look respectable. If it were always to be well and clearly understood, between every master and the servants to whom he gives livery, what shall be the number and kind of garments, to be given yearly, or otherwise, and that to be made a rule, from which no deviation should be made, it would prevent much of the unpleasant feeling on this subject, which has frequently been found to arise subsequent to the agreement.

The business of the footman below stairs being done, he next proceeds to clean the lamps in the best rooms. The oil in them should be fine and good, and changed once a week or ten days, and the cottons should be thick and closely woven, always kept dry, and cut even at the top, and soaked a little when fresh put in, by letting down the oil to them for a short time.

For cleaning boots and shoes, he takes care to provide himself with proper brushes and good blacking. In boots he will not clean the tops till he has finished the feet and legs, when it will be necessary to cover the legs whilst he is cleaning the tops.

Ladies' shoes are to be cleaned with milk, and other liquids, according to their colour, and merely the edges of the soles are to be blacked and polished, but in cleaning these and gentlemen's dress shoes, great care must be taken not to soil the inside linings.

Afterwards, the next business in rotation in the morning, will be to clean the mahogany and other furniture, in the parlour and best rooms. Whether the tables, side-boards, cellarets, chairs, &c. be of a light or dark colour, they must be cleaned with a preparation or oil of an appropriate colour.

In using the different compositions, have two pieces of woollen cloth for each, one to put it on with, and the other for polishing. Sometimes a hard brush will be required to lay on the paste, and a piece of soft cork to rub out the stains. Always rub the wood the way of the grain, and remember to dust the furniture before you begin to clean it.

If oil be used, let it be rubbed off as quickly as possible, and then polished with another cloth. When wax is used, let it be applied very sparingly, and polished off with another cloth.

The brass rods or other ornaments to side-boards, cellarets, &c. should be cleaned before the mahogany is touched. The dirt on these ornaments may be removed with flannel well soaped, and polished off with the plate leather. If any brass work has the lacquer worn off, it may be cleaned with brick-dust and leather.

Every article of furniture should be cleaned and rubbed in the middle of the room, when convenient, to prevent smearing and injuring the walls.

Looking Glasses being very costly, should be cleaned with great care. First, take a clean soft sponge, just squeezed out of water, and then dipped in spirits of wine; rub the glass over with this, and then polish if off with fine powder blue, or whiting tied up in muslin, quickly laid on, and then well rubbed off, with a clean cloth, and afterwards with a silk handkerchief. If the glass be very large, no more of it should be wetted with the spirit at a time, than can be cleaned off quickly.

The frames must never be touched with any thing wet or damp. Cotton-wool is the best thing to rub them with, as it will take off the stains and dirt without doing any injury; or, if the frames are varnished, they may be rubbed with the spirits of wine, which will at once take out the spots and dirt, after which they may be re-varnished. Picture-frame makers clean them with a soft brush and strong size waters. Fly spots may be prevented by rubbing frames with garlic or onion.

Pictures are best cleaned lightly with a wet sponge, but should never be touched with a cloth.

The attendance of the footman will now be required in the breakfast parlour, for which purpose, he must prepare by washing himself, and throwing off his working dress.

In the directions to the butler, we have given sufficiently at large, setting out the breakfast table, and waiting at breakfast, which in small families becomes solely the business of the footman.

After breakfast, he sets the parlour to rights by sweeping up the crumbs, shaking the green cloth, and laying it again on the table, making up the fire and sweeping up the hearth.

The footman now carries out such messages and cards as he is charged to deliver. When the footman is obliged to go out with the carriage, the butler or under butler usually undertakes to do such things in his absence, as he necessarily leaves undone.

In large families, the footman lays the cloth for dinner, and the knives and forks and glasses, and the butler arranges the silver articles, and sees that the whole is correctly laid out. When the hour of dinner approaches, notice is usually given, by the ringing of a bell by the footman, ten or fifteen minutes before the time; and during this time he is busy in carrying up every thing that he thinks may or can be wanted during dinner, so as to have every thing at hand, at that time. Again he rings the dinner bell, to announce to the family that dinner is going up, when the butler takes the first dish, and is followed by the under butler and footman with the remainder of the fish and soups, which the butler places on the table, and removing the covers, gives them to the footman and under butler, who convey them out of the room. The servants then take their respective stations,—the butler at the side-board, to serve the wines or beer when called for; the footman at the back of his master's chair, and the lady's footman, if any, behind his lady. When the soups and fish have been served round, the butler rings the dining-room bell to warn the cook to be ready with the removes, which are generally, solid joints of meat, or the first course, if no removes; the butler then removes the dishes from the table, and hands them to the footman or under butler, who carries them away.

A PLATED WAITER.

If wine or beer is asked for, the footman or under butler puts the empty glasses on a waiter, and the butler fills them. When a clean plate is wanted, the butler hands it to the footman, with a clean knife and fork, and the footman puts the dirty one in the proper place to be taken away.

When the butler sees that the first course is nearly done with, he again gives notice to the cook, and proceeds to take all the dishes off the table, and the footman and under butler take them away, and fetch the second course. The butler being employed, in the mean time, in setting the table in order, laying the mats, clean spoons, glasses, &c. The footman, with the assistance of the house-maids and others, having brought up the next course, the butler places the dishes on the table, takes off the covers, hands them to the footman, to be taken away, and again takes his station at the side-board, and during the whole dinner, the same kind of etiquette as before, is observed by every servant in attendance (of which, in some cases, there are several besides the butler, under butler, and footman; namely, the lady's footman, valet, and on particular occasions, waiters hired for the purpose). The third course (consisting of pastry, viz. pies, tarts, &c. with game at the top and bottom of the table, and the cheese and salads placed on the side-board), which being removed, as before, the butler with a napkin wipes off the stains and marks of the hot dishes on the tables, and places the dessert, as it is brought up by the footman and under butler. He also puts the wine on the table, and the under butler the wine-glasses, while the footman places the finger glasses before each person, and a plate, with a knife and fork and spoon on each plate, the butler putting other spoons for serving the fruits, jellies, &c. The butler takes his place behind his master's chair, at the foot of the table, and the lady's footman, behind his lady's chair at the head, to hand the wines, &c. and

A TIDE (A TIED) WAITER.

all the other servants leave the room, taking with them all the things that have been used.

The footman, as soon as all the things are carried down, repairs to the drawing-room, makes up the fire, sweeps up the hearth, and otherwise prepares that room. The butler also taking occasion to see that the lamps and candles are lighted, and the card tables set out, with candles and two packs of cards on each, and the chairs and sofas properly arranged by the footman.

The butler and footman then retire to their several avocations in the butler's pantry, where the footman is employed in washing and wiping the glasses, and the under butler cleaning the plate (which the kitchen maid generally washes). When the ladies have retired from the dining-room, and the drawing-room bell rings for coffee, the footman enters with the tray, the coffee being made below stairs, and the bread and butter, cakes, toast, &c. the under butler, or some other servant following, to take away the empty cups and saucers on a waiter or tray. At tea time, the butler carries up the tea-tray, and the footman the toast, muffins, &c. (which are prepared by the kitchen maid). Tea is announced to the gentlemen by the footman, and the gentlemen having joined the ladies, the tea and coffee is handed round by the butler, bread and butter, toast, &c. by the footman, the under butler following to take away the cups and saucers.

If there be no supper, the wine, when ordered, is carried in by the butler, and the glasses, &c. on a tray, by the footman; if sandwiches are introduced, they are carried up on a tray, covered with a clean cloth, by the footman, the butler attending in the room to hand the wines, &c.

The company being gone, the bed-room candlesticks are brought by the footman, and are handed to each person respectively as he wishes to retire to bed.

The footman then shuts up all the lower part of the house, if not before done, and retires to bed himself. The butler follows last, sees all safe, and retires also.

In going out with the carriage, the footman should be dressed in his best livery, his shoes and stockings being very clean, and his hat, great coat, &c. being well brushed; nothing being so disgraceful as a slovenly exterior. He should be ready at receiving directions at the carriage door, and accurate in delivering them to the coachman, and though he may indicate the importance of his family by his style of knocking at a door, he ought to have some regard to the nerves of the family and the peace of the neighbourhood. When the carriage waits at routs or public places, he should abstain from drinking with other servants, and take care to be within call when wanted. His expertness in letting down the steps and putting them up again, and his caution in shutting the door, so as not to injure any one, or the dresses of the ladies, are expected.

When he walks out behind his mistress, he should preserve a modest demeanour, and protect her, if necessary, from intrusion or insult; and on this duty he is expected to be particularly attentive to every part of his dress. In answering the door it is his duty to behave respectfully to all enquirers after his master or mistress, and never to presume on his knowledge of persons whom they ought to see or ought not to see, except in obedience to positive instructions.

[The Footman's wages are from 20 to 30 guineas, with two suits of livery, and two undress suits.]

Liquid for cleansing Boot Tops, &c.

Mix in a phial, one drachm of oxy-muriate of potash, with two ounces of distilled water; and when the salt is dissolved, add two ounces of muriatic acid. Then shake well together, mix in another phial, three ounces of rectified spirit of wine with half an ounce of the essential oil of lemon, unite the contents of the two phials, and keep the liquid thus prepared, closely corked for use. This chemical liquid should be applied with a clean sponge, and dried in a gentle heat; after which, the boot tops may be polished with a proper brush, so as to appear like new leather.

Another method of cleaning Boot Tops

Take of white vitriol, powdered, one ounce, acid of sugar one ounce, water, one quart. Mix together. Put a label on it, ''Rank Poison''. Sponge the tops with water first; then mix with the liquid, and then with water again.

To clean Mahogany Furniture

Take two ounces of bees' wax, scrape it fine, put it into a pot or jar, and pour over it enough of spirits of turpentine to cover it; let it stand a little while, and it will be ready for use. If the furniture is to be kept a dark colour, mix a very small quantity of alkanet root or rose-pink, with it.

To clean Furniture with Oil

Take a pint of cold-drawn linseed oil, and if you wish to colour it, take a little alkanet root or rose-pink, and mix with it: put a little on the furniture, and rub it well with a woollen cloth; do not let the oil stand long on the table before it is rubbed off.

To clean Japanned Candlesticks

Never hold them near the fire, nor scrape them with a knife; the best way is to pour water upon them just hot enough to melt the grease; then wipe them with a cloth, and if they look smeared, sprinkle a little whiting or flour upon them, and rub it clean off.

Be very particular in cleaning the patent snuffers, as they go with a spring, and are easily broken. The part which shuts up the snuffings has in general a small hole in it, where a pin can be put in to keep it open while cleaning it; be sure to have them well cleaned, that the snuff may not drop about when using them. The extinguishers likewise must be cleaned in the inside, and put ready with the snuffers, that the candlesticks may not be taken up without them.

German Polish for Furniture

Melt a quarter of a pound of yellow wax and an ounce of black resin, well beaten, in an earthen pipkin. Then pour in by degrees two ounces of spirit of turpentine. When the whole is thoroughly mixed, put it into an earthen jar, and keep it covered for use. Spread a little of it on the furniture with a woollen cloth, rub it well in, and in a few days the polish will be as hard and as bright as varnish.

To Warm a Carriage

Convey into it a stone bottle of boiling water, or for the feet a single glass bottle of boiled water, wrapped in flannel.

To Preserve Brass Ornaments

Brass ornaments, when not gilt or lacquered, may be cleaned, and a fine colour may be given to them by two simple processes. The first is to beat sal ammoniac into a fine powder, then to moisten it with soft water, rubbing it on the ornaments, which must be heated over charcoal, and rubbed dry with bran and whiting. The second is to wash the brass work with roche alum boiled in strong ley, in the proportion of an ounce to a pint; when dry it must be rubbed with fine tripoli. Either of these processes will give to brass the brilliancy of gold.

To prevent the Smoking of a Lamp

Soak the wick in strong vinegar, and dry it well before you use it; it will then burn both sweet and pleasant, and give much satisfaction for the trifling trouble in preparing it.

If for want of the above mentioned preparation any should escape, a wet sponge suspended by a string or wire over the flame of the lamp, at a few inches distance, will absorb all the smoke and disagreeable effluvia. Rinse it in warm water when wanted the next day.

To clean Water Casks

Scour the inside well out with water and sand, and afterwards apply a quantity of charcoal dust. Another and better method is, to rinse them with a pretty strong solution of oil of vitriol and water, which will entirely deprive them of their foulness.

To take stains out of Mahogany

Mix 6 ounces of spirit of salts, and ½ an ounce of rock salt of lemons (powdered) together. Drop a little on the stains, and rub it with a cork till it disappear. Wash off with cold water.

To remove Spots of Grease from Cloth

Spots of grease may be removed by a diluted solution of potash, but this must be cautiously applied to prevent injury to the cloth. Stains of white wax, which sometimes fall upon clothes from wax candles, are removed by spirits of turpentine, or sulphuric ether. The marks of white paint may also be discharged by the above mentioned agents.

To clean Candlesticks and Snuffers

If silver or plated, care must be taken that they are not scratched in getting off the wax or grease; therefore never use a knife for that purpose, nor hold them before the fire to melt the wax or grease, as in general the hollow part of the candlesticks, towards the bottom, is filled with a composition that will melt if made too hot. Pour boiling water over them; this will take all the grease off without injury, if wiped directly with an old cloth, and save the brushes from being greased: let them in all other respects be cleaned like the rest of the plate.

To render Leather Water Proof

This is done by rubbing of brushing into the leather a mixture of drying oils, and any of the oxides or calxes of lead, copper, or iron: or by substituting any of the gummy resins, in the room of the metallic oxides.

To clean Furniture

Keep the furniture paste or oil in a proper can or jar, that there may be no danger of upsetting when using it. Have two pieces of woollen cloth, one for rubbing it on, the other for rubbing it dry and polishing; also an old linen cloth to finish with, and a piece of smooth soft cork to rub out the stains: use a brush if the paste be hard. Always dust the table well before the oil or paste is put on; and if it should be stained rub it with a damp sponge, and then with a dry cloth. If the stain does not disappear, rub it well with the cork, or a brush the way of the grain, for if rubbed cross-grained, it will be sure to scratch it. Be careful to keep the cork and brush free from dust and dirt. When the dust is cleaned off and the stains have been got out, put on the oil or paste, but not too much at a time; rub it well into the wood; if oil, be as quick as possible in rubbing it over the table, and then polish it with another woollen cloth. If wax, put a little bit on the woollen cloth, with the finger, or a small stick; rub it well with this till the table has a high polish, then have another cloth to finish it with. Be very careful to have the edges of the tables well cleaned, and the oil and wax well rubbed off.

To Brush Clothes

Have a wooden horse to put the clothes on, and a small cane or small hand-whip to beat the dust out of them; also a board or table long enough for them to be put their whole length when brushing them. Have two brushes, one hard and the other soft: use the hardest for the great coats, and the others when spotted with dirt. Fine cloth coats should never be brushed with too hard a brush, as this will take off the nap, and make them look bare in a little time. Be careful in the choice of your cane; do not have it too large, and be particular not to hit too hard; be careful also not to hit the buttons, for it will scratch, if not break them. If a coat be wet, and spotted with dirt, let it be quite dry before you brush it; then rub out the spots with the hands, taking care not to rumple it. If it want beating, do it as before directed; then lay the coat at its full length on a board; let the collar be towards the left hand, and the brush in the right; brush the back of the collar first, between the two shoulders next, and then the sleeves, &c. observing to brush the cloth the same way that the nap goes, which is towards the bottom of the coat. When both sides are properly done, fold them together; then brush the inside, and last of all the collar.

To take out Grease from Clothes

Have a hot iron with some thick brown paper: lay the paper on the part where the grease is, then put the iron upon the spot; if the grease comes through the paper, put on another piece, till it does not soil the paper. If not all out, wrap a little bit of cloth or flannel round the finger, dip it into spirit of wine, and rub the grease spot; this will take it entirely out. Be careful not to have the iron too hot; but try it on a piece of white paper, and if it turn the paper brown, or scorch in the least, it is too hot. If paint should get on the coats, always have spirit of wine or turpentine ready, which, with a piece of flannel or cloth, will easily take it off, if not left to get quite dry.

THE LADY'S FOOTMAN

The chief business of this servant is to wait on his lady only, for whom he performs all the offices of a footman. He carries out all her messages and cards of invitation. He prepares the breakfast, and waits behind her chair both at breakfast and dinner—must be ready at all times to go out with his lady, either behind her carriage or on foot. For his more general duties, see the Directions to the Footman.

A genteel exterior and a good figure are principal recommendations of this servant; to which he should add great cleanliness in his person, and studied neatness in his dress. He is, of course, expected to assist the other servants in waiting at the dinner table, and to receive instructions through the lady's maid, in whose outdoor concerns he must officiate when required.

[Wages £18 to 25 guineas—two liveries and a working dress.]

THE UNDER FOOTMAN

In families where two or more footmen are kept, the under footman is expected, and indeed, engages to do that part of the business of a footman, which is deemed the most laborious; that is, he cleans knives and forks—boots and shoes—carries up the coals and attends all the fires above stairs during the day. He likewise carries out cards, messages, &c. and assists to carry up and wait at dinner, &c. &c.

[Wages, 16 to 20 guineas, with liveries.]

THE HALL PORTER

The duties of this servant are confined to the entrance-hall, and the door, where he is continually stationed. He answers every knock and ring, takes in all messages, parcels, letters, cards, &c. and immediately hands them to the butler, who conveys them to his master or mistress.

He trims the great hall and passage lamps, and opens and fastens up the doors and shutters every morning and night.

The public character of a nobleman or gentleman often depends on this servant. Rude or contemptuous language, to the meanest applicant, will frequently prove injurious to the interests of his master, in ways of which he cannot be a competent judge; and, therefore, his best qualities are patience and good temper, to which may be added, secrecy in regard to the affairs, connections, and intercourse of the family. A close tongue, and an inflexible countenance, are, therefore, indispensable, and he should practise the maxim of hearing and seeing all, but saying nothing. It is recorded of the porter of a minister of state, who died in the morning, that, on being asked in the afternoon if the fact were true, he replied that really he could not tell, but if the party would give him his card, he would make enquiry, and let him know. This was a well-trained porter, and such should be the system of all porters.

[Wages from £24 to £30 per annum.]

THE HEAD COACHMAN

THE UNDER, SECOND, OR LADY'S COACHMAN

THE UNDER COACHMAN

THE HEAD COACHMAN

On the sobriety, steady conduct, and respectable appearance of this important servant, depend the exterior appearance of the family with which he resides. Every genuine Coachman has his characteristic costume. His flaxen curls or wig, his low cocked hat, his plush breeches, and his benjamin surtout, his clothes being also well brushed, and the lace and buttons in a state of high polish. Care in driving his horses so as to preserve his own family and not injure other passengers on horse or foot, that he may not involve his master in law-suits, and wound the feelings of those he is driving, is of the utmost consequence. It is his business to have the carriage kept in repair, and to prevent his master being imposed upon by wanton charges; and in like manner to advise and assist in the purchase of horses, and in this delicate business, protect the interest of his employer. Much depends on his zeal, as to the annual expenditure of a carriage, with reference to the coachmaker, the horse-dealer, and the farrier; and he will do well always to make special contract, and leave as little as possible to the conscience of others. When only one coachman is kept, his duties generally include the whole of the stable business, as well as the cleaning, greasing, and examining the carriage; about which latter, he should never trust to chance; and consult the smith or coachmaker as often as he apprehends a possibility of danger. The following instructions apply to the coachman's duty when assisted by an establishment, but they apply to the coachman alone when there is no stable establishment, and whether the horses are jobbed or not, his anxious attention to their welfare is equally required.

If not fatigued by late hours on the preceding night, he rises to take care of his horses, at the same hour as the other men on the establishment, and they are attended in the same manner, by himself and his assistants, as is hereafter described, under the head *Groom*.

The necessary morning business of the stable usually occupies the servants till breakfast time, after which they all return to the stable, shake down the litter on each side of the horses, and put the stable in good order, in expectation of their master, who probably, pays them a visit after breakfast to inspect the horses, give orders, or make enquiries.

The helpers and assistants are now busily employed in looking over and cleaning such of the harness as was last used, and remains uncleaned. This, having been washed from the wet dirt, and clean sponged over-night, after the arrival of the carriage, and being now dry, is first brushed with a dry hard brush, and the brass ornaments cleaned, for which purpose see the receipts; or the silver ornaments may be cleaned with finely-powdered charcoal, and polished off with a soft brush.

The ornaments being cleaned, the leathers are to be blacked with the liquid mixture, which is a very valuable and excellent receipt for that purpose; the brushes to be used are, 1, a hard brush for taking off the dirt; 2, a soft brush for laying on the mixture; and 3, a polishing brush.

After breakfast, the coachmen, with their assistants, or each, if more than one, proceed to clean their respective coaches; first, well washing the carriage part and wheels with a mop and a water brush. The back straps and straps of the springs are to be blacked, and in short, all the parts, that are of leather, are to be blacked in the same way as the harness, the brass or other ornaments being first cleaned. The wheels and bed of the carriage are next to be greased or oiled, and the linch-pins securely put in.

The inside of the coach is then to be brushed, the glasses cleaned, and the lamps cleaned and trimmed.

The carriage, horses, harness, and the whole equipage being now ready, the coachman attends his master or mistress for *orders*, if not previously received.

When the time is nearly arrived at which the coach is ordered, the helper or assistants harness the horses and *put them to*, while the coachman is dressing himself. He then narrowly inspects the whole equipage—sees that the coach, horses, harness, and all things are in order; when taking his whip and the reins in his left hand, a man standing at the heads of the horses, he mounts the box, on the *near side*, and drives off to the door.

In due time, the coach and other carriages, as well as the saddle horses, return, when the coachman alights, unbuckles the reins, and giving the horses into the care of the helpers, takes his whip with him into the stable, and deposits it in its proper place. He then, if there be time and daylight, washes and cleans his coach.

At eight o'clock, if not otherwise engaged, he attends the regular stable duties, and waters, feeds, rubs down, litters, and racks up his horses, in the usual manner.

[The wages of the head or upper coachman, is from 25 to 36 guineas per annum, with generally two suits of livery—a box coat once in two or three years, two hats, and two pair of boots; also one or two stable dresses, consisting of overalls, jackets, waistcoats, and undress frock coat.]

To clean Brass Ornaments on Carriages and Harness

Take half a pint of turpentine, a quarter of a pound of rotten stone, a quarter of a pound of charcoal, finely powdered, and half a pint of the drippings of sweet oil. Mix them, and apply the paste with leather, and polish it off with powdered charcoal.

Black Dye for Harness

The colour of harness that has become rusty or brown by wear, may be restored to a fine black after the dirt has been sponged and brushed off, by using the following mixture: viz.

Boil logwood chips in three quarts of soft water, to which add three ounces of nut-galls, finely powdered, and one ounce of alum; simmer the whole together for half an hour, and it will be fit for use.

Liquid Blacking for Harness

Take 2 oz. of mutton suet, melted, 6 oz. of purified bees' wax, melted; ¼ lb. lamp black; 1 gill of turpentine; 2 oz. of Prussian blue, powdered; 1 oz. of indigo blue, ground; 6 oz. of sugar-candy, melted in a little water; and 2 oz. of soft soap. Mix, and simmer over the fire 15 minutes, when add a gill of turpentine. Lay it on the harness with a sponge, and then polish it.

To bring Horses out of a Stable in Case of Fire

Throw the saddle or harness to which it has been used over its back, and it will come out of the stable as tractably as usual.

THE UNDER, SECOND, OR LADY'S COACHMAN

The business of the *Under Coachman,* is precisely the same as that of the *Head Coachman,* as before detailed. He attends with the assistance of the helper, to the care and dressing of his horses, washing and cleaning the harness and the coach, which is always the second best, and is driven by him at night; whereas the best coach and the best horses, are driven by the Head Coachman by day.

[Wages from £20 to 24 guineas, with two suits of livery, a box coat occasionally, hat and boots—also one or two stable dresses.]

He is sometimes required to ride as postillion, or as courier, when the family travel *post*.

THE UNDER COACHMAN

If there be other Coachmen kept, their duties are similar to those of the first and second Coachmen, but their wages are somewhat lower, and the liveries, &c. not always quite so costly.

DOWN WITH THE DUST.

THE GROOM

THE GROOM AND VALET
OR
FOOTMAN

THE POSTILLION

THE COURIERS
OR
OUTRIDERS

THE STABLE BOY

HELPERS IN THE STABLES

THE GROOM

This, and indeed, every other person in the stable department, must rise about five in the summer, and six in the winter.

When the Groom has two or more horses under his care, with a chaise, or other vehicle or vehicles, he is generally allowed a boy to assist him in the stable.

We shall here insert the *general care and management of horses,* because in every stable establishment, however *small,* or however *large,* a Groom is to be found; and he ought to be fully competent to this branch of stable experience. In order to avoid repetition, we shall refer every other servant in this department, to this description of the usual care and management of horses.

The first thing, on entering the stable, is to give to each horse about a gallon of clean water in a clean bucket; then to shake up the best litter, under the manger, sweep out each stall, and clean out the whole stable. Every Coachman and Groom feeds his own horses;* and during the time of their feeding, he proceeds to *dress* them: thus each horse is first curried all over, with the curry-comb, to loosen the dirt and dust on its skin; then brushed with a whalebone brush, to take the dust off; next whisped with straw, to smooth and cleanse its coat; and again brushed with the brush and curry-comb, to take off what dust may remain; after which the horse is whisped again with a damp lock of hay, and finally, rubbed down with a woollen rubber, or a clean cloth. The horse is then turned round in the stall, and his head is next brushed well and whisped clean and smooth, with a damp lock of hay. After this, his ears are drawn through the hands, for several minutes, till made warm, and then the insides of the ears are wiped out with a damp sponge, to remove such dust and filth as may have accumulated there. The sponge after being washed clean, is then applied to the eyes, to cleanse them from dust, and any exudation that may have arisen in them. The nostrils are also sponged clean, and the whole head is afterwards finished by rubbing it with a cloth, in the same manner as the body had previously been cleaned. The horse is then turned round into its proper situation, the head stall put on, and the dirt and filth that may have accumulated under its tail, are then washed away with a sponge. The mane and tail are next cleaned and laid with a mane comb and water brush, used alternately with both hands; the head and body are again wiped over, and the body clothes are put on and fastened with a surcingle.

The Groom next examines the horse's heels, picks out the dirt from the feet, and washes its heels, with a water brush and plenty of water. If any horse has bad feet, they are then to be dressed and stuffed.

* Fourteen pounds of hay a day, or one hundred pounds per week, with three feeds of corn a day, is deemed sufficient for a horse that is not overworked.

Lastly, a due portion of hay* (about three or four pounds) is shaken into the rack, and then the horse is considered as completely dressed.

This is a summary of the whole process of cleaning and dressing horses of every description.

Horses thus attended to, and regularly managed, under the humane superintendance of a diligent and conscientious Groom or Coachman, will have healthy and beautiful appearance, and in a great measure escape from many diseases to which they would otherwise be liable.

When the master rides out before breakfast, the Groom rises so much the earlier, so as to be able to get the horses for himself and master ready, and at the time appointed. In this case, he gives the horses not more than two quarts of water each, and about half their usual feed of corn. On their return from the morning ride, the Groom sponges the eyes and nostrils of the horses, and under their tails; picks out their feet, washes their feet and heels, and then otherwise cleans and dresses them in the usual way, as already described. When thus far dressed, it is necessary to hand-rub their legs, downwards, for about ten minutes, to prevent wind-galls, and to strengthen the back sinews.

When horses have been ridden hard, or have been a long journey, bandages must be wrapped round their legs (from the knee to the fetlock joint), to prevent their swelling.

If their feet are heated, they must be stopped with the following mixture, called stopping: viz.

Mix equal quantities of cow-dung, clay, tar, and kitchen grease with urine, to the consistency of a stiff paste. This is usually kept in a small tub, or box, with a handle, to be ready when wanted.

The horses are then watered, fed, and littered down.

All horses when they come in, if they have sweated, or are very hot, must have their feet and legs first washed, and then be walked about ten or fifteen minutes, in the open air, till they are properly cool and dry; when they are to be well rubbed, and afterwards cleaned in the usual way. They should be encouraged to stale as soon as may be, by shaking a little straw under them, and whistling to them.

* The feed given to each horse, worked in the usual way is, a quartern of oats and a few beans, three times a day, with some chaff, or not, as may be desired. In the choice of oats, the shorter and fuller the grain the better; when bitten in two, they should be dry and mealy: they should feel hard in the hand, and when hard grasped should slip through the fingers; oats with thin bodies and long tails are the worst. When brought by sea, if they have lain long in bulk, they will have become heated, and have acquired a musty smell, to counteract which the corn dealers, when they are brought into their granaries, spread them thin on an upper floor, and turn them frequently, to cool, after which, they pass them through screens placed under holes in the floors, from the upper to the lower floors, which sweetens them much, and frequently enables the corn dealers to pass them off on inexperienced Coachmen and Grooms as fresh farmer's oats, which latter it will always be best to buy. As horses should always be fed with fresh clean corn, it would be well to rounce them in a hair bag, which takes off all the tails and filth, and they should afterwards be passed through a sieve, to free them from dust and other extraneous matter, at the time of feeding.

The finest-conditioned horses in England are fed thus: When at grass, equal quantities of oats and old white peas; when in the stable, two thirds oats and one third old white peas.

The saddles and bridles, with the bits and stirrups, are to be wiped when they are taken off, and are so left till the first opportunity, when they are to be thoroughly cleaned and put away.

If a gig, chaise, or other carriage has been used in the morning, it will require to be cleaned and got ready as soon as possible.

Such horses as are at home at twelve o'clock, are, at that hour, to be watered and fed again, and just wiped over, but not thoroughly cleaned, as in the morning; their manes and tails are, however, to be combed and properly *laid* with the mane-comb and water brush.

When the Groom's horses and carriages come in, in the evening, he attends to his horses first, washes their feet and legs and rubs them quite dry, before he cleans them. He afterwards cleans his gig, or whatever it may be by day-light, if there be time, or at any rate, he has to get his harness cleaned. About eight o'clock the stable man repairs to the stable, for the last time, cleans it out, waters, feeds, and rubs down the horses, litters them up, bandages their legs, stops their feet (if necessary), and racks them up for the night.

[Wages £22 to £25 with, generally, two livery suits, and two stable dresses a year.]

To make Oats prove Doubly Nutritious to Horses

Instead of grinding the oats, break them in a mill; and the same quantity will prove doubly nutritious. Another method is, to boil the corn, and give the horses the liquor in which it has been boiled; the result will be, that instead of six bushels in a crude state, three bushels, so prepared, will be found to answer, and to keep the animals in superior vigour and condition.

Sores and Bruises

Over the whole sore, or where the part is bruised, or where there is a tendency to suppuration, a poultice should be applied and kept on by suitable bandages. The poultice may be made of any kind of meal, fine bran, bruised linseed, or of mashed turnips, carrots, &c. The following has been found useful as a common poultice: Fine bran, 1 quart, pour on it a sufficient quantity of boiling water to make a thin paste; to this add of linseed powder enough to give it a proper consistence. The poultice may be kept on for a week or ten days, or even longer, if necessary, changing it once or twice a day; and cleaning the wound, when the poultice is removed, by washing it by means of a soft rag or linen cloth, with water not more than blood warm (some sponge is too rough for this purpose); or, where the wound is deep, the water may be injected into it by a syringe, in order to clean it from the bottom.

Ointment

In the course of a few days, when the wound, by care and proper management with the poultices, begins to put on a healthy appearance, and seems to be clean and of a reddish colour, not black or bloody; then there may be applied an ointment made of tallow, linseed oil, bees' wax, and hog's lard, in such proportions as to make it of a consistence somewhat firmer than butter. The ointment should be spread on some soft clean tow, and when applied to the sore, it ought never to be tied hard upon it (which is done too frequently and very improperly), but only fixed by a bandage of proper length and breadth (for a mere cord is often improper), so close and securely as to keep it from slipping off. This application may be changed once a day; or when nearly well, and discharging but little, once in two days.

Treatment according to the appearance of the part

When the wounded part begins to discharge a whitish, thick matter, and is observed to fill up, the general treatment and dressings to the sore, now mentioned, should be continued; and in the course of the cure, the animal, when free of fever, may be allowed better provision, and may take gentle exercise. If the animal be feeble, from the loss of blood originally, or from the long continuance of a feverish state produced by the inflammation attending the wound, or from weakness arising from confinement, or connected with its constitution naturally; and if the wound appear to be in a stationary state, very pale and flabby on its edges, with a thin discharge, then better food may be given to it; and if still no change should be observed, with the better food, the wound may be treated somewhat diffrently from what has been already advised. The ointment may be made more stimulant, by adding to it some resin and less bees' wax, or what would be still more stimulant, some common turpentine; for it is only in very rare cases that oil of turpentine can be requisite. The effects of an alteration in the mode of treatment should be particularly remarked, and stimulants should be laid aside, continued or increased, according as may be judged proper. Before changing the dressings applied to the wound, or before rendering them more stimulant and active by using heating applications, the effect of closer bandaging may be tried; for sometimes by keeping the parts a little more firmly together, the cure is promoted.

Food and Regimen

In the case of severe wounds, attention should be paid to the condition of the animal in other respects. There being always when such happen, a tendency to violent inflammation and fever, that may end fatally, means should be employed to moderate both. The apartment should be cool and airy, and so quiet that the animal should not be disturbed; the drink should not be warm, but rather cold, and given freely, though not in too large quantities at a time; the food should be sparingly given and of a poorer quality than usual, and should be rather succulent and laxative, than dry or apt to produce costiveness; bleeding may be employed either generally from a vein, or, in some cases, when it can be done, by cupping from the injured part, as in the case of a bruise (though this last will be seldom requisite or found convenient), and it may be done more than once or twice, as may seem proper; laxative medicines also ought to be given and repeated, as there may be occasion.

Bleeding in General

Bleeding is often the most useful and efficacious means of curing diseases in horses, &c. In inflammatory affections, it is generally the first remedy resorted to, and its immediate salutary effects are often surprising.

When it is necessary to lessen the whole quantity of blood in the system, open the jugular or neck vein. If the inflammation is local, bleed where it can be conveniently done, either from the part affected, or in its vicinity, as by opening the plate vein, superficial vein of the thigh, or temporal arteries.

In fevers of all kinds, and when inflammation attacks any important organ, as the brain, eyes, lungs, stomach, intestines, liver, kidneys, bladder, &c. bleeding is of the greatest use. It diminishes the quantity of blood in the body; and by this means prevents the ill effects of inflammation. The quantity of blood to be taken varies according to the age, size, condition, and constitution of the horse, and urgency of the symptoms.

From a large or strong horse, four or six quarts will be requisite, and may be repeated in smaller quantities if symptoms demand it. The blood, in these diseases, must flow from a large orifice made in the vein. A horse should never be suffered to bleed upon the ground, but into a measure, in order that the proper quantity may be taken. Young horses, also, while shedding their teeth, have sometimes much constitutional irritation, which bleeding relieves. But in these affections it is very rarely necessary to bleed to the same extent as in fevers, &c.; two or three quarts generally suffice to be taken away.

Fullness of Blood

Moderate bleeding, from two to three or four quarts, is also used to remove fullness of habit, or plethora, attended with slight inflammatory symptoms. In this case the eyes appear heavy, dull, red or inflamed, frequently closed as if asleep; the pulse small and oppressed; the heat of the body somewhat increased; the legs swell; and the hairs rub off. Horses that are removed from grass to a warm stable, and full fed on hay and corn, and not sufficiently exercised, are very subject to one or more of these symptoms. Regulating the quantity of food given to him, proper exercise and occasional laxatives, as the following powder, will be commonly found sufficient after the first bleeding, and operation of an aloetic purge. In slight affections of this kind, a brisk purge will often alone be sufficient.

Laxative and Diaphoretic Powder

Take of crocus of antimony, finely levigated, nitre, cream of tartar, and flour of sulphur, of each, 4 ounces: powder and mix them well together for use.

One tablespoonful of this mixture may be given every night and morning, in a mash of scalded bran, or a feed of corn moistened with water, that the powders may adhere thereto.

This powder will be found excellent for such horses as are kept on dry meat, whether they be in the stable, or travel on the road; also for stallions in the spring of the year, as they not only keep the body cool and open, but cause them to cast their coat, and make the skin appear as bright as silk.

Purging

In obstinate grease and swellings of the legs, accompanied with lameness of the joints, dry coughs, worms, diseases of the skin, farcy, apoplexy or staggers, affections of the liver, &c. &c., mercurial purges are of the greatest service. They purge; destroy worms; generally increase the flow of urine; operate upon the skin, liver, and other viscera in a peculiar manner; cause a healthful action in these parts; and remove many chronic complaints incident to the horse. Great caution is necessary during their operation, lest the horse take cold. The water given him must be warm, and when exercised he should be properly clothed.

Horses that are kept on dry meat, and are full fed, with little or no exercise, require regular purging every six months, with two or three doses each time, allowing proper intervals between each.

THE GROOM AND VALET, OR FOOTMAN

In small families, a servant is sometimes hired in the capacities of *groom and valet, or groom and footman*. The duties of this servant are given under the respective heads of GROOM, VALET, and FOOTMAN.

[The wages out of the house, about £50 a year, with the cast off clothes.]

THE POSTILLION

When the family travels post, the helper in the stables, and the stable-boy, generally ride as postillions: on other occasions, the boy or helper, rides and drives the chariot and other carriages; or if he be a regular servant, he has the care of a pair of horses.

[Wages from 16 to 20 guineas.]

His clothing is nearly the same as the grooms, only that he has a cap, and generally a jacket instead of a frock coat.

THE COURIERS, OR OUTRIDERS

Are generally selected from some of the persons employed in the stables—often, the under coachman and groom. Their business is to ride with the family when travelling, to guard them on the road—to ride forward with orders, and to pay the turnpikes, &c. &c. The outriders always take care of their own horses.

THE STABLE BOY

Assists the coachman and groom, under whose direction he is occupied in cleaning out the stables, cleaning the horses, washing and cleaning the harness and carriages, and making himself generally useful.

[The wages, when in the house, is from £8 to £21 per annum, and clothing, as may be agreed.]

HELPERS IN THE STABLES

The helpers are subordinate to the regular stable servants, and their business is to assist in cleaning the horses, harness, saddles, and carriages, cleaning out the stables, and assisting the coachman and groom in all the business of the stable that may be required of them. They are generally hired by the week, at from 16 to 21 shillings, out of doors, and have no liveries. If hired as regular stable servants, they are boarded in the house, and their wages and clothing are nearly the same as the groom's.

When the family travels, the helper is sometimes taken either as postillion or outrider.

THE HEAD GARDENER

THE UNDER GARDENERS

THE HEAD GARDENER

The gardener, to understand his business well, and to be capable of undertaking the management of a gentleman's garden and grounds, should not only be perfect in the ordinary business, and the regular routine of digging, cropping, and managing a kitchen garden, but should be also well versed in the nature of soils, manures, and composts, the best methods of propagating plants, shrubs, and trees, the management of the hothouse, greenhouse, conservatory, hotbeds; and the culture, not only of indigenous, but also of foreign and exotic productions.

The gardener, on first coming to his situation, will endeavour to ascertain the nature and present state of the soil. There are scarcely any of the ordinary esculent or culinary vegetables that will not require, at least, a depth of two spits of well cultivated earth; shrubs and trees much more; and this depth he should accordingly give it by proper digging, trenching, and other means. The substrata, or under soil, must also be considered, and articles fond of moisture should be planted where the substratum is of a clayey nature, and will not suffer the moisture imbibed from above to pass of; while those which require warm and dry situations, should be planted where the under soil consists of sand or gravel, and will the more readily absorb the moisture from above.

In small families, or in gardens not exceeding an acre, with a paddock of three or four acres for a horse or cow, it is usual to keep but one gardener, who, at an out-door salary of a guinea a week, performs all the necessary work in the garden, milks the cow, feeds the poultry, and, sometimes, takes care of the horse, his assistant being a jobbing labourer during a few weeks of particular duty. These gardeners generally consist of under gardeners from large establishments, or from market gardeners near large towns; and the only questions which arise between them and their employer, are the difficulties which they feel at first in accommodating the practice on a large scale to that on a small and economical one; but, when reconciled to this, no situation is more independent and comfortable than that of the solitary and accommodating gardener.

Gardeners generally prefer a sandy loam, of a nature not too binding in summer, nor too retentive in winter.

Perhaps the best practical rules that can be given are the following, from the best Treatise on Gardening.

1. *Perform every operation in the proper season.*
2. *Perform every operation in the best manner.*

This is to be acquired in part by practice, and partly also by reflection. For example, in digging over a piece of ground, it is a common practice with slovens, to throw the weeds and stones on the dug ground, or on the adjoining alley or walk, with the intention of gathering them off afterwards. A better way is to have a wheelbarrow, or a large basket, into which to put the weeds and extraneous matters, as they are picked out of the ground. Some persons in planting or weeding, whether in the open air, or in hot-houses, throw down all seeds, stones, and extraneous matters on the paths or alleys, with a view to pick them up, or sweep or rake them together afterwards: it is better to carry a basket or other utensil, either common or subdivided, in which to hold in one part the plants to be planted, in another the extraneous matters, &c.

3. *Complete every part of an operation as you proceed.*

4. *Finish one job before beginning another.*

5. *In leaving off working at any job, leave the work and tools in an orderly manner.*

6. *In leaving off work for the day, make a temporary finish, and carry the tools to the toolhouse.*

7. *In passing to and from the work, or on any occasion, through any part of what is considered under the charge of the gardener, keep a vigilant look out for weeds, decayed leaves, or any other deformity, and remove them.*

8. *In gathering a crop, remove at the same time, the roots, leaves, stems, or whatever else is of no further use, or may appear slovenly, decaying, or offensive.*

9. *Let no crop of fruit, or herbaceous vegetables, go to waste on the spot.*

10. *Cut down the flower stalks of all plants.*

11. *Keep every part of what is under your care, perfect in its kind.*

Attend in spring and autumn to *walls and buildings*, and get them repaired, jointed, glazed, and painted, where wanted. Attend at all times to *machines, implements, and tools*, keeping them clean, sharp, and in perfect repair. See particularly that they are placed in their proper situations in the toolhouse. House every implement, utensil, or machine not in use, both in winter and summer. Allow *no blanks* in edgings, rows, single specimens, drills, beds, and even where practicable, in broadcast sown pieces. Keep edgings and edges cut to the utmost nicety. Keep the shapes of the *wall-trees* filled with wood according to their kinds, and let their training be in the first style of perfection. Keep all walks in perfect form (whether raised or flat), free from weeds, dry, and well rolled. Keep all *the lawns* by every means, of a close texture, and dark-green velvet appearance. *Keep water clear and free from weeds*, and let not ponds, lakes, or artificial rivers, rise to the brim in winter, nor sink very far under it in summer.

TYPE OF PINEAPPLE.

To Sow Seeds with Advantage

This is the first operation of rearing. Where seeds are deposited singly, as in rows of beans, or large ruts, they are said to be planted; where dropt in numbers together, to be sown. The operation of sowing is either performed in drills, patches, or broadcast. Drills are small excavations formed with the draw-hoe, generally in straight lines parallel to each other, and in depth and distance apart, varying according to the size of the seeds. In these drills, the seeds are strewed from the hand of the operator, who, taking a small quantity in the palm of his hand and fingers, regulates its emission by the thumb. Some seeds are very thinly sown, as the pea, and spinach; others thick, as the cress, and small salad.

Patches are small circular excavations made with the trowel; in these seeds are either sown or planted, thicker or thinner, and covered more or less, according to their nature. This is the mode adopted in sowing in pots, and generally in flower borders.

In broadcast sowing, the operator scatters the seed over a considerable breadth of surface, previously prepared by digging, or otherwise being minutely pulverized. The seed is taken up in portions in the hand, and dispersed by a horizontal movement of the arm, to the extent of a semi-circle, opening the hand at the same time, and scattering the seeds in the air, so as they may fall as equally as possible over the breadth taken in by the sower at once, and which is generally six feet; that being the diameter of the circle in which his hand moves through half the circumference. In sowing broadcast on beds, and narrow strips or borders, the seeds are dispersed between the thumb and fingers, by horizontal movements of the hand in segments of smaller circles.

Dry weather is essentially requisite for sowing, and more especially for the operation of covering in the seed, which in broadcast sowing, is done by treading or gently rolling the surface, and then raking it; and in drill sowing, by treading in the larger seeds, as peas, and covering with the rake; smaller seeds, sown in drills, are covered with the same implement, without treading.

To Plant Shrubs and Trees

Planting, as applied to seeds, or seed-like roots, as potatoes, bulbs, &c. is most frequently performed in drills, or in separate holes made with the dibber; in these, the seed or bulb is dropped from the hand, and covered with or without treading, according to its nature. Sometimes planting is performed in patches, as in pots or borders, in which case, the trowel is the chief instrument used.

Quincunx is a mode of planting in rows, by which the plants in one row are always opposed to the blanks in the other, so that when a plot of ground is planted in this way, the plants appear in rows in four directions.

Planting, as applied to plants already originated, consists generally in inserting them in the soil of the same depth, and in the same position as they were before removal, but with various exceptions. The principal object is to preserve the fibrous roots entire; to distribute them equally around the stem among the mould or finer soil, and to preserve the plant upright. The plant should not be planted deeper than

GAILLARDIA.

it stood in the soil before removal, and commonly the same side should be kept towards the sun. Planting should, as much as possible, be accompanied by abundant watering, in order to consolidate the soil about the roots; and where the soil is dry, or not a stiff clay, it may be performed in the beginning of wet weather, in gardens; and in forest planting, on dry soils, in all open weather during autumn, winter, and spring.

To Water Gardens

Watering becomes requisite in gardens for various purposes, as aliment to plants in a growing state, to support newly transplanted plants, for keeping under insects, and keeping clean the leaves of vegetables. One general rule must be ever kept in mind during the employment of watering a garden; that is, never to water the top or leaves of a plant when the sun shines. All watering should be carried on in the evening or early in the morning, unless it be confined to watering the roots, in which case, transplanted plants, and others in a growing state, may be watered at any time; and if they are shaded from the sun, they may also be watered over their tops. Watering over the tops is performed with the *rose*, or dispenser attached to the spout of the watering-pot, or by the syringe or engine. Watering the roots is best done with the rose; but in the case of watering-pots in haste, and where the earth is hardened, it is done with the naked spout.

Many kitchen crops are lost, or produced of very inferior quality, for want of watering. Lettuces and cabbages are often hard and stringy; turnips and radishes do not swell, onions decay, cauliflowers die off, and, in general, in dry soils. Copious waterings in the evenings, during the dry season, would produce that fullness of succulency, which are found in the vegetables produced in the low countries, and in the Marsh Gardens at Paris; and in this country at the beginning and latter end of the season.

Watering the foliage of small trees to prevent the insects, and of strawberries, and fruit shrubs, to swell the fruit, is also of importance.

[Salary from £50 to £100 a year,—a cottage, generally, and vegetables and fuel allowed.]

THE UNDER GARDENERS

These men are entirely under the control and direction of the *head gardener*, and are employed by him, for the most part, in digging and trenching, wheeling, dunging, gravelling, hoeing, mowing, and other laborious work.

They are engaged as weekly servants and are paid according to their abilities, from 16 to 20 or 21 shillings per week, and vegetables. Some *under gardeners* have a cottage assigned for themselves and families, and others have also fuel allowed them for their fires.

The principal tools used by gardeners are, a light handy spade, a shovel, rake, with iron teeth, hoe, three-pronged fork, dibber, or setting-stick, line and reel, usually called a skillet, wheelbarrow, baskets, trowel, a pair of shears, scythe, hay-rake, hook, ladder, besom, or broom, beater, garden-roller, turfing-iron, hatchet, and hammer. The gardener usually wears a blue woollen apron, which, when he is pruning, he ties up before him, and then serves to hold his nails, shreds, scissors, hammer, and pruning-knife. He should also be provided with a light measuring rod, flat and narrow, painted and divided on one side into feet and half feet, and on the other into yards and half yards; with this he will be able to measure distances, to lay out his beds for sowing and planting, and to measure and lay down his gravel-walks, grass-plots, &c.

PLEASE, SIR, DID YOU WANT A STOUT ACTIVE LAD?

THE GARDENER'S CALENDAR

Containing useful Information for every Month in the Year

January

If the weather be open and dry, sow, upon warm compartments, small portions of peas, beans, cabbages, spinach, carrots, parsley, radish, lettuce, and onions, and preserve them from the cold by mats. Also, in hot-beds, cucumbers, melons, small salading, best early and red cabbage, kidney beans, and cauliflowers. Plant cabbages, horse-radish, beans, and mint roots. The cucumbers and melons this month require particular attention. They ought to receive air by small degrees, as often as possible.

February

Sow small salading, radishes, onions, parsley, spinach, lettuce, peas, beans, cabbage, cauliflowers, carrots, parsnips, fennel, &c. Plant cabbages, &c. as last month. The cucumber and melon plants raised last month, should be transplanted about the middle of this into new hot-beds. The ground should be prepared for planting asparagus next month.

March

Sow, in this month, principal crops of carrots, early turnips, radishes, onions, cabbage, celery, cauliflowers, spinach, lettuce, asparagus, peas, and beans. Sow asparagus for the new plantations of the next year. Make new asparagus beds, and fork the old ones.

April

Sow and plant, as in the former month, for a later crop. Towards the middle of the month dung should be prepared for ridges of melons and cucumbers. Snails and slugs ought to be killed, and weeds kept down; otherwise they will increase so fast as to render their destruction difficult.

May

The principal crops sowed and planted in the spring will now require weeding, hoeing, and thinning, and some transplanting. The melon beds require an equal degree of heat; and the glasses must be covered every night through the month with mats; but in the middle of the day they must be raised to the breadth of two or three fingers. Cucumbers in frames must receive a moderate supply of water, and be planted out under hand glasses.

June

Particular attention is now required in weeding, hoeing, thinning, and watering the principel crops, and pricking out and transplanting for autumn and winter. Sow savoys, broccoli, borecole, cabbages, turnips, carrots, spinach, coleworts, kidney beans, lettuce, endive, celery, cucumbers, radishes, peas, beans, and small salading. Plant cabbages, colewort, savoys, broccoli, borecole, leeks, beans, lettuce, endive, celery, cucumbers, radishes, peas, and beans. Melon plants must be shaded in the heat of the day, and receive a large portion of fresh air. Transplant endive for blanching, and prick out young broccoli plants, which were sown in April or May.

July

Prepare ground for the reception of succession crops, and some main crops for autumn and winter, and sow turnips, &c. as at the beginning of the year. The common radishes sown now will be fit to draw the beginning of September; and the cauliflowers sown in May must be planted out in spots where they are to remain. The beds of carrots sown now will be fit to draw early in April. Spinach for winter may now be sown, and onions taken up if the leaves wither.

August

Asparagus beds planted in March must now be cleared, celery transplanted and earthed, and the heads or suckers taken from the March artichokes. The early cabbage seed must not be sown later than the 12th of this month; but lettuce seed may be put in as late as the 24th. The cauliflower seed will not do without covering, and the spinach sown last month will require hoeing.

September

Sow spinach, lettuce, onions, radishes, cabbages, colewort, chervil, corn-salad, borage, coriander, turnips, and successions of small salading. Plant savoys, cabbages, coleworts, broccoli, borecole, lettuces, leeks, celery, endive, and perennial, aromatic, and pot-herbs. Make mushroom beds, and cut down the haulm of asparagus, clean the beds and dung them if necessary. Hoe your turnips, and weed onions. The cauliflowers of last month must be weeded out, and cabbage-plants pricked. Of the lettuces sown last month some may be put into warm borders for spring use, and others planted under frames for pulling in December and January. The different seeds must be gathered as they ripen.

October

Sow a small crop of radishes and lettuces, successions of small salading, and a few early peas to come in next summer. Plant crops of cabbage, cauliflowers, late broccoli, celery, lettuce, early beans. Keep uncovered night and day, for the greater part of this month, such cauliflowers as are planted in frames. All spare ground should be dunged and trenched.

November

Most of the processes used last month will also be appropriate for this. Such as giving air to lettuce and cauliflower plants that are under frames. Cut down the leaves of artichokes and earth up the plants.

December

Forward the digging, manuring, or trenching vacant ground, preparing hot dung, making hot-beds, and earthing and tying up plants. Sow a few early peas and radishes on warm borders, and small salading and cucumbers in hot-beds. Plant early beans, strong cabbage-plants, and coleworts; and plant in hot-beds, cucumbers, mint, tarragon, and asparagus. The small salads may be sown every ten days, under frames; and such radish seed as may be put into the ground this month, should be covered on cold nights with fern, or long litter.

THE SERVANTS' HALL

In large establishments, the housekeeper, the lady's maid, and the men servants out of livery, usually take their meals by themselves, in the housekeeper's or steward's room; but when they take their dinner together, they preserve an order at table like the following:—The housekeeper usually takes her seat at the head, and the butler at the lower end of the table; the cook at the right of the housekeeper, and the lady's maid on her left; the under butler on the right, and the coachman on the left of the butler; the housemaid next to the cook, and the kitchenmaid next to the lady's maid; and the men servants always occupying the lower end of the table. The dinner is set on the table by the cook, and the beer is drawn by the under butler.

The servants' table is usually provided with solid dishes, and with ale and table beer; and it is the business of the superior servants to see that their accommodation is comfortable and in plenty, but without extravagance, or waste and riot. In well-regulated families, the servants' hall is distinguished by its decorum, good order, and even good manners, which the servants who wait in the parlour imbibe, and convey to the kitchen. Servants of coarse manners, vulgar habits, or profane discourse, and malicious dispositions, are shunned by others, and never make good their footing or rise in first-rate families, where all the good and bad qualities which belong to the superior ranks of society operate as much to their advantage or disadvantage as in any station of life. In truth, the servants' hall is a little world by itself, in which the passions, tempers, vices, and virtues, are brought into play, and contribute their full share in promoting that welfare and happiness, which it is the object of this work to fix and improve.

COMING IN FOR THE PLATE.

INDEX

and 15, Albion-street, Hyde-park-square, at 4 p.m.

INFANTS' NEW FEEDING BOTTLES.—From the Lancet:—"We have seldom seen anything so beautiful as the nursing bottles introduced by Mr. Elam, of Oxford-street. They are adapted to milk, biscuits, and all kinds of food; and, whether for weaning, rearing by hand, or occasional feeding, are quite unrivalled. —BENJAMIN ELAM, 196, Oxford-street. 7s. 6d. The bottle and mouthpiece are stamped with my name and address.

WANT PLACES.—All letters to be post paid.

WET NURSE. Strong, healthy, age 24. Good character. Baby five weeks old.—A. B., 6, Jewin-street, city.

WET NURSE, a healthy woman, from the country, with a good breast of milk. Age 22. Baby seven weeks old.—M. Porter, 19, Adam-street east, Portman-square.

NURSE (HEAD), in a gentleman's family. Five years' character.—M. M., 37, Windsor-terrace, City-road.

NURSE (UPPER) in a gentleman's family. Age 30. Four years' good character.—E. P., Evans', 134, New Bond-street.

NURSE (UPPER), in a nobleman's or gentleman's family. Age 39.—J. B., 7, Upper Grafton-street, Fitzroy-square.

NURSE (UPPER) in a gentleman's family. Good character. Can take an infant from the birth. Good needlewoman.—H. J., New London Coal Company, 1, Providence-row, Finsbury-sq.

NURSE (UPPER). Middle-aged. Well experienced. Can take an infant from the month, and bring it up by hand. No objection to the country.—Y. Z., 18, New-street, Dorset-square.

NURSE (UPPER). Can take the entire charge of an infant and make children's dresses. One year and nine months' character.—N. F., Woodhouse's, 3, Alfred-terrace, Bayswater.

NURSE (UPPER), where there are two or three children, or to a lady with her first child. Good character.—Miss James, 104, Oxford-street.

NURSE (UPPER). Experienced. To take an infant from the month. Good needlewoman. Good character.—A. B., 7, Stafford-terrace, Loughborough-road, Brixton.

NURSE (UPPER), in a nobleman's or gentleman's family. Lived 15 years as upper nurse. Can take a baby from the birth, &c. 3 years' character. Age 38.—A. B., 7, Upper Grafton-st.

NURSE (UPPER). Age 30. Has been accustomed to children, and can take a baby from the month.—E. L., 55, John-street, Oxford-street.

NURSE (UNDER), or to assist another. Age 16. Good character.—E. W., 14, Thornton-street, South-street, Walworth.

NURSE in a gentleman's family, to one or two children. Age 25. Town preferred.—C. S., 63, Union-street, Clarendon-sq.

NURSE, or Housemaid in a gentleman's family. 2½ years' unexceptionable character.—U. K., Peak's, 113, Goswell-rd.

NURSE. Age 26. Three years' good character. Town preferred.—A. B., 7, Lambs' Conduit-street, Holborn.

NURSE in a gentleman's family, or to wait on an invalid lady.—A. B., 7, Seymour-crescent, Euston-square.

NURSE to an invalid lady or gentleman.—E. C., 9, Lower Porchester-street, Connaught-square, Hyde-park.

NURSE, a married woman, without encumbrance. Can take an infant from the month. Good needlewoman. Well recommended.—J. P., Beddiscomb's, 5, Chenies-street, Bedford-square.

NURSE in a small family, to take charge of one or two children. Age 21. Good character. Can work well at her needle. No objection to travel.—M. A. E., 78, Westbourne-street, Pimlico.

NURSE to one or two children, or Under Housemaid in a gentleman's family. Age 20. Good character.—E. B., 6, Fell-street, Wood-street, city.

NURSE. Is capable of taking a baby from the month, and has a slight knowledge of dressmaking.—A. G. R., 12, Downham-road, Kingsland.

NURSE, to take the charge of two or three children. Where no baby preferred. Age 35.—J. B., 10, Park-street, New-street, Dorset-square.

NURSE to one or two children out of arms. Age 21. Not been out before. Good references.—E. M., 16, Wellington-street, Goswell-road.

NURSE to one or two children, in a gentleman's family. Can take a baby from the month. Age 27.—H. L., 60 Beaumont-street, corner of Weymouth-street, Portland-place.

NURSE, in a gentleman's family. Age 24. No objection to travel or go abroad. Can take a baby from the month. 14 months' character.—M. C., 32, Broad-street, Golden-square.

NURSE, in a gentleman's family. Steady. Good needlewoman. Age 30. Country preferred.—J. H., Piercy's, grocer, Stephen-street, Tottenham-court-road.

NURSE, to take the entire care and management of children, and wait upon the lady. Steady. Speaks French fluently. Highly recommended.—G. P., Beck's, 24, St. Martin's-le Grand.

NURSE, in a gentleman's or tradesman's family. Age 22. Good character.—E. L., 12, Clifton-place, New North-street, Finsbury.

NURSE, to take a baby from the month if required. Age 35. Good character.—A. B., Shaw's, collarmaker, Kennington-lane.

NURSE, to attend upon an invalid, a middle-aged person. Understands insanity.—A. B., 21, Wilton-terrace, Wilton-road, Pimlico.

NURSE, a young woman, who can take a baby from the month, or bring it up by hand if required. Five years' good character.—E. G., 5, George-court, Piccadilly.

NURSE (UNDER), or Housemaid in a small family. Age 19. Highly recommended. Country objected to.—A. Z., 1, Archer-street, Camden-town.

NURSE (UNDER) in a gentleman's family, or to take charge of one or two children. 6½ years' character.—H. Hines, 5, Acton-street, Fox-lane, Kingsland-road.

HOUSEKEEPER in an hotel or club-house. Experienced. Undeniable reference.—M. C., 16, Hinde-street, Manchester-square.

HOUSEKEEPER and GENERAL SERVANT to a single gentleman. Middle-aged. Good reference.—R. M., 54, Upper John-street, Fitzroy-square.

HOUSEKEEPER to a single gentleman or tradesman. Aged 40. Qualified to take the charge of a motherless family.—E. T., 33, Surrey-place, Old Kent-road.

HOUSEKEEPER, or Housekeeper and General Servant to a single gentleman or widower. Age 26. Good character.—D. F., 14, Alfred-place, Newington-causeway.

COOK and HOUSEKEEPER. Good reference.—A. B., Watts', baker, Shepherd's-bush, Notting-hill.

COOK and HOUSEKEEPER to a single gentleman, or in a house of business, or to take charge of chambers. Middle-aged. Good reference.—E. H., 27, Doughty-street, Mecklenburg-square.

COOK and HOUSEKEEPER to a single gentleman, or in a small family. Four years' good character.—M. C., the lodge, Dorchester-house, Park-lane.

COOK and HOUSEKEEPER to a single gentleman, or Plain Cook in a small family. Good character.—B. Puzey, tailor and clothier, Holloway.

COOK and HOUSEKEEPER, or Cook, where the lady is her own housekeeper.—M. B., post-office, Sussex-place, Hyde-park-gardens.

COOK and HOUSEKEEPER to a single gentleman, where another or man servant is kept; or Charge of Chambers. Middle-aged. 2 years' character.—C.B., 6, Balmes-road, Southgate-rd., Kingsland.

COOK and HOUSEKEEPER, or Cook where the lady is her own housekeeper and a kitchenmaid is kept. Understands her business. Good character.—A.D., 6, Lower Seymour-st., Portman-sq.

COOK (PROFESSED) and HOUSEKEEPER, or where the lady is her own housekeeper, and a kitchenmaid is kept. Understands confectionery. Age 36.—J. K., 49, James-street, Oxford-street.

COOK (PROFESSED), where the lady is her own housekeeper, with kitchen and scullery maid. Thoroughly understands her business.—N. C., 93, Park-street, Grosvenor-square.

COOK (PROFESSED), where a kitchenmaid is kept. Middle-aged.—X. Y. Z., 12, Cockner-terrace, Wellington-road, St. John's-wood.

COOK (GOOD) in a gentleman's family. Town preferred.—F. W., 5, Chenies-street, Bedford-square.

COOK (thorough GOOD), where a kitchenmaid is kept. Understands her business.—E. J., 145, High Holborn.

COOK (thorough GOOD), with or without a kitchenmaid. Good character.—M. M., 21, King-street, Regent-street.

COOK (thorough GOOD) in an hotel or tavern, or respectable house of business, where a kitchenmaid is kept. Age 36.—C. C., Fisher's tea warehouse, Compton-street, Brunswick-square.

COOK (GOOD) in a gentleman's family, in town or suburbs, where assistance is given. Age 40. Good character.—J. S., Mr. Dean's, 7, South-street, Manchester-square.

COOK (thorough GOOD). Has had many years' experience. Understands baking and dairy if required. Three years' unexceptionable character.—A.B., 34, Princess-street, Portman-market.

COOK (thorough GOOD), with or without a kitchenmaid. Good character.—A.B., Oliver's, fishmonger, Dorset-street, Glocester-place.

COOK (thorough GOOD), where a kitchenmaid is kept or assistance given. 1½ year's good character. No objection to the country.—M. W., 10, Seymour-place, Bryanston-square.

COOK (thorough GOOD) in a gentleman's family, where a kitchenmaid is kept, or Cook and Housekeeper. Experienced. Good character.—S. E., 6, Charles-street, Portman-square.

COOK (thorough GOOD), where a footman or parlourmaid is kept. Age 30.—F. G., Phicard's, 3, Holland-place, Kensington.

COOK (thorough GOOD), with or without assistance. No objection to a job. Good character.—R.R., 12, Great Chesterfield-street, St. Marylebone.

COOK (thorough GOOD) where a kitchenmaid is kept, or Cook and Housekeeper. Experienced. Good character.—A. B., 6, Charles-street, Portman-square.

COOK (very GOOD PLAIN) in a private gentleman's family, where a man-servant is kept, or in a respectable tradesman's family. Four years' good character.—M. R., 72, Piccadilly.

COOK (GOOD). Town or country. Understands dairy and baking.—H. M., Walter's toyshop, Clapham Old-town.

COOK (GOOD) in a gentleman's family, where a footman is kept.—A. S., Tubb's, 313, Regent-street.

COOK (GOOD), in a house of business, a middle-aged person. City preferred.—Y. Z., 5, Melville-terrace, Caledonian-rd.

COOK (GOOD), in a quiet family. 15 months' good character.—M. W., 18, Brand-street, Blandford-square.

COOK (GOOD). Middle-aged. Good character.—A. B., 3, Bride-lane, Fleet-street.

COOK (GOOD). Understands made-dishes. Three years' character.—A. H., 84, Fore-street, city.

COOK (GOOD), in an hotel or tavern. Long character.—E. C., 224, Piccadilly.

COOK (GOOD), in a gentleman's family. Age 30. Two years' good character.—C. B., 8, Park-street, Camden-town.

COOK (GOOD) in a tradesman's family, or on a job. City preferred.—A. B., Willent's, 67, Welbeck-st., Cavendish-sq.

COOK (GOOD), in a small family, where a footman is kept. Town or country.—A. Z., 2B, Wilton-road, Pimlico.

COOK (GOOD) in a gentleman's family, or Cook and Housekeeper to a single gentleman. Middle-aged. Good character.—M. R., 6, Cross-street, Finsbury.

COOK (GOOD) where a man is kept and trust and confidence are required, or Housekeeper to a single gentleman. Good character. Age 35.—G. L., 40, Milton-street, Dorset-square.

COOK ... tleman. Age 35 ...
Little Sussex-place, H...

COOK (PLAIN) ...
country, age 26. ...
street west.

COOK (PLAIN) ...
Accustomed to ba...
Molyneux-street, Brya...

COOK (PLAIN) ...
family. Good ch...
Golden-square.

HOUSEMAID (U...
there is a footm...

HOUSEMAID (U...
years' good cha...

HOUSEMAID (U...
part of the h...
Smith's, 3, Lamb's Con...

HOUSEMAID (U...
family. 12 mon...
Molton-street, Hanove...

HOUSEMAID (U...
required. Can ...
Lower Porchester-stree...

HOUSEMAID (U...
family. Midd...
New-street, Hampton, ...

HOUSEMAID (U...
family where a ...
—S. S., 1, Torrington-p...

HOUSEMAID, in ...
family.—A. M., ...

HOUSEMAID in ...
her needle.—...

HOUSEMAID, or ...

HOUSEMAID, or ...
6, Mybill's-...

HOUSEMAID, in ...
age 25.—A. B...

HOUSEMAID, wh...
ter. Age 30...

HOUSEMAID, wh...
good character.—...

HOUSEMAID wh...
—G. R., ...

HOUSEMAID, a ...
A. B., Stansmor...

HOUSEMAID, w...
woman.—E. T...

HOUSEMAID, wh...
character.—T. ...

HOUSEMAID, in ...
character.—N...

HOUSEMAID, wh...
racter.—M. C., E...

HOUSEMAID, in ...
character.—E. S...

HOUSEMAID in ...
kept.—W. M., Ha...

HOUSEMAID wh...
good character.—...

HOUSEMAID, or ...
character.—E. ...

HOUSEMAID, a y...
character.—C. ...

HOUSEMAID, wh...
Good character.—...

HOUSEMAID, wh...
a good needlewom...
33, George-street, Portma...

HOUSEMAID, in ...
man is kept. A...
country.—E. W., Sturch...

HOUSEMAID, wh...
A good needlew...
toria-street, Paddington...

HOUSEMAID in a ...
man or parlourma...
H. X., 14, Hartland-road...

HOUSEMAID, in ...
footman is kept. ...
John-street north, New-...

HOUSEMAID, to ...
needle. Can get ...
chester-terrace north.

HOUSEMAID, or ...
country. Three ...
St. Martin's-court, St. M...

HOUSEMAID in a ...
the country. Good...
road, Hoxton.

HOUSEMAID, wh...
Three years' goo...
Manchester-square.

HOUSEMAID wh...
good character. ...
Marsh-street, Walthamst...

HOUSEMAID in a ...
is kept, a young wo...
racter.—M. F., 19, Hind...